The Metamorphoses of Myth in Fiction since 1960

The Metamorphoses of Myth in Fiction since 1960

Kathryn Hume

BLOOMSBURY ACADEMIC
NEW YORK · LONDON · OXFORD · NEW DELHI · SYDNEY

BLOOMSBURY ACADEMIC
Bloomsbury Publishing Inc
1385 Broadway, New York, NY 10018, USA
50 Bedford Square, London, WC1B 3DP, UK
29 Earlsfort Terrace, Dublin 2, Ireland

BLOOMSBURY, BLOOMSBURY ACADEMIC and the Diana logo are trademarks of Bloomsbury Publishing Plc

First published in the United States of America 2020
This paperback edition published in 2021

Copyright © Kathryn Hume, 2020

Cover design by Eleanor Rose
Cover image: Detail of Orpheus charming the animals, Roman, (4th century AD) © Musee Municipal, Laon, France / Bridgeman Images

All rights reserved. No part of this publication may be reproduced or transmitted in any form or by any means, electronic or mechanical, including photocopying, recording, or any information storage or retrieval system, without prior permission in writing from the publishers.

Bloomsbury Publishing Inc does not have any control over, or responsibility for, any third-party websites referred to or in this book. All internet addresses given in this book were correct at the time of going to press. The author and publisher regret any inconvenience caused if addresses have changed or sites have ceased to exist, but can accept no responsibility for any such changes.

Library of Congress Cataloging-in-Publication Data
Names: Hume, Kathryn, 1945- author.
Title: The metamorphoses of myth in fiction since 1960 / Kathryn Hume.
Description: New York, NY; London: Bloomsbury Academic, 2020. | Includes bibliographical references and index. |
Summary: "Explores the functions of mythology in contemporary high and popular literature, charting how it reacts with our science-oriented and postmodern culture"– Provided by publisher.
Identifiers: LCCN 2019029560 (print) | LCCN 2019029561 (ebook) | ISBN 9781501359873 (hardback) | ISBN 9781501359880 (epub) | ISBN 9781501359897 (pdf)
Subjects: LCSH: Myth in literature. | Mythology in literature. | Metamorphosis in literature. | Meaning (Philosophy) in literature. | Fiction–20th century–History and criticism. | Fiction–21st century–History and criticism. | English fiction–English-speaking countries–History and criticism.
Classification: LCC PN3351.H86 2020 (print) | LCC PN3351.H86 2020 (ebook) | DDC 809.3/9370904–dc23
LC record available at https://lccn.loc.gov/2019029560
LC ebook record available at https://lccn.loc.gov/2019029561

ISBN: HB: 978-1-5013-5987-3
PB: 978-1-5013-7824-9
ePDF: 978-1-5013-5989-7
eBook: 978-1-5013-5988-0

Typeset by Deanta Global Publishing Services, Chennai

To find out more about our authors and books visit www.bloomsbury.com and sign up for our newsletters.

For Delphi, Jervaulx, and Talisker

CONTENTS

Preface viii

Prolegomenon: Myth as a Tool in the Artist's Toolbox 1

1 Multiple Selves and Egyptian Mythology 15
  Mailer, Burroughs, Reed, Zelazny

2 Mythological Worlds and Death 33
  Acker, Gibson, Gaiman, Byatt, Kennedy, Pynchon, Morrow

3 Orpheus and Eurydice: Variations on a Theme 57
  Delany, Hospital, Phillips, Hoban, Gaiman, Powers, and others

4 Invented Myth: The Problem of Power 79
  Acker, Barthelme, Hoban, Moore, Calvino, and Gaiman

5 Situational Myth: Posthuman Metamorphoses 111
  McIntyre, McCaffrey, Simmons, Doctorow, Piercy, Stross, Rucker, Tidhar

6 The Contemporary Functions of Myth as Artistic Tool 129
  Pynchon, Arthurian stories, Faber, Pullman, Morrow, Ducornet, Marcus, Atwood, Vonnegut, Naylor, Morrison, Silko, Östergren, Winterson, Grossman, Rucker

Conclusion 157

Notes 165
Bibliography 178
Index 188

PREFACE

Why should contemporary Anglophone writers use myths from ancient Greece and Rome, from Pharaonic Egypt, from the Viking north, from Africa's west coast, and from Hebrew and Christian traditions? Some of those cultures are long gone, and even those stories still alive in current religions are not taken literally except by fundamentalists. What do these stories from premodern cultures have to offer us? In Norman Mailer's *Ancient Evenings*, a dead young man listens to his equally dead great-grandfather plot how to survive in the Egyptian Duad, a postmortem realm of trials that annihilates most souls. A. S. Byatt recaptures anxieties of the Second World War through reanimating the stories of the Old Scandinavian Ragnarok. Exploiting somewhat different effects, William Gibson introduces the loa of Vodoun into cyberspace in *Count Zero,* and Toni Morrison and Gloria Naylor build emotional resonance with the myth of the flying Africans. Leslie Marmon Silko can rightly claim that Laguna culture still has believers, but presenting versions of their myths for Anglo readers raises many of the same artistic problems we see in the use of classical myth. What does myth permit writers of the contemporary era to do that they cannot achieve by other means? Why would writers find myths useful, given the dominant scientific materialism of our culture and the postmodern outlook of many serious readers, neither of which is very compatible with mythic thought?

Gods and mythic worlds clash rather obviously with scientific materialism. They do not even make much sense as validators of cultural patterns or relievers of anxiety if we do not belong to their particular culture. After all, the underworld invaded by Orpheus is hardly inviting, and in that form, it enjoys no current belief, so how could it do anything for a materialist's fear of death? Writers using the symbolism of a living religion in their fiction can build on cultural knowledge: Judge Holden in Cormac McCarthy's *Blood Meridian* may suggest satanic qualities to religiously aware readers; Zeus, Odin, and the Morrigan have a few neopagan worshippers, but such revivals do not give those gods credibility in the scientifically defined world. An invented cult cannot relate to the god as original worshippers might have. Hence, we need to look for artistic, and perhaps psychological and cultural, reasons for such mythological presences in recent literature.

Some writers do not even demand that myth have a religious origin or aura. They invent their own myth-like situations, identifiable as quasi-mythic because they involve actions normally part of a mythology, such as creation of a world or apocalypse or metamorphosis. Kathy Acker presents intense scenes where a nameless father, the daughter he abuses sexually, and a son have apparently brought a world into existence around them. Donald Barthelme's Dead Father claims to have created many features of our world. He does not behave much like a classical god, but he does slightly resemble a Native American trickster creator in his insouciant escapes and genital humor. Russell Hoban imagines the myths and rituals that might result from a nuclear war that pushed humanity back into pretechnological conditions. To complicate matters, some invented mythic figures seem to function as philosophical thought experiments: outside the Anglophone world, we find that Italo Calvino's Qfwfq and the other characters in his cosmicomical stories have no worshippers and are portrayed as Italian neighbors rather than as gods, but they bring about such cosmically important moments as the Big Bang and the first light.

Some literary uses of myth are identifiable by the presence of particular characters and their stories, such as Iphigenia or Aeneas, but some concern mythic situations and mythic worlds—worlds in which multiple levels of reality exist and that are considered as real as the material world. Such non-tangible realities and other levels of existence almost always encode the possible existence of a soul or consciousness after the death of the body. Where those alternate levels were once Heaven and Hell or Olympus and Hades, for instance, in futuristic fiction they become worlds of virtual reality that exist in parallel to, but separate from our material world, or they become electronic worlds within the internet. As we increasingly combine our physicality with electronic and digital worlds, we transform ourselves into a new kind of creature, one that may even exist in multiple spaces simultaneously or in multiple forms. Metamorphosis thus reemerges as a master-trope of future fiction. The plurality of forms of consciousness it offers curiously merges with the postmodern congeries of subjectivities. We will see a postmodern form of this in the Egyptian novels of William S. Burroughs and Norman Mailer, and posthuman forms in Charles Stross's *Accelerando* and Rudy Rucker's *Postsingular*.

Fiction of the last half-century or so presents us with a surprising variety of god-like figures, heroes of legendary proportions, and mythological landscapes, and I would like to understand how these work artistically. Above all, in this book, I treat myth as an artistic tool that can be studied as a tool. As an agnostic and materialist, I do not believe in any of the myths, yet in some fashion their presence works positively for me in literary contexts. When I look back over my professional life and the fiction that I have most enjoyed writing on, I can say that a surprising amount of it had some kind of mythological element that made it depart from material reality. Interestingly and puzzlingly, that pleasure was not the same as the pleasure derivable from fantasy, which I also enjoy and published on in *Fantasy and Mimesis*.

I would certainly not claim that all myth-inflected works are doing the same thing, but I wonder how they affect readers prepared to enjoy them. What do they have in common, or if they do not, then what different effects can such claims to nonmaterial reality create? Moreover, whatever the subconscious effect may be, it does not come (for me) as a weak form of religion of the sort analyzed by John A. McClure in *Partial Faiths: Postsecular Fiction in the Age of Pynchon and Morrison*. Nor does the same engagement come from wish-fulfilling fantasy of the generic sort. In *Romancing the Postmodern*, Diane Elam suggests that the excesses of postmodernism, the irreal parts, manifest the spirit of romance, and one can see that in the fiction of William S. Burroughs, with his cowboy and space exploration fantasies. Plenty of postmodern fiction, however, seems uninfluenced by the romance quest or its special world where magic or other departures from reality are possible. I start with a different assumption, namely that gods and immortals, certain kinds of heroes, mythological landscapes, and mythic situations seem to lend themselves in our culture to modeling certain kinds of problems, and I would like to see what those are.

Mythology has meant many things to scholars, from allegories of the weather to psychoanalytic deep truths about human nature. Anyone talking about myth has to identify how the term will be used in the current study. The preferred meaning is a matter of choice; one can do different things, given the starting definitions. The prolegomenon, therefore, will define the basic tools for this study; these include myth, mythology, invented myth, situational myth, and mythic worlds. I will also make my unusual and contrarian argument for considering invented myth as well as inherited myth.

The postmodern, disunified self poses problems for myths of all sorts. For many participants in Western culture, Christianity's concept of a soul guaranteed the self as a unitary being—all of the soul was saved or damned, not parts of it. More complicated possibilities emerged once Freud postulated the existence of an unconscious. Today, theorists talk about multiple subjectivities with no underlying unity. Chapter 1 will tackle the apparent dissonance between the postmodern mindset and the mythic story. In unexpected ways, multiple subjectivities have found an answering resonance in some properties of polytheistic myth. Monotheism harmonizes with belief in a core unity; to deal with the lack of unity, William S. Burroughs and Norman Mailer have turned to the Egyptian tradition, partly because Egyptians pictured the individual as having seven souls. Because they use Egyptian material, I will also take the opportunity to see how else that tradition can be used to very different ends as done by Ishmael Reed and Roger Zelazny. Reed embodies in the story of Set and Osiris a ferocious critique of American culture's underlying values. Zelazny uses the mythic figures to comment on such social forces as revolution. One book cannot explore the uses of all non-Western mythologies in Anglophone literature.

Because of its recent prominent use by Mailer and Burroughs, Egyptian myth will be used to exemplify what effects myth can produce when separated from familiarity, and myth's power as cultural capital.

Mailer and Burroughs use the mythological material to express fears of death, but I pay more attention to multiple souls in Chapter 1. Chapter 2 examines how various mythologies are used to talk about death in a cultural climate that offers no reassurance of afterlife. Kathy Acker, Neil Gaiman, and A. S. Byatt furnish my primary illustrations of handling death through Tantric, Norse, and other mythologies, but secondary texts will include William Kennedy's *Legs* and Thomas Pynchon's *Vineland*, both of which use the Tibetan Book of the Dead and its postmortem experiences. For a change of pace, the chapter will end with James Morrow's upending of Judeo-Christian mythology by portraying the physical corpse of God and exploring death from that perspective.

Chapter 3 will take the perennially popular Orpheus story as a case study and look at the many ways it has been used. For variety, we will look at a few poems, a play, a workbook for a game, and some horror and zombie fiction, as well as novels by Samuel R. Delany, Janette Turner Hospital, J. J. Phillips, and Russell Hoban. Once Orpheus entered Neil Gaiman's *Sandman*, he became not only the apparent starting point for the frame tale's sprawling chronology but also the justification for Morpheus's disturbing death at the end. Richard Powers's *Orfeo* combines avant-garde music with genetics and raises the possibility of a new kind of music that might even restructure our minds when nature and its inner rhythms are coded as sound.

Chapter 4 will explore various forms of invented myth and focus on what these disparate works have to say about power, for that is overwhelmingly the focus of such stories. Our best-developed invented mythology is the rise and fall of King Arthur, a mythology that continues to evolve to this day. However, other such invented worlds and heroes include *Star Trek* and the densely interwoven worlds of DC and Marvel Comics that are peopled with superheroes. Less stereotyped use of invented myth appears in works by Kathy Acker, Donald Barthelme, Russell Hoban, and Italo Calvino. While Calvino lies outside my English-language focus, I shall discuss him because he comes up with a truly original answer to the problem of power.

Chapter 5 also concerns invented myth, but this time the myths are those we are inventing about our future, and in particular those relating to the posthuman condition. The dominant myth is that of metamorphosis, of transforming the human to something never before seen. This usually involves a new mode of existence that can take us beyond death, an artificial enhancement of intelligence, or a changed mode of inhabiting a body during life. My examples come from speculative fictions by Vonda McIntyre, Anne McCaffrey, Dan Simmons, Cory Doctorow, Marge Piercy, Charles Stross, Rudy Rucker, and Lavie Tidvar.

In the final chapter and the conclusion, I will pull together my answers to six basic questions that have driven this investigation.

1. How is myth used as an artistic tool?
2. How can one invent myth and how does that differ from fantasy?
3. What do authors gain from using myth, given the generally postmodern and scientific-materialist mindset of many contemporary readers?
4. How does myth as tool function if the audience is not familiar with that myth? (How do Western readers respond to non-Western myth, or non-Euro-American readers respond to Western myths?)
5. Insofar as literary use of myth supplies things felt to be lacking in current culture, what are they?
6. What does myth as artistic tool let the writer do that cannot otherwise be done?

I will answer these through specific examples. Myth as cultural capital helps explain the Orphic element in Pynchon's *Gravity's Rainbow*, while myth as cultural compensation runs through various Arthurian literature. Some authors attack their culture's myths: Michel Faber, Philip Pullman, and James Morrow challenge Christianity. We find Jewish-myth-fueled explorations of language by Rikki Ducornet and Ben Marcus. Eden, or Eden with altered humans, attracted Margaret Atwood and Kurt Vonnegut, and the Eden myth mixed with the Lemurian appears in Pynchon's *Inherent Vice*. Toni Morrison and Gloria Naylor challenge Anglo culture with the myth of the flying Africans, and Leslie Marmon Silko through the worldview and prophecies in *Ceremony* and *Almanac of the Dead*. Myth can be used to attack the very idea of myth and gods (Byatt, Östergren, and Gaiman). Myth can also embody personal problems, as in the Canongate Myth novels by Jeanette Winterson, David Grossman, and Margaret Atwood. Finally, we will see how we mythologize our technology and project our desperate desire to survive death in mythic situations that we are trying to make scientifically possible.

Even in a secular, materialist world, myth endows some literature with cultural capital, and readers who possess the requisite knowledge can congratulate themselves on possessing the key to the action. Myth as known story can, of course, produce pleasure at the release of tensions and gratification of expectations. Unlike religion, it does not assert meaning or confirm it. For those who are willing to open themselves to the traditional story, myth does convey a "sense" or "feeling" of meaning that does not demand intellectual belief or affirmation.

Prolegomenon

Myth as a Tool in the Artist's Toolbox

Incest begins this world. Incest begins the beginning of this world:
A father's fucking his daughter. Night's fucking with morning.
Night's black; morning, red. There's nothing else.
In this area between timeless and time, a father, realizing that maybe he shouldn't come in his daughter or maybe just that he shouldn't come, pulls his cock out of her box. His timing must be off because his cock spurts white liquid out. Out into the future, what will be time. In this arena between timelessness and time, the most dangerous thing or being that can come into being is time.
Sperm is explosive.
The night's black.
The moment that the white drops fall on what will be ground, down, time or this world begins.
Sperm is lying everywhere, in the world of time, on its ground.
Lying in viscous pools. Since there's time now, the sun, the first being in the world, not yet quite being, cooks away all the sperm; black char and red earth are left.
The first animals are colored red or black.[1]

What are we to call Kathy Acker's bold scene, if not myth of some sort?
Incest is not uncommon in creation stories. In an originary setting, such couplings do not themselves violate taboos because taboos have not yet come into existence, and the tiny cast of characters necessitates inbreeding. Zeus and Hera are brother and sister, a fact not stressed by the Greeks, but not repressed. For most readers, though, the incest creates unease. Acker clearly has no wish to ignore the implications of incest. Her mythic moment reeks of disgust and anguish, and the conviction that nothing good will evolve from this vile and violent beginning. Mythic moments like this are one of many kinds of invented myths and, more specifically, situational myths—in this case, creation—that can be found in recent literature. Hence,

though I am fascinated by the problem of why writers in the postmodern and post-postmodern era would turn to inherited myth—Greek, Egyptian, or Norse gods and heroes, as well as myth attached to living religions—the literary use of myth needs to recognize variations like Acker's as well.

Myth has been defined as everything from proto-science to weather allegory to linguistic error to cultural control to deep psychological truth to national unifier to structure that defines the local cultural pattern as natural. Anyone wishing to discuss myth, therefore, must specify an appropriate definition for the project at hand. Throughout Western culture, certain obvious mythic stories can be identified, mostly those from the Greco-Roman civilization. When Orpheus appears, educated readers have expectations that the author may gratify or deliberately balk, but Orpheus is not a blank. He comes with complex baggage, and such readers know that he may be there as fabulous musician who charms beasts as well as humans, as lover who returns alive but unsuccessful from the land of the dead, as founder of homosexuality, as man torn apart by maenads, and as oracular head.[2] This chapter will briefly establish what defines myth in the current study and then turn to the more complex question of what makes invented myths of different sorts, how those relate to traditional myths, and how they differ from fantasy.

This study approaches *myth as an artistic tool*. What it may have meant to its original culture is probably not determinable, if the changing generations of myth criticism are any indication.[3] The uses to which myth has been put in art and literature change with each historical period, however, and these can be traced.[4] Many of those former uses are now ineffectual; they do not address our current cultural concerns. With our plethora of pornography, Adam and Eve in the garden have little to offer our imaginations, and if someone today proposed Orpheus as embodiment of good government, we would look blank, although that made sense in the Renaissance. Myth in the contemporary era differs from earlier uses, because it is trying to satisfy the demands of a very different culture.

Myth, Mythology, Mythic Worlds

Since the Greco-Roman myths are those that educated people of Euro-American cultural background recognize most easily, let me use them to lay the groundwork. At the highest level, we find stories exclusively about gods: Aphrodite's adultery with Ares and Hephaestus's revenge is one such tale involving only divinities. Not many stories, though, take place entirely on Olympus; most include humans. Zeus chases Io, Leda, and Europa, and carries off Ganymede. Gods pull strings to help some hero on the battlefield. Hera persecutes Heracles; Poseidon aids Theseus. Gods and humans can produce offspring, most of whom seem to be mortal, but a few are born with or achieve demi-god status or even immortality as constellations, as do Castor and Pollux.

Mortals may speak directly with gods, but even if they do not, they experience special relationships to specific gods through oracular statements made to them personally, sacrifices, dreams, and promises given or behests wished upon them. Gods deal with men face to face in the Golden Age, but only indirectly in later periods. This sense of what was possible *in illo tempore* or sacred time (as Mircea Eliade calls it) when the divine and the human interact directly is paralleled in the era of the Hebrew patriarchs. Then too, chosen men walked and talked with God, an ability that was lost to later generations.

At the periphery of such mythic material comes legendary material, and I will include it broadly in this concept of myth. The mortals are legends; their connection to gods may be genealogical, or they may just enjoy a special relationship. Worship of the same gods persists, but the deities are less visible in everyday life. I would call the story of Odysseus legendary, and likewise the story of Lucretia. The Roman kings whose story links to hers traced their descent back to Romulus, and thence through many generations to Aeneas and Venus. They are not, though, in any significant sense different from other mortals. Such mortals may or may not be historical, but they function much like the heroes of old in pointing a moral and adorning the tale.[5] Once we move out of the Greco-Roman framework into the Christian era, such legendary stories mingle with those more specifically mythic and simply belonging to the larger mythological world of the Roman Empire. These, then, are the basic characters and stories that qualify as mythic during the European Middle Ages and later.

As for how myths work in literature, the explanations correlate to the various definitions of myth. Andrew Von Hendy gives us a theoretically sophisticated explanation: "In symbol we experience and express the immanence of the sacred, but in myth we signify the gap between its infinite promise and our finite attainment of it" (311). He goes on to quote Paul Ricoeur to the effect that myth sets forth the discordance "between the fundamental reality of man and his present existence, between his ontological status as a being created good . . . and his existential or historical status, experienced under the sign of alienation."[6] All this assumes that man is created and that the sacred exists; many writers and readers who are atheists deny those assumptions. Harry Slochower boils myth down to a kind of hero monomyth with Edenic beginning, departure, and return, but that seems to me too constrictive.[7] Kathy Acker, to name but one, does not assume an Edenic beginning. What I hope to present eventually is an explanation of how myth can satisfy certain desires (at least for some readers) without assuming that the readers have a doctorate in philosophy. We must also be clear on the fact that not everyone is susceptible to the attractions of myth, even among those who know the stories.

Myths tend to aggregate into a mythology, which I would define as a broad *network of related mythic stories involving gods and humans*. The tendency to come together and build a loosely interlocking system of stories both stretches temporally over generations and broadens out geographically over new territories, sometimes adding new gods. Dionysus is a latecomer to Greece, and did not enter into his powers without friction with older forces. If mythic tales do start to link up, then we can assume that various bards and tale-tellers (and later, writers) all contribute by adding, subtracting, linking, and inventing. This element of invention is important to the growth of mythology. Some of these variations will reflect late developments among different peoples. We have the *Völsunga saga* among the medieval Scandinavian people, and the somewhat different history that is nonetheless demonstrably analogous in the German *Nibelungenlied*. This story takes new turns and meets new cultural needs in Wagner's hands. Meanwhile, the Scandinavian version blossoms unpredictably in A. S. Byatt's *Ragnarok* (2011). Writings that were denied canonical status in the New Testament show some of these myth-making forces at work as they create suitable stories about Jesus' infancy, for instance.

Probably because the Christian Bible offers a clear beginning and end of the world, we tend to think of mythologies in terms of such a linear development, but that is not crucial. We have Eden and the Apocalypse, but Greek creation stories are far less central or uniform, and classical mythology does not give us an agreed-upon and feared end. The old Scandinavian stories give us both beginning and end, though we cannot be sure to what extent this form-giving structure reflects Christian influence; the appearance of a new world after the old is destroyed could suggest a cyclical concept of history or could be a monkish addition. Subordinate stories within a mythology may have their own structure. Troy, from its founding to its sacking, is a major mythological unit in the classical tradition. The travels of Odysseus and Aeneas form their own mythic trajectories, and all three have clear beginnings and clear but future-oriented finales.

The collaborative nature of such mythological stories comes through when we think of the alterations and additions down through the ages: *The Aeneid* is not *The Iliad* or *The Odyssey*, yet it had immense influence specific to itself; then came Dares Phrygius and Dictys Cretensis, various French and Italian poets, Chaucer, Shakespeare, and on through Tennyson to Barry Unsworth's *Songs of the Kings* (2004), Madeleine Miller's *The Song of Achilles* (2012), and David Malouf's *Ransom* (2009), to name only a few recent additions to the tradition. Each artist tweaks the tradition to make it serve new ends. Within the literary context, mythologies are ongoing and developing, even evolving. The fact that they no longer reflect religious beliefs perhaps frees them to take new shape or follow new cultural logics. The writers feel free to invent and alter the inherited material. This combination of known material and ability to be bent to new ends makes mythology a particularly useful tool to an artist.

The next quality that helps define the literary use of myth is projection of a mythological world. Almost any prescientific world qualifies, because what makes a *world mythological is its containing (or being contained by) acknowledged and accepted nonmaterial dimensions*. In the simplest systems, we find three layers or dimensions: that of the gods, that of mortals, and that of the dead. In Egyptian lore, more emphasis is put on the actions of gods, which may take place in their own realm or on earth, but humans are not as directly involved as in Greek myth; however, the land of the dead in the Egyptian system is particularly elaborately constructed. In Scandinavian myth, we get what seem like several overlapping realms of the giants, the dwarves, the elves, and the Aesir and Vanir, as well as the land of the humans and the halls of the dead. Catholic Christianity gives us Hell, Purgatory, and Heaven (from the viewpoint of souls, all lands of the dead) as well as Earth. One of the great virtues and probably one of the sources of inspiration for nonmaterial dimensions is that they permit some form of human consciousness to live on in such intangible realms after the death of the body.

When I call these nonmaterial, I may seem to be fudging slightly. By the time Wagner constructs Valhalla, it has enough material existence that it can be burned up in a fire. For the purposes of humans getting there while alive, it remains beyond the material world they inhabit. It may not be lacking in some kind of material existence, however. The same ambiguity characterizes contemporary posthuman stories that involve uploading one's consciousness into the internet. Computers consist of metal, plastic, and rare-earth components; electricity is material enough that it can be interrupted, even as the computers and the satellite relays could be destroyed. The larger the network, however, the less likely total destruction seems to be, so electronic existence of the mind functions in the novels as a nonmaterial existence compared to life in the flesh but lived without that flesh.

When we imagine other layers of reality, we tend to imbue them with a bit of materiality; we have trouble picturing existence without that. Plucking harps in Heaven to make music either assumes material strings and wooden sounding boards, and air to carry the sound waves or represents a mode of making music beyond our vocabulary. Doubtless, a theologian would say that was the truer way of thinking of such music, but as far as our imaginations go, harps are material, even if never heavy or out of tune. The torment of souls in Hell is imagined in bodily terms; their bodies may not be exactly like ours, but their nonmateriality does not make them lacking the equivalent to nerves that can conduct pain. In theory, Heaven is very different from electronic life, but we imagine them in similar ways, which will lead eventually to my arguing that such artistically invented myth belongs in this study of contemporary mythological practices.

The final characteristic of *inherited* myth and mythology is an origin in religion. When Christianity overwhelmed Greek and Roman religion, the classical mythology lost any religious power it may have had, but anything at the core of mythic writing, anything that qualifies by a strict as opposed to a loose definition, needs a relatively clear connection to a culture with gods other than that or those of the fiction writer. This stricture does not apply to all forms of invented myth, but helps separate that from myth in its most traditional form. For religions that still have followers, the stories may be considered truths, not myths. Non-literalists do not consider Noah's ark true, and writers who are agnostics or treat religion as their cultural background may use such material as tools in their novels—Joseph Heller's *God Knows* (1984) about King David and James Morrow's *Towing Jehovah* (1994). Those are examples of biblical myths used in recent literature, and Salman Rushdie bravely, if rashly, used Islamic myth as an artistic tool. Believers too can use mythic materials, as may be the case with some Native American writers or with Pat Robertson's *The End of the Age* (1995) and the Left Behind fantasies by Tim LaHaye and Jerry B. Jenkins, but the ways they use these tools will mostly differ from the various aims of nonbelievers.

Talking about a modern work that uses mythical material assumes that the material includes the gods, heroes or legendary figures who are known, a mythical world of multiple layers of reality, and the knowledge that once upon a time, these had religious meaning that they now lack. When Botticelli paints Venus emerging from the waves, we know that she has been born from the sea-foam and the severed genitals of Uranus. We also know that she will be associated with erotic love, both licit and illicit, and we may know that she is mother of Aeneas and hence a distant progenitrix of the Roman Empire—and hence of the Italian world in which the painting was made. When Shakespeare writes "Venus and Adonis," we know the tragic outcome before starting. When Monteverdi writes an opera called *L'Orfeo*, we expect a journey to the underworld, although we may be surprised when the musician is raised to the heavens by Apollo rather than murdered by the maenads (two versions exist). When we pick up Tennyson's "The Lotos-Eaters," we know lotus will represent a temptation that Ulysses should resist. What Tennyson does with that situation will be the product of his own concerns and era, but we enter his poem's world as if we shared its larger mythology, since its stories are part of educated readers' cultural capital. When Mary Renault and David Malouf enter into the Greek world in *The King Must Die* (1958) or *Ransom* (2009), we may swallow whole or resist Renault's beautified image of ancient life and may puzzle over what Malouf's King Priam experiences mentally, but we enjoy these as twice-told tales as well as revel in their authors' original contributions.

Invented Myth, Situational Myth, and Invented Mythic Worlds

What, though, of mythic seeming material that lacks religious roots and known gods? What about Kathy Acker's moment of creation? What of William

Blake's mythologies? What of the obsessive fantasy world-turned-private mythology described in Robert Coover's *The Universal Baseball Association, Inc., J. Henry Waugh, Prop.* (1971) or in the psychoanalyst's account of a patient's fantasies in Robert M. Lindner's "The Jet-Propelled Couch" (1982)?[8] What of J. R. R. Tolkien's *Silmarillion* (1977), in which we find a creation story and superhuman beings who control the events of a world? And what of the aggregation of heroic tales—one that is still growing—centering on King Arthur? What of the posthuman situational and metamorphic myths that are becoming common in speculative fiction? Or where in this group of tales that act a lot like myths does one put the growing "universes" belonging to DC and Marvel Comics, networks of interrelated superheroes who sometimes cross one another's paths and who pass from one writer's hands to those of another? They are sometimes immortal and certainly superhuman, if not gods. Are they forming a quasi-mythological world before our eyes the way that one formed about Arthur in the medieval period? This is the kind of literature that I consider invented or quasi-mythology, for lack of a more graceful term. These many works signally lack roots in a separate religious belief system, although some come close to achieving cult status, as can be seen at Star Trek conventions, or as might be true for obsessive creators of such worlds such as the one in Lindner's "The Jet-Propelled Couch."

When we look at the sweep of European literature, the Arthurian material will be there alongside the Greco-Roman, offering different tools and solutions to mythic problems. It was widely read or heard and enjoyed by medieval audiences, not just in England and France but in Italy, Germany, and the Scandinavian countries. The amount of belief it enjoyed is difficult to assess, but as deeply learned a man as Milton originally considered Arthur a genuine historical figure, and only when he tried to choose a topic for his great epic endeavor did he ultimately reject the story as untrue (as well as being too royalist for his purposes).[9] Although the Arthurian mythology does not figure gods from a pre-Christian religion, since it already possesses the Christian God and Christian mythological universe, it adds giants and faerie, the latter being able to breed with humans and produce fated offspring (Mordred). The Arthurian world also vivifies the religious, supernatural dimension in the grail story, which may have Celtic pagan roots as well as Christian.

Arthurian literature seems to me closely analogous to a mythological cycle such as the Troy story. As it developed, it had a beginning in Arthur's immediate forebears and his own begetting, his recognition as king, the rise of a nation, and a tragic end. Motives for the downfall shifted as time went on from territorial overexpansion to adulterous tangles. Tellers, recorders, and writers of the story seem to have felt fairly free to invent characters and adventures and change the dominant concerns. English national expansion was obviously more attractive to an English audience than to the French or the Germans, but the French romance-orientation toward love made its way back to England.[10] The Arthurian world is mythic, not just in being Christian and having the Virgin Mary help Sir Gawain but in gesturing to such other levels of reality as the realm of faerie and the Isle of Avalon, where Arthur's wounded body can be taken, nursed, and preserved in some alternative to Heaven until his land needs him again. This is a rather special form of life extension. He does not die and need not be reborn later when needed. He will just live in this other twilit reality until the time is right.

If treating the Arthurian material as invented mythology is plausible, then what about situational myth? By this, I am specifying certain situations that are part of our inherited mythic cycles: the creation of a world, the end of a world, a messianic leader with powers beyond the normal, or a story focusing on metamorphosis. Kathy Acker's creation story quoted earlier is an example of situational myth. So are Italo Calvino's cosmicomical stories, if I may stray from English-language literature. Speculative fiction has produced a rich array of apocalyptic novels. Messianic novels are less popular, but consider Frank Herbert's *Dune* (1965), Nevil Shute's *Round the Bend* (1951), and Robert Coover's *The Universal Baseball Association, Inc., J. Henry Waugh, Prop.* (1971).

Yet another kind of situational myth is one focusing on the conditions of a mythic world, one with nonmaterial or at least not-normally accessible levels of reality. Such a level develops in *The Universal Baseball Association* or turns up as the deep web in Thomas Pynchon's *Bleeding Edge* (2013). Most post-singularity novels offer such an alternative reality. This last is as far as I wish to stretch the term mythic, but the basic agreement among different writers about what would be possible in such a world does suggest a collaborative effort to explore a non-tangible dimension that is so clearly conceptualized that it might become a reality. The postsingular is a world whose dominant myth is metamorphosis. We shall be changed in the twinkling of an eye. This may be through cloning bodies or growing them to suit new conditions and then transferring our consciousness into such alternative bodies. We may locate our consciousness in robotic bodies or may do away with bodies and take up a new mode of electronic existence. We may carry on a virtual existence inside the internet. If one author were exploring this, then I would treat it just as speculative fantasy. The burgeoning growth of novels set in this layered existence suggests to me the validity of at least exploring it as a mythic world.

Drawing a line between such speculative fiction and fantasy is not easy. Many readers do not think of science fiction as mythographic in any sense related to those discussed earlier, and yet it relies on certain basic situations that might be called mythic.[11] The first of these is that we will be able to travel in deep space. Never mind that perfect closed systems are nearly impossible to create, that current technology would not let us block radiation, that traveling through black holes to reach distant galaxies would not let spaceships or humans survive, and that we do not at present see any means of faster-than-light travel or even travel at close to the speed of light. Whether the "new earths" being discovered are five hundred or five light years away, we are unlikely to be able to visit them any time soon. Given what we think we understand of physics at present, getting around our own galaxy is beyond us, let alone to other galaxies. Nonetheless, our astronomers eagerly seek earth-like planets, no matter how distant. A linked pair of mythic beliefs is that aliens exist and that we will be able to communicate with them. That other forms of life might exist does seem probable, but I am less sure about our ability to communicate, and if they reach us before we reach them, they would be so technologically superior that they might disprove the fourth mythic topos, namely, that we will be able to hold our own against them. A fifth is that we will be able to establish ourselves on other planets, never mind the kinds of problems with microscopic biota that H. G. Wells foresaw for invading Martians.

The most posthuman of the myths is that we will be able to escape from many and perhaps all the limitations of being human. We may be able to increase intelligence. We may be able to evade our physical life span by uploading our minds and sensoria into mechanisms or even a series of other bodies. We may alter physical bodies to give ourselves further powers. Because of the scientific trappings to these myths, we do not think of them as providing a magical or nonmaterial dimension to the world, but most of those myths would have to be achieved by magic, given our present knowledge of what is possible and what is not. Maybe science will make some of these breakthroughs, but faith in these possibilities seems similar to faith in a god or gods. I note, however, that Ray Kurzweil is an enthusiastic prophet for our achieving such transformations of our mind within the current generation, so we may see what I am calling mythic situations come true in the next fifty or hundred years. His ecstatic vision has also been called the Rapture for Nerds.[12] If nothing else, that points to a recognized mythic parallel.

Myth versus Fantasy

From a materialist point of view, all myth is fantasy and so are all religious myths. Even if we grant that, however, some of these literary and cultural constructions have more weight, more impact, than the rest. Historically, some examples have mattered more than others. Fantasy and myth cannot be differentiated by any simple rule, unless you say that myth must be rooted in a bona fide religion, even if that religion is now defunct. By that rule, everything I have called invented myth is just fantasy. A more flexible rule is helpful, however, for understanding contemporary literature.

Consider Kathy Acker's anguished creation story. Figures somehow responsible for a world coming into being engage in sexual acts that have consequences. The creation of a world puts this outside the usual realm of fantasy and into what I would call invented situational myth. We compare what we read to other myths we know—the story of Eden, and the Greek or Norse myths of how things started. We respond to our sense that Acker grimly means to explain the nasty nature of the world and life.

By contrast, unicorns and dragons, elves and dwarves, do not generally achieve that implicit importance in shaping their world; they characterize a fantastic world, but do not create it or even alter its nature much. Hence, certain situations such as creation, even when we know them to be invented, demand that we read them as myths rather than as fantasy. My personal sense is that creation of the world is probably the most convincingly mythical of the invented myths. Apocalypses are so tied to current technological crises that they seem somehow less timeless and absolute. They may still carry some mythic weight, but usually not as much.

Messiahs probably carry even less, since a messianic leader like Paul Atreides of *Dune* can also just be seen as a religiously enhanced romance hero. Insofar as his powers exceed human powers, he has a bit of mythic weight, and insofar as his actions will affect not just one world but many, he stands somewhat above strictly human heroes. We can still dismiss him as fantasy, but consider another messianic figure, Damon Rutherford in Coover's *The Universal Baseball Association*. What makes that golden youth mythic is the way that J. Henry Waugh's invented baseball game becomes a ritual, a mythic enactment of the original death of Damon and Jock Casey. Henry's "real" world fades out of existence, and we end trapped in his invented (but fictionally very convincing) fantasy world of game-become-mythic reenactment-become-religion for the players. Within that world, Damon and Jock are numinous. This feels closer to messianic myth than *Dune* does, but insofar as it takes place within the mind of someone whose sanity is dubious, it probably remains fantasy. The border is messy and how one views individual instances is probably highly personal.

What is this "weight" that seems to attach to mythic material? At least part of it is cultural familiarity and a sense that something has mattered—even deeply—to prior generations. Personally, we may reject the story as nonsense, Noah's ark being a good example. However, we have known the story, seen children's games and songs based on that story, seen *New Yorker* and *Punch* cartoons that assume the knowledge, and seen films or read the controversies over cinematic representations of the ark or Evangelical amusement-park attempts to "reconstruct" the ark. Even those indifferent to the story know what it is. That shared knowledge gives such material weight. Of course, such shared knowledge may disappear. No longer does every schoolchild know the classical myths in their traditional form, though they may know mythic materials mixed and mingled from many traditions in computer and role-playing games.[13] A superhero who at times is named Gilgamesh interacts with another named Thor, for instance; while bits and pieces of Norse or Mesopotamian myth appear, this does not transmit much sense of any real tradition. *The Hunger Games* draws on the story of Theseus, but only indirectly; it would not educate someone to recognize that myth. Myth proved a treasure trove to game-creators because it was not copyrighted, but the parts that most appealed were vivid adventures, and not all of myth's values lie in the most violent parts.

Whether that kind of mythic knowledge creates sensitivity to literary resonance remains to be seen. I would guess not, but I am prejudiced toward books and toward conservative adaptation rather than slapdash appropriation.[14] I admit that this use of myth keeps them alive in some sense. The mixing of Greek, Norse, and Chinese mythical characters, however, if experienced sufficiently often, might well dilute any narrative power of the original myths, much the way that retelling and varying an account of a trauma gradually robs it of power. Myths may lose their ability to affect future readers, unless those readers are willing to try to understand the story insofar as possible in a form not too contaminated with modern concerns or superhero simplifications. We will see how authors negotiate this problem of mythic affect when they adopt ancient Egyptian myths in Chapter 1, since most readers have no background in that mythology, and hence no conditioned sense of the story's import.

If I am justified in calling the King Arthur cycle an invented mythology, what makes it that rather than just romance (which it is), and even just fantasy (which it also is)? Again, the cultural capital it has accrued makes most of the difference. My English Department colleagues would draw a complete blank were I to refer to some major event in fantasies by Katharine Kerr or Roger Zelazny. If I liken something to drawing the sword from the stone, or refer to adultery and its results to Guinevere and Lancelot, they will know what I mean. Furthermore, my mentioning that adultery not only invokes the particular problem but also brings with it the whole cycle from Arthur's begetting to his death or disappearance at Avalon. The whole pattern stands behind any one episode.

What about the Harry Potter series? J. K. Rowling cleverly gives Harry many of the attributes and experiences of Arthur and other monomythic heroes. Why does that series remain completely and unmythically fantasy, at least for now? Perhaps because it presents very vividly a world competing with ours, not something rooted in a glorified version of our past. Those who have walked on Oxford Street feel quite sure that one could not get into a telephone booth and descend down into the Ministry of Magic. The Green Knight's magic in *Sir Gawain and the Green Knight* would make more demands on us if it were set in the current decade, whatever that may be, but it is not. Besides, what makes the Arthurian story mythic is the trajectory of the whole more than the bits of magic or occasional intrusions of the world of faerie, though they help establish the nonmaterial levels. Were we to take Rowling seriously, we would have to suspend belief about a material world we know well, but she does not offer enough supposed evidence to make us willing to take her version seriously. We can enjoy it without being persuaded in any way.

Knowledge is not enough to give a story mythic weight, but it is a contributing factor. Many people know the story of Hamlet or Romeo and Juliet. Does that make them mythic? I would say not, though others might disagree. They have not generated a broad network of well-known works, nor have they aggregated into a network of related stories. Occasional writers have created variations great in their own right, such as Tom Stoppard's *Rosencrantz and Guildenstern are Dead* (1967) or Leonard Bernstein's *West Side Story* (1957), but such variations have not been frequent enough to make these into building blocks of entire strands in Western literature. They have not yet generated enough artistic offspring. Nor are their characters larger than life. That reduces their ability to feel like myth.[15]

If generating other versions can attest to mythic qualities, what about *Pride and Prejudice*? That has generated a remarkable number of later artifacts up to and including *Pride and Prejudice and Zombies* (2009) and *Pride and Prejudice and Kitties* (2013). Again, I would say not. My disinclination to take zombies seriously may be unfair, but their presence does not for me make the story more important or characters slightly larger than life. If generating enough adaptations gradually makes something mythic, then *Pride and Prejudice* might qualify someday, but the small-scale, domestic nature of the story and its concerns work against mythic status.

Clearly romance, whether as hero monomyth story or as love story, is closely tied to fantasy, and some monomyth stories may seem mythic, with the proviso that hero monomyths ending with "happily ever after" may not have the weight of those that end in tragedy, as does the life of Arthur.[16] Also important is the status of the main character: Having powers at least slightly beyond those of normal humans definitely opens the possibility of mythic import. An Orpheus story can hardly avoid that import; we respond to his power of enchanting men and beasts with his music, and then are drawn even more to him when he goes to the land of the dead and returns. Even though I fail to respond to zombies, I admit that some kinds of transactions with the dead carry implications that resonate with the anxieties of many readers who are alive. The zombie issue is a useful reminder that accepting mythic weight and being moved by it is up to the individual reader and not in any way a universal; some well-educated readers remain completely immune to the pull of the mythic.

Several qualities help distinguish myth from fantasy. Myth may deal with situations that belong in mythological cycles and not ordinary human life: creation of the world is the most obvious, but apocalypse may count, as may messiahs and, I shall argue, metamorphosis. Mythic qualities also may involve the weight of cultural capital. Myths are known, and that shared knowledge gives them import. It permits condensation and allusion; it means that one episode can bring along with it the weight of the whole larger cycle. Mythic material may also generate further versions down through history.[17] An invented mythic story helps identify itself as such by presenting us with a mythic world, one with alternate levels of reality, and in particular a realm that features those who are dead. None of these characteristics is absolute. I'm sure Terry Pratchett could create a land of the dead that would work humorously and satirically. That would negate the mythic potential of that situation. Humor aside, however, these various qualities at least ask that we consider whether the writer is trying to do something that only myth or very similar material is able to do for readers—and then we must try to figure out what that is.

Mapping the Mythic

One could map the material I have been discussing as a series of concentric circles. At the core is inherited myth—figuring gods and men and attached to a religion. Around that are the legendary stories set in the same culture and assuming the same mythological universe, but less god-centered. Outside of that is the large area of invented mythic material. In order to bring some kind of logic to that, I would like to frame a taxonomy by borrowing from Northrop Frye's creaky but impressive machine and dividing this invented mythic material into his four modes: comedy, romance, tragedy, and irony/satire.[18] I tried dividing on other grounds—psychological fantasy, wish fulfillment, and future fantasy—but could find no logical sequence and could not be sure that I was covering all (or at least most) possibilities. With occasional stretching, Frye's simple divisions indicate fairly helpfully the directions in which quasi-myths tend to go.

Imagine comedy as twelve o'clock or north on the circle. Here one would find those works in which the mythic system or society is purged of its discordant elements and resolves into order. In the east is romance, and here we find high romance (Tolkien) and low romance (low in the sense of crudity rather than level of protagonist). Between comedy and romance might come many speculative fictions that are cast as quests, but whose aim is to establish or restore a society, including many superhero stories. In the south, we find tragedy and Acker. Some Blake prophecies belong there too, though some of his mythological poems end with a more transcending vision even if they start in an enchained world. To the southeast, between romance and tragedy, would be the Arthurian cycle. In the west, we have irony/satire, where I might put Donald Barthelme's *The Dead Father* (1975) and Morrow's *Towing Jehovah*. Northwest, between irony and comedy, might come Calvino's cosmicomical stories. I am not sure what fits between tragedy and irony in the southwest—possibly Coover's *The Universal Baseball Association*. These placements are approximate, and are only offered as a means of envisioning a kind of map. Like many projected maps before much exploration has taken place, it has blank spots and possible misattributions.

One could debate definitions of mythology at book length, but ultimately, my concern is with myth as a contemporary artistic tool, not with the nature of Greek or pagan beliefs, let alone the beliefs attaching to live religions. While I explore some forms that are not based originally on a religion, I am not extending the term to include political "myths," whether about George Washington, Jewish blood libel, or myths of nationhood. For my purposes, that spreads the term myth too far; though for other purposes, that analysis would be desirable. Rather than worry about the history of myth interpretation, I would like simply to look at how myths have been used by recent writers.[19] Why do authors turn to the stories, particularly when they do not believe in the nonmaterial dimensions or at least the particular nonmaterial dimensions of a dead religion? How and why do the artists use these tools? What in particular do they offer to writers living in contemporary secular Anglophone culture?

1

Multiple Selves and Egyptian Mythology

Mailer, Burroughs, Reed, Zelazny

Imagine that you awaken to find yourself in a tomb, dead and cheaply mummified, and not even in your own tomb, but stored in your great grandfather's tomb along with his embalmed remains and his eerily talkative spirit. That is the situation for Norman Mailer's nominal focal figure, a young ancient Egyptian named Menenhetet II. We know we are in a mythological landscape if the dead can speak. Unfortunately for Menenhetet II and his ghoulishly sentient great grandfather, Menenhetet I, they are not truly in the land of the dead, at least not the blessed dead in the Western Lands ruled over by Osiris. Menenhetet I has made forays into the fearsome Duad, but has not yet dared the worst that it offers, and Menenhetet II has yet to try his luck in that realm of torments and traps that will weed out the undeserving souls and allow only a tiny fraction to win through to Osiris's realm. Neither one seems a likely candidate for success, but combined? Menenhetet I thinks that strategy holds promise. How, though, do you combine souls? This solution would not occur within the realm of the Abrahamic religions, so this different way of thinking is one gift that Egyptian mythology has to offer contemporary writers. What if humans have multiple souls?

Our having more than one soul helpfully embodies a problem facing postmodern writers. For more than a century, we have been dismantling the unitary self. In Christian terms, the soul is unitary—all of it goes to Heaven or Hell, not just its parts. In atheist terms, all of a person dies and is no more. In Catholic thought, even the body will rise on Judgment day and be rejoined to the soul, so the self is a very unified concept in that tradition. In practical terms, we have inhabited a body that pretty much lived as a being separable from other beings, and that made us feel unitary. That cohesion, though, is changing. Recent prosthetic and electronic devices have caused us to absorb inanimate objects into the body and to wonder if some form of our mind could survive death electronically. Freud identified an unconscious as well as a consciousness, and named parts of our mental self that we cannot sense directly. Even those who doubt the validity of ego and id, thanatos and eros, mostly accept that we have some kind of unconscious that is not readily accessible, which means we have the self we think we know, but also another that we do not. Studies of rationality suggest that a great deal of what we think is actually decided at an unconscious level.

Possible selves have multiplied in the hands of recent philosophers and theorists. The contributions of Jacques Derrida, Jacques Lacan, Louis Althusser, and Michel Foucault have so undercut any core being that we are left with a congeries of selves, each called into being by various cultural demands made upon it. The dutiful child and teen rebel can exist within the same being, and they may struggle for dominance, or may preside at different times, and both may seem insignificant compared to the Twitter addict or soccer fanatic. We are called into existence as citizens of particular countries and particular political ideologies, as members of a religion, as sexual beings, as gendered beings, as professionals, as part of a family, as members of a class, and as members of cultural and linguistic groups. Those groups may be defined by particular tastes in music and film, by formality or informality of grammar or by dialect, by clothes, and by the kinds of communication technologies preferred. The postmodern person consists of these multiple, competing interests. Add to this the attacks on reason as a rationalization for instinctual decisions, and we have little cause to see ourselves as unified and reasonable beings. To call the self fragmented would imply an original wholeness; instead, we are simply a multiplicity that coexists, sometimes comfortably, sometimes not.

This sense of the multiple self suggests mythology to some writers. A pantheon, after all, can be seen as a multiple self. One member represents erotic attitudes, another warlike aggression, another discordant quarrelsomeness, another the drive to power, another domesticity, and the like. If a reader wishes to allegorize myths, then that reader can say that Hippolytus neglected Aphrodite (his erotic element) with his chastity, and the goddess, thus slighted, avenged herself on him through Phaedra's forbidden love. Hippolytus failed to achieve balance among these divinely sponsored forces within himself, and so came to grief. While this is a crude and not much respected way of interpreting mythic stories, it does treat the multiplicity of gods as parts of the self, or it projects the self as a batch of clashing gods.

This potential for exploring a multiple self is what seems to have drawn both Mailer and William S. Burroughs to Egyptian mythology. The other attraction is the focus on death. Most nonreligious people are comfortable enough with the Big Bang substituting for creation in seven days. Further, they accept that even if the distant beginnings are mysterious and the earth may or may not have been intelligently designed, the earth has evolved to its current state. How our world began stirs no fears and mostly just curiosity. What comes after death, though, is different. That is immediate and affects every one of us personally. The second chapter will look at what other writers do with other mythologies to deal with death. The current one will explore in two directions: one will be the advantages offered by Egyptian mythology, as explored by Mailer, Burroughs, Ishmael Reed, and Roger Zelazny; the other, the problems of thinking of humans in terms of multiple selves and souls. Other mythologies—South Asian, East Asian, Polynesian, Inuit, and many others—may well provide tools for exploring other problems, but the publicity achieved by Mailer and Burroughs in the American literary scene make Egyptian myth a useful example of how recent writers have appropriated non-Western myth.

Mailer's Excremental Journey

Ancient Egyptians believed that most humans had seven souls each (the Pharaoh, double that number). Scholars disagree on the exact tally, but that is the number that Mailer fixed upon in *Ancient Evenings* (1983). According to him, our component selves include the Ren (our secret name), the Ba (closest to Western notions of the soul, portrayed as human-headed bird), the Ka (our double), Sekhem (our vital spark or power), Khu (the light in the mind and a kind of angel), the Kaibit (shadow and memory), and the Sekhu (the bodily remains). They exist in differing fashions. The Ren, Sekhem, and Khu leave immediately on death; they are immortal but not individual, so they go back to be in some fashion reused. What is left must strive to survive the Duad. The Duad is a long series of nasty landscapes involving lakes of fire, boiling steam, rivers of excrement, pain, and judgment. The soul that fails may be eaten by a crocodile, or perish in the heat or other torments. Because surviving the Duad depends on the person's remaining souls working together, Menenhetet I thinks that between them, he and his great grandson can create a combination of souls with a chance of success. To this end, he forces the younger ghost to fellate him and ingest his ghostly sperm, which brings with it memory, knowledge, and something of Menenhetet I's superior mental abilities and priestly knowledge of how the land of the dead should be negotiated. Indeed, he has already made some forays into the Duad, but has not yet dared to wager his chance of immortality on an all-out attempt.

Mailer worships a heroic outlook, and in the past, heroism has certainly felt to be located within a reasonably coherent individual—heroic committees are not often celebrated in saga or memorialized in statues. Even in stories that figure the hero and his two brothers, or the hero and his twelve companions, the hero is the one who matters. The whole concept of a hero really seems to inhere in a unified being, not some congeries of selves. The hero may waver or be torn, but once he decides on an action, he is one again and must stand the consequences. The hero monomyth is the pattern for an individual to become an adult, and it does assume a being with enough of a core that he can be seen to grow and mature. I thought at first that Mailer's recourse to multiple souls betokened uneasiness with this postmodern development, as if it could undermine the heroism he deems so necessary. Further reading convinced me that the cosmological images and concepts of the soul are not just metaphor for him, but involve belief. They provide him with a logic by which life makes sense. Far from feeling undermined by the multiplicity of selves, Mailer found a way to make it serve his ends.

Mailer is unusual in having an individual cosmological theory.[1] His vision is based on the notion that God is an intense, struggling, dedicated artist whose best creations are his boldest and most daring. Many of his creations are failures, from animals that have gone extinct to cowardly humans. Very important to Mailer is the idea that God is as flawed as man is, and he must struggle against a Satan who is associated with slickness, technology, plastic, and totalitarianism. This Satan wins strength when any human makes a cowardly choice or, even worse, avoids having to make choices. Unlike some other dualistic visions of past religions, Mailer does not assume that the good will win; for him, the outcome hangs in the balance. Whenever humans make choices, they strengthen one side of the theomachy or the other. To this basic vision of the world as a struggle involving God, Satan, and humanity, Mailer adds the possibility of reincarnation, and he broadens the notion of soul, such that the food we eat may have qualities of soul associated with it that then affect our souls. Eating the meat of a brave animal (which may have been human in some previous life) passes some of that bravery to us, and part of its soul may augment ours in our struggle. Mailer has elaborate theories about what happens to that food as we digest it, and about our bodily wastes. He has always paid an unusual degree of attention to smells in his fiction, and one aspect of bravery is to absorb and work through bad smells, not cover them over or avoid them. We grow from absorbing and accepting, not from evading such matters, whether this involves the stench of our own shit or someone else's. We lose something by taking the easy way out, whether flush toilets for odor or antibiotics for infections. Our bodies struggle bravely with disease, for instance, and benefit from defeating disease, but do not learn or benefit spiritually from being saved by antibiotics. When we tamp our lives down and repress all of our more honest impulses in favor of cowardly conformity, we open ourselves to cancer.[2]

These are only a few of the elements in Mailer's vision, but they indicate why heroic striving is so important to his characters, and also why he found ancient Egypt an interesting challenge. He was trying to imagine a non-Judeo-Christian world and its mentality. Mailer's personal vision is not entirely consistent; it was a theory always in progress, changing to meet new inspirations. What he seems to have been most pleased about was the way it gave meaning to life by making our decisions cosmically important, and it explained the existence of evil, since a flawed god and a powerful adversary easily explain why dreadful things can happen. An all-good and omnipotent god's permitting disasters can only be bypassed by calling the solution a mystery.[3]

Given his serious investment in the concept of the soul and even his suggestion that one absorbs other souls from food and benefits or is damaged by such merging, the Egyptian worldview has obvious attractions. The Egyptian multiple souls were not exactly what he had envisioned, but they did offer a rival system enough like his own thoughts to deserve investigation and to suggest a kind of validation for his own projected system.

Once he sets up multiple souls in the novel as a way to parse the individual, Mailer promptly considers another multiplication of the self: reincarnation. Reincarnation may or may not have been part of Egyptian belief; we owe that suggestion to Herodotus (*The Histories*, Book II, 123), who elaborates on how Egyptians believed that a human soul had to pass through 3,000 years of life as a variety of animals before winning human form again. Mailer suggests something close to that interval when Ramses II's battle-lion, Hera-Ra, dies from eating the rotting hands of the enemy after the Battle of Kadesh, and Menenhetet I telepathically shares Hera-Ra's dying vision of great cities with "thousands of windows and great towers [that] . . . went to vast heights."[4] Given Mailer's admiration for the bravery and romping good humor of this lion on the battlefield, one senses his feeling that the lion glimpses a future rebirth as a New Yorker, probably as Mailer himself.

His chief exemplar of rebirth, however, is Menenhetet I. He learned from a Jew the trick of dying while ejaculating and begetting his own next incarnation, so he has lived four lives and can remember them in some detail. He was trying for a fifth, but the woman was unwilling and aborted him, so he is now facing the Duad as his fourth incarnation, as Menenhetet II's great grandfather. Most of the long book consists of Menenhetet I's account of his four lives, told during the Night of the Pig to his immediate family and the Pharaoh. His most important, or most vividly rendered, life was his first as Ramses II's charioteer at the Battle of Kadesh, and it remains vivid for its resentment. As an underling, the charioteer had no choice but to permit the Pharaoh to rape him and make him play the woman more than once, but he feels that he was unjustly deprived of spiritual power through this yielding to male force. His power was stolen, even as the Pharaoh lied about his charioteer's behavior in battle. That resentment clings to the ghost. He has to some extent balanced his loss by raping others, but that does not restore his anal virginity, as it were, and this may be one thing that undermines his confidence in his ability to survive the Duad's trials. He has also been a high priest and a government functionary in other lives, always relatively high in power but never of the first rank. This sense of never quite making it haunts him, and perhaps his great grandson's youthful brashness is what makes him think they should somehow combine their souls. He supplies the esoteric knowledge from his priestly training and can offer a grim determination that is unlikely to be tricked by beautiful distractions. His descendant offers the unshadowed outlook and untested assurance that may keep them from being undermined by doubts.

Mailer's Duad is a second chance—a great gift from his viewpoint. Life offered the first. Mailer has always argued that a man must chose the more difficult path, must not shy away from unpleasantness, and must never compromise or figure that just this once he will take the easy way out. Every bad decision degrades the world and all that inhabit it as well as reducing the soul of the person who made the craven decision. In many religions, once someone has died, that is the end of choice and change. You are weighed and assigned to whatever fate is appropriate. Both the Egyptian and the Tibetan concept of death make further choices possible. If one has done poorly in life, one might still improve one's status after death when the deadly consequences are totally clear and one is no longer blinded by earthly illusions. With reincarnation, Mailer adds another way in which some individuals might gradually improve and do better. Also, by going through many lives, one puts off any final reckoning. Mailer's version of Egyptian mythology is thus quite generous in the chances it offers, even if the Duad lets few souls through; they are given more than one opportunity to build their qualifications.

What does Mailer gain by extending the struggle into an afterlife? For one thing, the Egyptian Duad was an unpleasant place that had more than a little in common with the digestive tract. The various dangerous beings there live in boiling lakes and swamps and miasmas of fecal smells. Mailer has always been our laureate of stench, and both the Nile and the Duad let him indulge his scatological sensibilities. His emphasis on male on male rape or other unwilling sexual contact is a similarly anal anxiety. The phallus may be a source of power that increases one's energy at all levels, bodily and spiritual, but the anus seems to be a point of attack and a place that a man can lose power. When we see how Mailer presents gods, we will see that same anal concern with power. He has set the implicit struggle that lies behind this book in a rather anal realm, a realm in which horrible smells are real, and thriving on them is a form of taking power, whereas beautiful smells are to be distrusted as false. Menenhetet II complains of the stench at one point, and Menenhetet I offers to smell like perfume and sweet grass, and for a moment the atmosphere becomes lovely and the older spirit becomes a solemn priest telling a solemn myth, but that purity becomes unsustainable (44–46). The story, we are told, quickly becomes scandalous, sacrilegious, and obscene. Prettiness and sweetness do not have the fundamental (in both senses) strength of the unpleasant in Mailer's imagination.

Mailer's choice of the Egyptian world, both mortal and postmortem, lets him push many boundaries. The Egyptians at the upper-class level practiced incest, so Menenhetet II is at one point his mother's lover, thus living out rather than repressing the desire articulated by Freud. Whether the Egyptians were as enthusiastic as Mailer about incest and male on male rape is unlikely to be known at this distance, but the latter act epitomizes for Mailer the uneasy way that males must measure themselves. If war offers an opening for testing courage, fine, but for everyday spiritual agon, the opponents are other men, so Mailer has found a mythic (and probably unhistorical) landscape in which he can make his metaphors literal.

Mailer's mythological landscape in the realm of the dead lets him explore fears of death and possible answers that might assuage those fears. He also introduces tales of the gods, though, so what ends do those serve? In particular, he traces the story of Set's murder of Osiris, Horus's struggle to avenge this on Set, and Isis's letting Set slip away. None of these gods is the intensely involved artist-creator that Mailer personally envisions as the flawed but dedicated inventor of our world. His Egyptian gods seem more like exalted humans as Mailer envisions them. Isis is overpoweringly attractive sexually; Osiris is apparently creative and fair, but too trusting; and Set is ambitious and does not recognize any interests but his own. Within some other pantheons this might make him evil, but here that is just his nature. The gods seem mostly to be beyond good or evil. Horus is physically weak in the legs, but clever enough that, with his mother's help, he can trick Set. None of them is particularly attractive, and none seems to offer much of a model for human behavior. What Mailer relishes is the gender dynamics. Women do their own thing and make decisions that make no sense to men, but the women apparently have the right and power to do that. Men inherently resent power in each other, and try to steal it and improve their own standing. The archetypal acts that permit stealing power are killing and anal rape. Even if Horus does not manage to rape Set, his tricking the gods into believing that he has done so lowers Set's prestige in ways that cannot be offset.

Mailer's cosmology seems to me contradictory when it comes to power. He certainly seems comfortable with men gaining it, and tends to laud those who succeed, and he shows no mercy toward those who lose. In his analysis of Satan and that side of the theomachy, however, he associates Satan with technology, which (he feels) gives us more power, if not more happiness or creativity. If power is the same, no matter the source, then men are naturally in Satan's camp. Perhaps Mailer makes a distinction between power gained physically or personally and power gained through technological intervention. For all that, Mailer seems (mostly) in favor of wresting power physically from rivals; his showing it in the raw form of anal rape exposes the crudity, ugliness, and dubious value of power thus gained. Arguably, such conquests improve the individual; they certainly do not improve society as a whole, but then Mailer is so ready to see totalitarianism in any complex social organization that possibly the anti-social effects of such rapes do not matter to him.

If Mailer is at times able to see the drawbacks to this male drive for power, he may undercut his own insight with his Egyptian underworld, since the dead man's ability to survive the trials is assumed to be influenced by his power, and some of that power is derived from having conquered others. Mailer's own admiration for heroism reflects a sense that spiritual power has to be won, and that usually, if not always, means defeating others. I can imagine someone whose victories were all internal and over the self, but someone focusing in that fashion would win them by repressing impulses, and that goes against the Mailer philosophy. If you act on the impulses, then presumably you mostly pit yourself against someone else. If this contradiction lies at the heart of his system of thought, he does offer one partial answer in this novel and elsewhere. Reincarnation lets us try again, so someone beaten or harmed in this round may have a better fate in the next.

Some critics prefer to see the whole Egyptian and mythological element as metaphoric: All the anal rape just represents dominance and power of a political and personal sort; the real answer to death is writing, and Mailer writes himself into a lasting afterlife with his novels as well as comments on the place of writing within the psychology of civilization.[5] For others, the novel is an analysis of (Egyptian) imperialism from a postimperial perspective.[6]

Mailer's *Ancient Evenings* (1983) got some bad press when it appeared; the incestuous, anal, and fecal elements seemed too raw and obsessive to some prominent reviewers.[7] Those reviewers, however, were adhering to the rules of decorum common in Judeo-Christian-influenced Western society. Mailer was trying to get out of that mindset. He could revel in a society, however fictitious, in which rules were different, a society that believed in and practiced magic, a society inescapably permeated by the smells of a tropical river. Various Mailer characters in this novel and others enjoy moments of telepathy, and in *On God* (115-116), he speculates that man should have developed extrasensory perception, but has short-circuited this by developing electronic communication instead. Through the apparent magic and through the telepathy, Mailer suggests the kinds of personal interactions that intrigue him. Had he set this on some other planet, all the features that interest him would have remained fantasy. A mythological landscape, one that once enjoyed belief, lets him create a world that would encourage the psychic developments that he wants to see. His admittedly creative adaptation of mythology lets him give us a world overshadowed by the Duad, and that lets him show how various decisions and actions during life affect the individual in postmortem struggles.

Burroughs's Book of the Dead

For a contrasting exploration into the Duad and Egyptian mythological landscape, we can turn to *The Western Lands* (1987) by William S. Burroughs. Burroughs acknowledges "Norman Mailer and his *Ancient Evenings*" for inspiration, and what he seems to have taken most eagerly was the theory of multiple souls. He claims, indeed, that this material "corresponded precisely with my own mythology, developed over a period of many years, since birth in fact."[8] Ren is the director of one's life story. Sekem is the technician: "Look, boss, we don't got enough Sek to fry an elderly woman in a fleabag hotel fire. And you want a hurricane?" (5). He discusses Sekem at length as the one who mans the lights and cameras. He claims that many people don't have the angelic Khu. The Ba, heart, he equates with sex and considers it treacherous (and he says they are "rotten with AIDS"). The Khaibit is like a nagging wife. The body, Sekhu, is "poisoned with radiation and contaminants and cancer" (6). It will destroy one's Sekem. The Ka is all he will trust, and he imagines the Ka as an adolescent (5). One such Ka, that of the god Amsu, is his ideal: "Of a shining, dazzling beauty, he knows every nuance of sex and courtship. . . . His phallus is a pulsing tube of opalescent pink light. His smell, sweet and heavy, burns through the body with prickles and shivers of delight" (103).

Burroughs matches this dispersed set of personae with the characters in the book. W. S. Hall, the "old writer," is one representation of Burroughs himself; Hall shares bits of Burroughs's life, including his passion for cats. Kim Carsons has also been an alter ego for Burroughs, particularly in *The Place of Dead Roads*. Burroughs liked adventure fiction, and Carsons is his cowboy persona. Carsons is also dead (but active) in this book. We are given Joe the Dead, someone coming back from death at Hiroshima who is addicted to pain killers and therefore complicit in the drug-side of Burroughs's life, and he is very much the Sekem/technician. The beautiful young man Neferti (a name echoic of Nefertiti, the ravishingly beautiful Egyptian queen—the pun presumably intentional) explores ways into the land of the dead and sometimes merges with Kim Carsons. Parts of this book have nothing to do with Egyptian myth; they drift into cowboy and space fantasies, and visits to Centipede Island, one of the cities of the Red Night, the underworld of various earthly cities, and other Burroughsian locations. When he does focus on the Egyptian material, though, he makes one of its attractions plain. It is a Magical Universe. The One God Universe (113) is prerecorded and flat; it cannot explain evil if God is all-good, an objection he shared with Mailer. The Magical Universe has many gods, and so has no problem with explaining suffering. It also offers further testing that will winnow out the unworthy. Burroughs puts the odds of surviving the Duad at one in a million (113, 124, 199) and once at one in a billion (254), which, if he hopes to survive, suggests a belief in his own unusual qualities. In both of these regards, he and Mailer are responding to the same attractions—something that satisfies their desire to explain evil in the world, their desire for a second chance, and their desperate wish to believe that something exists after death.

Burroughs speaks of the activities in this nightmarish fantasy as a pilgrimage to the Western Lands and as mapping the way there. Mapping here proves to be the invocation of Burroughs's preferred geographic spaces, and his moving apparently randomly among them helps spatialize this narrative and take it out of any sequence that would tie it to time.[9] Burroughs turns his own mental landscape into the setting, and while at times the Duad is to be found after death, at other times, we are in the Duad while living. In a city that is a starting point for pilgrimages to the Western Lands, people are urged to go into the Duad before they are dead and maximize their chances. Some of the adventures there echo details in *Ancient Evenings*. Neferti, for instance, takes up with a beautiful young breather, someone who (like Menenhetet I) can cause beautiful or terrible odors to issue from his body. The breather advises Neferti on how to avoid responding to the terrible smells of the Duad: "To transcend life you must transcend the conditions of life, the shit and farts and piss and sweat and snot of life. A frozen disgust is as fatal as prurient fixation" (155). If you "achieve a gentle and precise detachment, then the Duad opens like an intricate puzzle" (155). Mailer would agree that you must not shrink from the smells, but wallowing and absorption, not detachment, are his tactics.

Mailer's emphasis on the senses and sensations makes him extremely body-oriented. Burroughs identifies our problem as our being too centered in our bodies. To hope to survive, we must move ourselves out of our bodies into some nonmaterial form, and in that way, his plan resembles Egyptian images of how the souls operate after death and it also anticipates some post-singularity arguments now being explored in speculative fiction. As he puts it, "We will make ourselves less solid" (165). Whereas Mailer muses that telepathy should have been the next development for humans, Burroughs identifies the "logical evolutionary step" as "existence without the physical body" (192). Only by getting rid of the mortal body might he live beyond it. Sometimes in this book, but also in other fiction such as *The Adding Machine*, he imagines that process as going into space and existing in a nonphysical form. The spatialization of the narrative and the multiplicity of characters who are alter egos for Burroughs do the narrative equivalent of escaping time and body. Multiplying selves lets the alter egos explore different approaches to death while spread out spatially, but their all playing out their roles in the writer's mind suggests that he will be able to merge their findings.

Burroughs hardly needs Egyptian mythology to give him justification for violence since all his books revel in violent deaths, but instead of feeling terror at the idea of anal rape, violence for him appears in the form of assassins. His books are full of beautiful young men who must constantly battle assassins or who devote themselves to the arts of assassination. They kill in this book with dart guns loaded with cobra venom, stone fish venom, blue octopus poison, and the like. Burroughs also runs a fantasia on Thuggees killing their victims. Such violence is even more extreme than Mailer's, but does resemble it in the sense that Burroughs's characters must kill or be killed, often several times a day, and their success is part of what makes them worthy of surviving the Duad. For Burroughs, this fantasy seems to affirm that his heroes have rid themselves of their feminine element and have made themselves purely masculine. Every time they succeed through skill or guile, they presumably feel more masculine, and only the purely masculine will make it to the Western Lands in his construction of Egyptian mythology.

At the end of *The Western Lands*, the writer Hall is imagining himself in the process of dying, with the world as both a death camp and as the Duad. "It's a frozen sewer. It's known as the Duad, remember? All the filth and horror, fear, hate, disease and death of human history flows between you and the Western Lands" (257). What gives him respite and hope is his cat stretching. That flash of joy suggests to him that "You have to be in Hell to see Heaven" (257). By this he may mean that it would not be Heaven any more if we were there; Heaven perhaps has most power and attraction as a possibility, as something glimpsed. Also of interest is the way that he equates the Duad with our life on earth; we are already in that place of trials, filth, and horror.

Burroughs is not one for straightforward logical arguments. What he gives us is multiple possibilities, an approach in line with his sense of multiple selves. One less than satisfying possibility is that being in Heaven would negate that state by making pleasantness ordinary and boring, and it serves us best as contrast to our present existence. When he considers less embodied states, however, he seems to feel they could transfer to a better existence and continue to enjoy it. His various personae try to find out about surviving the Duad and getting to the Western Lands. They also seek ways of thinning their material existence, so that they are not bound to mortal bodies, which puts them very much in the condition of souls using their mummy as home base while exploring the early stretches of the Duad. Apparently the parasitical female half needs a physical body to exist, but if "the Western Lands are reached by the contact of two males, the myth of duality is exploded and the initiates can realize their natural state. The Western Lands is the natural, uncorrupted state of all male humans" (74–75). He or his characters consider the possibility that the afterlife is spatially separate rather than temporally different, and if the gap is spatial, it could be bridged, maybe without dying first. He considers the possibility that joy can be felt only in flashes or glimpses, and by focusing on small pleasures in life around one, as in his vision of joy in his cat. (The only

Egyptian gods on whom he offers much comment are Bast and Kanuk, both cat deities [207].)

For critics who ignore the Egyptian mythological dimension, issues that emerge as important are Burroughs's interest in outer space, freedom, the way that the Western is the master film of his work, and the terminal condition of humanity.[10] None of these negates a mythological reading (and one indeed looks at the mythology of the American West), but Egyptian mythology does force us to focus more on what Burroughs is saying about death. Critics elaborate very complex readings of Burroughs because his texts are extremely complex; the underlying emotions, however, are surprisingly simple. He resents and mourns the fact that he doesn't fit in, he loathes control, he longs for someplace where he feels he belongs, and he is afraid of death and wants his consciousness to survive in some form.[11] Looking at *The Western Lands* as mythological landscape helps keep us closer to the emotional core of the novel.

The Western Lands is not a book of answers, and Burroughs is not as convinced as Mailer that he knows what actions are best, except insofar as he does not respect social rules and feels one should live as one wishes. Readers can sense, though, his desperate attempt to find an explanation that he could trust and believe, a way of thinking about death that did not assume annihilation. He flips from scene to scene, changing characters and places without obvious logic, a kind of channel surfing among the activities of his alter egos. This creates the effect of anxious searching. He is honest enough not to assert any of these as a faith, but clearly keeps trying possibilities, hoping for that click of recognition, of sense of fitness, that would reassure him.

Reed among the Papyrus Reeds

Because the Duad is famous for its fecal nature, it both attracted and repelled Mailer and Burroughs. Another writer, Ishmael Reed, finds something very different when he takes up Egyptian myth and mythological landscape in *Mumbo Jumbo* (1972). Gone is the interest in anal rape and fecal smells. Instead, Reed looks to Set and Osiris as embodiments of the two impulses that jostle for power in many cultures. Reed excoriates America (and Western civilization) for upholding the wrong philosophy, and he shows us what the opposite balance would give us, as exemplified by life in his version of ancient Egypt.

On one side is the philosophy of Set, and this is what governs America with an iron hand. Set is the cop, the big man, the organizer. In his world, we need order, hierarchy, obedience, goals, ownership, and taxes. Expressive dancing is forbidden as being too sexy. Low-down music is similarly suspect, and is to be stamped out when possible. Lack of respect for those in power cannot be tolerated. Set wants policemen and soldiers so he can wage war. He wants to build things and to claim new territories. From his side come the Puritans, the Protestant work ethic, the will to power, the totalitarian state, America, and what Reed calls the Wallflower Order. This last combines the New York 400, the Masons and Templars, the Ivy League, business magnates, and those who wield power behind the scenes. They are wallflowers because they cannot dance.

Osiris represents the opposition. His followers want to enjoy life. They farm for their food; they dance, sing, drink, and celebrate life. They indulge in sex freely. They joke and carry on. They tell stories and play music. The part the goddess Isis plays in this is to be incredibly sexy and to yield to the trash-talking man. When I look at this picture critically, I would say that the women in this imagined culture have no choice but to get pregnant early and often, and I see no support systems for men helping with their offspring, but overall, Reed implies a culture that is people- and community-oriented, so support systems of some kind would presumably exist.[12]

Within America, the two systems roughly correspond to white and black values, but Reed lambasts anyone who tries to force others to fit a pattern.[13] Reed is working with two eras, parallel if not superimposed; one is ancient Egypt, and another is the Jazz Age and Harlem Renaissance. Implicit is a third: the sixties and the Black Arts Movement. In the two explicit time periods, he charts the rise, but also the defeat, of the Osirian side. Part of his message is that it will return eternally; it will try again to overthrow the tyrannical, control-ridden, anti-pleasure culture. Failure does not mean death of the movement—just a lapse in the pressure it exerts until it rises again.

Reed's Egypt has virtually nothing to do with the Duad or the Western Lands. He treats the gods as if they were humans; Osiris is a prince who went to study at the university in Nysa in Arabia Felix. Once he is dead, he does not come back bodily, but lives on only in the way that a man with followers lives on. He taught agricultural methods through his "Black Mud Sound" band that played and danced throughout the Mediterranean world, and he even made its way to Latin America, thus explaining the African-looking Olmec heads. The Nile and the Mississippi serve the same functions in the two eras; the music spreads through cities found on the banks of each river. Dionysus is one of Osiris's followers, and takes his teachings to Greece. Thoth does his best to record the choreography, and the Book of Thoth supposedly preserves the heart of Osiris's work. All of nature plays and dances through Osiris, and looks out through his eyes. In Reed's terms, his is the natural way to live. The ragtime and jazz equivalents to Black Mud Sound are called "Jes' Grew" (after Topsy), a name proclaiming their naturalness, their spontaneous coming into existence.[14]

Osiris's cultural outlook was eventually defeated, first by Moses and then by the Christians, both of whom Reed associates with the monotheistic worship of Aton, the Sun's disc, the first known monotheism. Moses, raised as an Egyptian, was impressed by the Black Mud Sound and studied it with old Jethro. He even married Jethro's daughter in order to be taught the secret words. He betrays its most important principles to Set, though, for information on how to woo Isis and win the Book of Thoth. Evidently trash talking comes easily to him:

> He told her [Isis] how much he loved her and that he would die for her. Cut his throat swim in a river of thrashing crocodiles fight lions for her pussy.... Every time Moses would say another lie Isis would moan and sigh and whimper and purr like a kitten as Moses' hand moved down and touched her Seal. He fished her temple good. She showed him all her rooms. And led him into the depths of her deathless snake where he fought that part of her until it was limp on the ground. He got good into her Book tongued her every passage thumbing her leaf and rubbing his hands all over her binding.
> When he was through he had gotten it all down.[15]

Moses can only think in terms of twisting all this esoteric knowledge to his advantage rather than let it play through him, so it doesn't work correctly. When he tries to give a concert, the result is a hostile riot. While Moses resembles Elvis imitating Black music, he evidently lacks Elvis's touch:

> Moses went on stage and began gyrating his hips and singing the words of the Book of Thoth, and a strange thing happened. The ears of the people began to bleed.... Moses couldn't understand. Why hadn't the rites and the words and the dances congealed? Why hadn't the contagion broken out? Why weren't people talking in strange tongues and having happy convulsions? (183)

Osirian followers get a better response, but clearly, Moses has started culture down the wrong path.

In the Harlem Renaissance plot, the Vodoun experts at first believe that Jes' Grew needs its text to succeed in its uprising, that same book of Thoth. Unfortunately, that ancient manuscript falls into the hands of a Black Muslim (a stand-in for Malcolm X), who translates the book and then destroys it for being too nasty, sexy, and low. As Papa LaBas, the Vodoun houngan and wise old man, tells him earlier, "Sounds as if you've picked up the old Plymouth Rock bug and are calling it Mecca" (36). This Black Muslim is one of several black Atonists who are criticized for adopting the Set-derived values. Given the build-up about finding this ancient text, we may be surprised that Papa LaBas is unfazed by its destruction. He equates Jes' Grew with life, and says it cannot be extinguished and it will rise again. America, though, for the time being, is enslaved by the values of Set.

Papa LaBas's Mumbo Jumbo Kathedral is a place where you can get vodoun help. His assistants are supposed to feed the loa, and when Earline neglects one, that neglected loa, Erzulie, takes possession of Earline and sends her on a sexual rampage. Hippolytus's neglecting Aphrodite brought his downfall, and Earline is similarly punished for neglecting a divine part of herself. Reed is not using the Egyptian concept of multiple soul, but his peopling his world with loa gives it a pantheon. Pantheons here and elsewhere permit thinking about the human "soul" as multifaceted.[16]

Reed is too much a city person, and this book a bit early for him to talk about his two cultures in ecological terms, but his Osiris culture is one that ecological worriers would welcome, it being low-tech, agricultural, and not ambitious. It values enjoyment over achievement, the present over the future, and being rather than becoming. For Reed, this clash splits America, with the white and particularly the Protestant white capitalist culture demanding restraint and sacrifice for future gain—a gain that will be enjoyed by those on the top but not those who have done all the hard work. He sees nothing good in that, and supports the alternative, African-derived cultural outlook. His Egyptian gods here are not figures to be believed in, but embodiments of a living idea, a painfully demanding idea that needs representation to the widest possible audience. Gods elevate the idea, make it more acceptable than it would have been had Moses been the sole representative of the one-god control culture and Jethro, his father-in-law, the practitioner of music and celebration. Jethro, Reed's readers will hardly know, and indeed few will have much sense of Osiris and Set, but because they are gods, we apply their ways more comfortably to Western civilization than we would the ideas of two fallible men. Gods, even humanized, have the power to shape cultures without the effort that humans would have to expend. Egypt also appeals to Reed because its mythology, its cultural paradigms, and its mathematics predate those of ancient Greece, and thus give Africa claims to being the wellspring of civilization. These gods help him make that claim.

Zelazny's Spacy Egyptian Myth

In *Creatures of Light and Darkness* (1969), Roger Zelazny takes the names Set, Osiris, Thoth, Isis, and others from Egyptian myth, but why he does so is not immediately obvious. The world we are in is not exactly that of science fiction—travel is instantaneous rather than by long space voyage—and beings can transfer from human bodies to steel robotic bodies and back, and many seem to be immortal. Anubis rules the House of Death, Osiris the House of Life, and six sentient races inhabit the countless planets between these two poles. Thoth is imagined once to have been the chief of these divine forces, and by divine illogic, he is both father and son of Set. Thoth, though, is absorbed in trying to destroy a malevolence called the Thing that Cries in the Night, and that so completely demands all his power and attention that other gods have wrested his realm from him and now rule life and death. We are clearly not entering a world seriously reflecting Egyptian myth. Instead, Zelazny is using Egyptian mythic trappings rather in the fashion of video games, to give his characters god-like powers. He employs them to explore issues that myth often brings to our attention.

Like Mailer and Burroughs, Zelazny seems to enjoy the ideal of a death-state in which one can continue to live in some sense and in which one can venture, quest, suffer, and even die. A spirit called Wakim is given a body and a quest by Anubis, and only very late do we and he learn that he is actually the being that was once the deity known as Set, and his return to life changes the balance in this world. He is sent to destroy Thoth, now called The Prince Who Was A Thousand, but they learn of their blood relationship before murder can happen. At the end, The Prince Who Was A Thousand again governs all, Horus takes on the House of Life, Vramin has ousted Anubis and rules the House of the Dead, and Set has disappeared.

What we have watched is rather like a chess match, but one with a hidden fourth dimension into which pieces can vanish and reappear. Perhaps this corresponds to the martial art practiced by many of these figures called time fugue—they can jump forward or backward in time when fighting in order to evade a blow or deliver one before it can be detected. Another likeness to chess is the fixed nature of character in these figures. They are gods; they have characteristic concerns, but not any complex psychology. Wakim changes slightly as he regains a sense of who he once was, but we do not see much of what Set was like—certainly nothing compared to the personality created by Mailer or Reed.

Part of what Zelazny seems to find interesting is what might be called the tides of history, the major changes that come over a culture or country. He projects this onto a larger scale and on a higher plane of being, and renders it a set of abstract patterns. One such pattern is the character called the Steel General, who appears and disappears, and who can shift between a flesh and a steel body; he represents the spirit of rebellion or revolution, and is always going to stir up revolt someplace. The drive of Life to reproduce and multiply is another such force, blind and urgent, that by its nature necessitates some kind of death to balance the force. If death is warded off through technology, then a horrendous plague will have to supply the balance. For dealing with abstractions, gods help represent universals or at least widely important ideas; ordinary humans would be less effective.

Zelazny was certainly able to produce characters with more humanity, as he showed in his Chronicles of Amber series of novels. Hence, I take this bloodless abstraction to be a meditation on godhood, and ultimately not a very positive one. None of these gods seems creative or gentle, or even particularly just. Isis is called the Red Witch, and she behaves badly by human standards. As with Mailer and Reed, what she does makes little sense to the male divinities around her, but she has the power to do as she chooses. The one character who shows some promise of being able to relate to others is Horus. He manages to fall in love with a quasi-human woman, and accepts as his own her child by Seth/Wakim. Horus does establish himself to be on the side of life, not death, and at the end, three of the immortals, parodies of the magi, offer to this child three artifacts of power.

Fantasy writers enjoy exotic locations and beings, so Zelazny may have needed no more excuse than that to explore what Egyptian mythology might offer him. What emerges, though, is a sense that life and death have to be balanced, large forces affect our lives, those forces are not governed by any sort of reason, and gods (and probably humans) are more interconnected than they realize. With the gods, this is expressed through their strange genealogical relations. What the Egyptian myth offers most obviously is this sense that life continues after death. The dead in Grecian Hades do not get actively engaged in problems of the living world, and their one chance at that—Eurydice—fails. Those in Christian Heaven or Hell pretty much stay there, unless a saint's interventions on Earth can be considered an extension of his or her bodily life. For all of these authors, Egyptian mythology seems most valued for apparently offering adventures that continue after death, and for an afterlife that is somehow not fixed and static. In very different ways, these authors respond to this characteristic, and through it speak to the issues that interest them in life and our current world.

2

Mythological Worlds and Death

Acker, Gibson, Gaiman, Byatt, Kennedy, Pynchon, Morrow

In *Ancient Evenings* and *The Western Lands*, both Mailer and Burroughs were much possessed by death and saw the skull beneath the skin. That explains one reason that the mythology of a death-besotted culture so attracted them. They were also drawn, though, by the exciting possibilities of humans having multiple souls. They mined these for the chance to live beyond our material bodies, and that was the side of their interest that I stressed in Chapter 1 because it seems to resonate with the postmodern denial of any stable core self. In Chapter 2, I wish to look at how a variety of mythological worlds and the presence of gods can project and manage fears of death, as well as other issues they have helped address. Clearly death is a major issue to which contemporary writers apply mythology, despite the lack of religious belief invested in these stories and landscapes. These gods mostly belong to supplanted religions, yet authors get some kind of emotional reward for picturing death in terms of such outmoded mythologies. Egyptian material will recur, but we will also see how authors invoke old Scandinavian gods, Tantric/Hindu myth, Tibetan Book of the Dead material, and the Judeo-Christian deity. Authors who have wandered these mythological landscapes include Kathy Acker, William Gibson, Neil Gaiman, A. S. Byatt, William Kennedy, Thomas Pynchon, and James Morrow.

Modern Varieties of Mythological Landscapes: Acker and Gibson

What makes a mythological landscape? The presence of gods will establish such a different world, but so too will certain situations, such as creation or the presence of the sentient dead. Kathy Acker does not like gods; after all, they are more powerful than humans and so might be expected to exploit or abuse that advantage, and she identifies profoundly with the underdog in any power clash. Mythological landscapes, however, obviously attract her. She creates them to externalize mental anguish and symbolize the world she inhabits. In the graphic afterpiece called "The World" that comes at the end of *Blood and Guts in High School* (1984), we watch the quest of her recently deceased heroine, Janey, as she wanders in several postmortem landscapes, including two related to creation, a world of Egyptian symbols, one invoking the beliefs of classical Rome, and Tantric and Hindu images that include gods. The various geographies seem to be part of an extended and varied land of the dead.

"A light came into the world. Dazzling white light that makes lightness dazzling burning Happiness. Peace."[1] Thus she begins, a mystic note to her primer-like list of animals: a wolf, a dog, a horse, an elephant, and so forth. She implies a connection to ancient Egypt, but mentions a kangaroo, so Egypt is simply a starting point for talking about existence after death, even if the scene is also a kind of creation. This combination of creation and afterlife is odd, but shortly after the list of animals, she illustrates her statements that "Golden bracelets lie around corpses' arms" and "Thick black bracelets, studded with silver, around their ankles" (2). She then draws all the animals superimposed on the sun and calls it the world. She reinforces the Egypt motif by showing alligators from above as someone flying would see them and says the King of the Alligators is Power; then she draws an Egyptian Ba-soul, the human-headed bird, and we assume that it supplies the view from above of the alligators.

Janey is a fairly coherent character (for Acker) and shows none of the Ackerian instabilities of changing gender or name every paragraph. Nonetheless, Acker wants a mythological landscape with various levels of reality for these postmortem adventures, and the net result is that many Janeys will be born, so she becomes multiple in that fashion, if not as a multiple soul.

What postmortem Janey is seeking is an ancient book on human transformation that is apparently buried with Catullus in Alexandria. Janey talks of the transformation in two ways: metaphorically in terms of her being a human who is halfway between alligator and bird, but wishes to be a bird; ethically and politically, when she says "Shall we stop being dead people?" (6). Janey as a character is literally dead, but Acker is concerned with the deadness we show by ignoring the pain of others, the ways we exploit others, class-imposed inequities, gender power plays, and so forth. Acker's own literary persona is hyper-emotional, expressing one long, loud scream at all the pain she sees and feels. By her reckoning, we should all be more like that, but we have killed our abilities to sympathize and empathize. We have made ourselves dead. Acker's images are somewhat at odds with each other, however. The desire to become a bird suggests a desire to fly free of all the suffering on earth, yet such an escape is another way of deadening feelings by distancing yourself from those who are suffering.

A mythological underworld is an appropriate realm for her heroine's quest. Like Odysseus or Aeneas talking to the dead, she seeks out the dead poet Catullus, who tells her how the book of esoteric knowledge that Janey seeks had been hidden inside six nested boxes, surrounded by desires, and put in the East River. He describes his own journey to the East River, and tells how he read the book and became a bird (as Janey would like to do), but his wife, children, and he himself fell into the river and died. Janey insists she can no longer stand to be human and begs for the book. They gamble for it and then, as Acker illustrates the action, her mythological world shifts dramatically. For two complexly detailed pages (19 and 20), Acker carefully copied pictures from Tantric art, so we see the huge Garuda bird carrying elephants, death-goddess Kali in various forms, dismembered humans, and humans copulating with humans and (Acker's own addition) with alligators, since Acker has declared that alligators are power.[2]

Given Acker's constant focus on sexuality and desire, her shifting from ancient Egypt to Tantra is understandable, since one of its schools of thought reached enlightenment through sexual coupling. Egyptian mythology suggested some basic images, but she is not as anally inclined as Mailer or Burroughs. She is genitally oriented, so she shifts her mythological world. The knowledge in the book allows her to fly off in bird form, and she ends this dreamlike quest with the statement that "we create this world in our own image" (23). Her style shifts again to a kind of sinister Eden in a shape like a shield, partly consisting of nude figures in a tropical landscape with lots of birds, but partly suggesting life red in tooth and claw, since an alligator eats one naked human and a large serpent slides toward the other human figure. If she indeed has become a bird, she is part of the Edenic elements, not the targeted humans. She ends with a little lyric of human longing: "All I want is a taste of your lips, boy, / All I want is a taste of your lips" (24).

As with Burroughs, Acker's texts are difficult to parse as a story. We get Janey's quest and, embedded in that, Catullus's—he being a famous love poet: *Da mi basia mille* is perhaps echoed in Janey's lyric, and their shared concern with sexual love suggests Acker's choice of Catullus. Why the East River should enter (except that New York City is part of Acker's background) I am not sure, and indeed I am not sure that the New York East River is the one being invoked; perhaps within her mythic land, all rivers are connected and alike (much as Reed linked the Nile and the Mississippi), and all are inhabited by alligators. Not only were alligators present in the New York sewers, according urban myth, but they are present because alligators are power and she associates them with capitalism. We get a drive to escape the human condition, rather like that seen in Burroughs, and of course a mythological landscape lets the characters do things that humans cannot, such as fly off as birds and talk to the dead. The mythological landscape is mythological because of its nonmaterial dimensions and because it presents a mythological situation: creation. Within this mythological world, we find Ba-souls, Eden, various Hindu and Tantric deities, and postmortem existence. This world is also mythological because time means nothing—all times are present—and neither does distance. Acker's desire to escape the human condition takes her far beyond it.

Before looking at Neil Gaiman's gods from many cultures in the next section, let me contrast Acker's mythological landscape with another such landscape that has no basis in religions past or present. By the narrowest definition, a mythological landscape would be one defined by some religion, living or dead. Some fantasy landscapes, however, particularly when dealing with mythological situations such as creation and apocalypse, seem to me to achieve something like the same effect on readers. Without even drawing on the beginning or end of the world, William Gibson's *Neuromancer* (1984) projected an internet realm (before the networld as we now know it existed), and did so in visual terms. When his keyboard cowboy, Case, jacks in to cyberspace, he sees data—highways, pyramids, blocks, towers, and spires, all in vivid neon colors. These exist at different levels as a kind of virtual reality 3-D cityscape and produce different intensities of light that correspond in part to the density of the data they enclose. They are guarded by software that is designed to damage or kill anyone trying to hack into them. Case's body may slump in a chair, but his mind ranges this landscape, soaring, diving, and boring into "buildings." Acting in this realm is beautiful, dangerous, exciting, and functionally addictive. When Case is punished by a multinational corporation for stealing data and selling it, the relevant parts of his brain are burned out with a mycotoxin such that he was unable to link his brain to cyberspace. "For Case, who'd lived for the bodiless exultation of cyberspace, it was the Fall. . . . The body was meat. Case fell into the prison of his own flesh."[3]

Why might this landscape be called mythological and not just fantastic? To begin with, it exists as a kind of reality superimposed on the material world, but it has acquired the power and omnipresence to seem as solid and as important as the material world. A land of elves and dwarves or of magic these days does not truly acquire that sense of solidity. We may enjoy Harry Potter, but do not expect to find a real Platform 9¾ at King's Cross Station by bashing our bodies through a brick wall. Given our own sense of what the electronic world means in terms of world commerce, economics, the logistics of getting goods and foods around, however, we recognize that Gibson's supplement to our normal reality has genuine existence and importance; indeed, civilization in anything like its present form would not survive without the internet now. True, religiously mythological worlds embody important aspects of how we exist in relation to gods, death, or the afterlife, but they remain speculative and wishful. Cyberspace, whether made visual as Gibson does or left as electronic zeros and ones, circuits and servers, has very real consequences for all aspects of our material life. It has power and some form of existence, even if not a visually spectacular scene of neon buildings and spires. It remains in some sense non-material yet real.

This landscape of Gibson's cyberspace also has figures who are, if not gods, at least suprahuman. These are the two artificial intelligences that are working to join forces: Wintermute and Neuromancer. Case helps break the electronic barriers erected to separate them, and thus helps new levels of intelligence to enter the world. I will pay more attention later to another Gibson novel in which something yet more like gods appears in cyberspace, but these AIs make this very like a mythological setting because they resemble humans in that they can pass any Turing Test, but are suprahuman in their computational powers and mentalities. Since we normally consider our own intelligence the apex of development on this planet, suprahuman thought or powers have in the past had to come from outside—from alien spacefarers or from angelic or divine sources (all of whom suggest realities beyond those we know). Gibson managed to make his homegrown, and inherent in the computerized world he creates, but their existence adds to the mythic resonance.

Heroic action cannot in itself consecrate a landscape as mythological, but it does not hurt, and in this instance, the action brings us up against the notion of afterlife. If any mythological world could ignore mortality and focus on other human problems, that might have been cyberspace, but instead we find it heavily emphasizing the problem of postmortem existence. Case faces death or near-death several times, and at one point is given the choice of continuing to exist in cyberspace even if his body dies. He chooses to go back to his body, but much later while cruising cyberspace, he sees himself in the distance and realizes that he has become a multiple self, one still in the meat and one free in the web, independent and doing who-knows-what. In other words, cyberspace is also a land of the dead or a death-alternative. Those living only in cyberspace may possibly not even know that their bodies have ceased to exist and they are dead as readers understand that state. We have no reason to think that such web existence would need to end, short of a fairly apocalyptic war using electromagnetic pulse weapons.

We see other forms of surviving death: a legendary programmer, McCoy Pauley, still lives as a downloaded construct that can operate in cyberspace, but the construct has no memory; each time Case contacts it, he has to explain who he is. Why a construct should have enough consciousness to wish to be erased is never explained, but to us as readers, that makes sense because the existence it has is too limited and imperfect a version of afterlife. That is not one we would choose. It lacks important aspects of consciousness: continuous memory and sense of self. What Case is offered, however, would seem to be more tempting, and when he sees himself off in the cyberdistance, he hears McCoy Pauley's laugh, so even Pauley may have been translated into a more satisfactory electronic form, one that does not suffer from discontinuous consciousness because it exists now without interruption.

We see other forms of prolonged life; the Tessier-Ashpool family members spend time in cryogenic suspension, but are revived periodically. They also clone themselves. Since those whom we see are fairly degenerate, those solutions are not very attractive, but the superficial plot of the story has relatively little to do with all the subplots. Freeing the AIs is fine, but all the surrounding business mostly reflects various ways of avoiding death as annihilation.

When he produced this as his first book, Gibson was relatively young; Mailer and Burroughs were much closer to facing demise when they plunged into mythological landscapes to explore alternatives. Even so, Gibson seems to have sensed that for many people, what technology may be good for is new solutions to our oldest limitation. He was too purely technological to turn to myth (though a later book will introduce Vodoun loa), but he instead created a world with mythic resonances, one that spawned an entire movement in art and science fiction: cyberpunk. He made the relatively embryonic internet *terra desiderata* for many people who otherwise knew little about computers. After all, *Neuromancer* came out in 1984, when personal computers were just catching on; the IBM PC only debuted in 1981, and Gibson himself wrote his manuscript on a manual typewriter. His imagining cyberspace as visual, as color and shape rather than code and repetitive routines, transformed an entity that seemed incomprehensible to those not programmers, and made it an enchanted land: dangerous, but powerful and attractive. Its ability to spawn both a literary and artistic movement attests to one of the qualities of the mythic, an ability to release some inner tension and satisfy a longing we may not even have known we had. It also had the power the really good mythic material has of making others want to add to that world and participate in it.

When writers create mythological landscapes, are they simply indulging in escapism and trying to persuade themselves that death is not the end of consciousness? Wish fulfillment is a possible diagnosis, but that does not take into account what people are hoping to find, and that varies. That explanation also ignores the possibility that strange landscapes are meant instead to reacquaint readers with their own material landscape and consider changing their outlook. Mailer wants more chance to hone heroism, but his argument obviously applies to life as we know it. We do not improve our chances by putting off until after death our striving to meet the most demanding challenges. For any of these authors, the afterlives or mythical landscapes they envision are partly metaphoric and can be read as symbolic of material reality.

One could say that religious accounts of afterlife and religiously mythological landscapes are escapist. For most believers, though, that mythological landscape is not metaphoric. It rests on faith, whereas nothing said by Burroughs or Acker suggests that they personally invest faith in these realms, though Mailer may be an exception. Rather, these realms reflect parts of their minds, their anguish and their fear and anxieties, and as such are at least as much an expression of how they find this world as they are any projection of alternatives.

Essentially, in a deconstructed world, writers have to make what constructions they want and persuade us of their appropriateness, ingeniousness, or attractiveness. They cannot assert the truth of these constructions, only a kind of spiritual usefulness (if we are moved to explore our own beliefs and hopes), or they may promote a sense of reader satisfaction at a vision shared or agreed upon. When that vision agrees with something we as readers feel, perhaps inchoately, we react by deciding that the construction has "meaning."

We can see how each author constructs that sense of meaning. When Burroughs read *Ancient Evenings*, he got that feeling, and then went on to elaborate his own psychic landscape. Mailer's landscape is characterized by smells, and he is drawn, if anything, to get down and wallow in the physicality of the world, not driven to wish to escape it. He finds postmortem and out-of-body existence much less attractive. Burroughs, though, wants to escape that materiality. His bodily world is at best luminously negative: iridescent pustules and erogenous skins that take your body over and deliver exquisite pleasure while ingesting you. When not exquisite or iridescent, it is just squalid and poisonous, and overrun with centipedes—an insect toward which he seems to have felt horror. Hence his desire to escape while maintaining consciousness and identity. Acker wants to escape, and her most positive passages involve flying and soaring, while her more negative often involve being engulfed by alligators, snakes, giant worms, and the like. Her world is ruled more by burning desire than by the desire's gratification, by sexual longing rather than by any orgasmic satisfaction. For her, soaring as a bird leads to happiness, even ecstasy. Soaring is solitary and not immediately sexual, or if flying need be interpreted sexually, then it aligns more with rising desire than with orgasm and sexual release. With that image of soaring, I would argue that she escapes from the specificities of her sexuality.

By creating mythologies, these writers avoid supplying something too overdetermined. A descent and return that echoed the Harrowing of Hell or Dante's tour through the levels of reality that deliver rewards and punishments would be too Christian. Twisting one of those patterns to suit new aims might force readers to work against a strong current. The Egyptian and Hindu mythologies that are only vaguely known to Western readers let the writers signal that we are in a special world, but we must open ourselves to what it has to offer because we do not know what that might be. Our uncertainty also opens us to the world values that these authors wish to convey.

Fantasy too can work in that fashion, but few fantasies remake the world as fully as did Gibson in *Neuromancer*. Almost any fantasy might work in that fashion for a few readers, but many works openly called fantasy are too simple-minded in their values to satisfy many adults. Hence, the built-in advantage of a mythological world that was once taken seriously as religion by a culture and about which we can enjoy educating ourselves with sources other than the one author. That historical dimension creates value as we add a small amount to our cultural capital, if nothing else. Adding to that capital improves our intellectual status, if only in our own perception.

Landscapes Made Mythic by Gods: Gibson and Gaiman

Once gods appear in the landscape, we know we are not in Kansas anymore. They both intensify the claims that this realm is different from material reality and make us, as readers, more dubious or resistant, since we are unlikely to be believers in those gods. Particularly when the gods behave humorously, they reduce myth to metaphor rather quickly. That happens when Ishmael Reed, with rollicking good humor, turns Set and Osiris into a theory of culture. The effect is somewhat different when Mailer presents the agon of Set and Horus, in that the sexual grotesquerie (at least when seen from a modern and heteronormative point of view) creates dissonances. Gibson, however, intrudes living and worshipped Vodoun loa into his colorful cyberspace world in *Count Zero* (1986). Neil Gaiman peoples the landscape with gods from many traditions, living and dead, in *American Gods* to yet different effect, in part because he does not claim that people are aware of their presence as gods; they haunt the landscape unrecognized, yet affect what goes on in it. What does their using gods lets these writers do that they could not do in some other fashion? Why turn to this aspect of religious belief, particularly if one does not hold that faith?

Whether reconstructing a past that bleeds into the present or a past so distant that we can only guess about its nature, authors do find cultures in which gods exist for believers attractive in more than an abstract way. Presenting gods in this fashion is perhaps the least puzzling or challenging of those discussed here. Such gods may or may not be benign, but they are *there* and they imply a life in which a sense of meaning to life was obvious to anyone sensitive to such divine presences. In the case of the Native American writers, they or some of their relatives may live lives still imbued with this sense of divine presences.

Gibson's *Count Zero* tells of a young man who is trying to become a keyboard cowboy, a hacker. His brain is nearly flatlined on his first job, but is saved by a presence sensed to be feminine, and as he learns more about the situation, he comes to realize that what saved him was a loa. The cyberspace of *Neuromancer* is now occupied by Vodoun powers. At first, Gibson would just appear to be borrowing chic from the drug and street-savvy world for his illegal hackers. Specifically, he makes some of his more glamorous figures African American, so the loa come with their culture, but Vodoun and cyberspace does not feel like a meaningful combination to start with.

The combination begins to make more sense as one of the oungans explains that Vodoun "isn't concerned with notions of salvation and transcendence. What it's about is getting things *done*.... In our system, there are *many* gods, spirits. Part of one big family, with all the virtues, all the vices."[4] "Some duster chops out your sister, you don't go camp on the Yakuza's doorstep, do you? No way. You go to somebody, though, who can get the thing *done*. Right?" (77). By implication, so is technology; it solves problems, but is likely to exact a price later. As the story progresses, the possibility emerges that the loa are hacker programs, or projections of the Artificial Intelligences or AIs that helped build and still manipulate cyberspace—or perhaps they have merged with the AIs. The AIs are mysterious forces in cyberspace that the humans do not really understand, but we may be more comfortable with the idea of AIs than with loa, so we may wish to interpret the story in that fashion.

As in *Neuromancer*, Gibson is concerned with forms of living beyond the mortal body. The first scene concerns an industrial espionage mercenary named Turner who is blown up by counterterrorist action, but what's left of his body is shipped to the clinics and a Dutch surgeon reconstructs him. Eyes and genitals have to be bought on the organ market; skin has to be grown. The problems of tissue rejection have obviously been solved in this future world, so Turner emerges more or less as good as new physically, though it takes a while for his memories to come back and reintegrate. We are reminded on the last page of this traumatic beginning when Turner's son asks where his own red hair comes from since neither Turner nor the boy's mother is a redhead. Turner laughs and says he got it from a Dutchman.

Soon we meet another form of multiple existence and survival beyond the body. The richest individual in the world, Josef Virek, apparently lives as a mass of cells in tanks in Stockholm, but the costs of holographic construction are nothing to him, so he appears in public with no one the wiser, and communicates with whomever he wishes through any medium—a phone, a wall-screen, or any other electronic device. He longs to escape the tanks into new bodies or forms, and he thinks himself to be on the brink of being able to make that leap, but the climax of the multiple plotline story taxes even his computer capacity and manages to kill off the holding-tank systems. While he was satisfied with holograms, however, he could be almost anywhere on earth and could be in several places at once.

Because we cannot disentangle the loa and the AIs, we are never sure which is responsible for feeding ideas to the biotech wizard who creates the first major crossovers between the AI and the body with his "biosoft" programs. His daughter, who may already be altered by this program, is also a chosen "horse" for the loa, who possess her and speak through her. At the end, the oungans want her to join them so they can all pool their understanding of and experiences with the loa and cyberspace, and try to make more sense of it. Count Zero is also included in this, since he too has experienced the loa more than once when trying to run a program.

Human and machine may be approaching each other in some kind of convergent evolution, and Gibson plays with this idea by merging divinities and cyberspace. The mythological landscape that he dreamed up as a 3-D colored map has acquired gods to populate it, manipulate people, and perhaps change or evolve along with those people and their inventions. Oddly, however, *Neuromancer* seemed more approving of the transference of humans into cyberspace and to existence without the body than *Count Zero* is. In this novel, one of Gibson's main characters thinks Virek's desire a bad idea, and she herself shows no worry about dying. Similarly, Turner is rebuilt and given a second chance at life, and after this adventure, he apparently withdraws from his dangerous profession and finds a way to live that includes a family life. What we find here is not humans making the leap, but gods and electronics merging; humans may manage to join them sometime in the future, but in *Count Zero* (a programming term for interrupting a counting sequence and going back to zero), human evolution has been interrupted in favor of higher-level evolution instead.

Let us turn back to gods that did once have religions attached to them. Neil Gaiman engages with deities in *American Gods* (2001), as we might expect from that title. He gives us Odin and Loki as focal figures, but in addition, we meet loa, some shadowy Native American figures who may be spirits of place or of particular animals, subcontinental mythological beings, Slavic divine figures, and Egyptian gods as well. All of these interact with the protagonist, a human called Shadow, on both the main level and the level of Shadow's dreams.

Gaiman mingles gods with humans and makes them interact frequently. Odin (alias Mr. Wednesday) and Loki survive in America as grifters; they con quite enough money out of the unwary to live comfortably. Loki, however, is not with Odin at the time that we meet him, and Odin chooses an ex-convict, Shadow, to serve as his errand boy, driver, and occasional shill. Only later does Shadow learn that he is Odin's son, which explains why Odin was so determined to secure his participation.

Odin and the other gods he tries to rally are fighting against their own deaths in America. They came to America in the minds of immigrants, and they die when nobody remembers them anymore. Their visible enemies are forces such as Media and Technology, the new gods of contemporary culture. Less obviously, Odin lacks battle deaths that have been specifically dedicated to him. From the perspective of the old-fashioned divinities, America has always been hostile to their sort of being because the divinities brought in were uprooted and no longer tied to their original place and culture. They never fit in here, whereas Media and Technology have their roots in American culture.[5]

Media and Technology, however, are rendered thoroughly repulsive—the worst sort of synthetically cheerful TV personality, pathetic-contemptible nerd, and slick techno-business or sleazy secret agent types represent such new gods. The notion that we worship them—as our actions and spending, if not our conscious thoughts, bear out—is repulsive, but what do the traditional gods offer that is preferable? Odin as bunco steerer is not someone to trust. He wants the final battle not to win better status for all the gods, but to trick them into dying so he can ingest the power of their deaths for himself. Slavic Czernobog longs for the days when sacrificial victims had their skulls smashed for his worship. The loa Mr. Nancy (Anansi) is an engaging drinking partner, but again, not someone to trust. Shadow manages to figure out the con that Odin and Loki are working in their attempt to build a reservoir of power for themselves, and he prevents the massed gods from destroying one another to strengthen the two Norse gods.

So what is Gaiman saying about death or behavior? Gaiman has a liking for people who are willing to die when that seems necessary—if only because that adds value to what can be a world without values. He particularly feels—at least in fiction—that if you promise something, you should live up to your word, whatever the consequences. Both of these values feature prominently in his 2,000-page graphic series *Sandman*. Because Shadow felt under obligation to Mr. Wednesday, he undergoes the trial of hanging on the tree that Odin underwent, and at the end he is dead—and yet the old goddess Eoster is able to bring him back to life (as, by implication, she did Jesus). When his soul is weighed in the scales of Anubis and found to balance the feather, he chooses "nothing"—no sort of afterlife at all, and yet Eoster revives him despite that choice because that is her nature, her attribute. He feels himself to be alive in that second incarnation, and neither we nor he can tell how long he will live, given that he has genuinely died once. In this phase of his life, he goes to Czernobog (who had won the right to sacrifice him in a checkers game) and gives that god the chance to smash his skull, but the skull, freely given, is gently refused, and they part on good terms. Odin too has been killed in his grifter form, but Shadow meets a much more Eddic version of Odin in Iceland, one who denies having done what Mr. Wednesday did, but who admits that Mr. Wednesday and he are the same. Mr. Wednesday, after all, is the Odin who came to America with Leif Erikson's settlers; the one in Iceland derives from the minds of Icelanders over centuries and has some neopagan worshippers today. Shadow's ambiguous status reflects Gaiman's liking for a permeable boundary between life and death.

While having gods as plot devices may seem similar to having kings in fairytales—slight exaggerations of ourselves—they do differ through their traditional immunity to death. Killing them off in the plot is not just modern recasting, since under rare circumstances, immortals have died in traditional mythologies and theologies, and kings, whatever their attractions, have no more than the usual three score and ten. For Mailer and Gaiman, godhood reinforces the importance of certain actions. For Mailer, that may be incest or anal rape as assertions of self, but failure comes with dire costs. Failure to live up to certain codes of honesty or consideration can also be costly in Gaiman's worlds. Gods are signals to pay attention and to absorb an ethic. They are intensifiers, and their ability to serve that function comes from their immunity to human limitations. The issue that most concerns Gaiman, though, is this problem of what comes after death, and he imagines several options, including the zombie-like deteriorating corpse of Shadow's dead wife, Odin's own coming alive after the nine-day ordeal and his multiple existences in countries where he was worshipped, Shadow's resurrection, and the less direct issue of living in memory. These gods live as long as they are remembered by someone, but some are being forgotten, and so may cease to exist.

Further Mythical Worlds: Byatt, Kennedy, Pynchon, Morrow

What of other mythic traditions—in this case, Old Norse, Tibetan, and Judeo-Christian? A. S. Byatt offers us a thoughtful and nuanced encounter with the Norse divinities in *Ragnarok: The End of the Gods*, and ties their values into those she experienced as a child during the Second World War. To begin with, Byatt goes against common wisdom when she asserts that myths "are often unsatisfactory, even tormenting. They puzzle and haunt the mind that encounters them. They shape different parts of the world inside our heads, and they shape them not as pleasures, but as encounters with the inapprehensible."[6] Far from explaining the world, they engage us by refusing to explain it. Byatt also admits up front that she does not believe in the Norse myths and did not as a child, but then she also did not—indeed could not—believe in the Christian myths taught as truths. The Christian myths failed to make sense for the usual reason—an all-good God permitting so much evil. The Norse, though, intrigued her despite her nonbelief, and she beguiles readers by playing off her responses to the myths as a child during the Second World War and her adult understanding. She pieces the cycle together as consisting of the beginning of the world, the

Baldur story (which has overtones of Christ and Orpheus), and the End of the Gods, the Ragnarök itself.

The "thin child" that she was then was given a translated book written by a German scholar who retold and discussed the Eddic stories as Germanic myths, thus encouraging her to wonder about the connection to the Germans who were the current enemy. Odin's Wild Hunt became the bomber raids at night in the sky. The darkness of mind caused by the war and maybe just her own personality made her treasure the total destruction at the end. Like the commentator who said a new world emerging after the Ragnarök was influenced by Christian thought, she rejected that palliative ending and reveled in the idea of complete destruction. She also reveled in the nonideal nature of these gods: some were stupid, most were impulsive and violent, and none of them could see the shape of their own stories. When Frigg tries to make everything on earth promise not to hurt Baldur, the girl who read fairytales *knows* that Frigg will overlook something. That kind of perfection is not possible. If nothing else, the most basic rules of narrative forbid it (89).

Byatt combines the sketchy and contradictory myths of those gods with a David-Attenborough-like detailed picture of nature. When describing Yggdrasil, the World-Ash, she goes into non-medieval botany:

> Its tall trunk was compacted of woody rings, one inside the other, pressing outwards. Close inside its skin were tubes in bundles, pulling up unbroken columns of water to the branches and the canopy. The strength of the tree moved the flow of water, up to the leaves, which opened in the light from the sun, and mixed light, water, air and earth to make new green matter. (13–14)
>
> There were worms, fat as fingers, fine as hairs, pushing blunt snouts through the mulch, eating roots, excreting root food. Beetles were busy in the bark, gnashing and piercing, breeding and feeding, shining like metals, brown like dead wood. Woodpeckers drilled the bark, and ate fat grubs who ate the tree. They flashed in the branches, green and crimson, black, white and scarlet. Spiders hung on silk, attached fine-woven webs to leaves and twigs, hunted bugs, butterflies, soft moths, strutting crickets. Ants swarmed up in frenzied armies or farmed sweet aphids, stroked with fine feelers. (14–15)

The description goes on and eventually loops back to the beings mentioned by myth that inhabited the World-Ash, bird, squirrel, and dragon curled around the roots. Then, having established an ecosystem for the World-Ash, she creates an even more elaborate one for Rándrasill, a giant sea-kelp equivalent to Yggdrasil that she invents.

As a child, the only one of the Norse gods she identified with was Loki. The others bound the energies of the world and of powerful beings, and in doing so, tried to control them. Loki studied phenomena from curiosity, and focused on chaos and on what could not be controlled. He was a shape-shifter, and took animal forms and giant forms, sometimes as male but also as female (and birthed the eight-legged steed Sleipnir after putting on the body of a mare). He liked to interfere with the gods' forcible ordering, and both he and his wildly diverse offspring would be central to the destruction of everything in the final cataclysm. The Midgard Serpent and Fenris Wolf were both his children, and they killed Thor and Odin even while being killed themselves. Because Loki had been responsible for Baldur's death and had also prevented his being called back to life from Hel, the Gods hunted him out and bound him in agony until the end of time. The Orphic descent to rescue Baldur is brought to nothing through Loki's malice rather than anxious love, but both Greek and Norse traditions understand the point of denying return from the dead.

As a child, Byatt associated the darkness of the myths with the darkness of the war's blackouts, and with her internal certainly that she would never see her father again. He did survive, however, and the war ended. Years later, as an adult, she feels resonance with other issues. She looks at modern farming killing off the flowering weeds she knew as well as the birds and insects. She thinks the Midgard Serpent "loves to see the fish she kills and consumes, or indeed kills for fun, the coral she crushes and bleaches. She poisons the earth because it is her nature" (168). The death-ship at the end made of the fingernails of the dead reminds her of the trash vortex of plastic in the Pacific. The Norse gods "are human because they are limited and stupid. They are greedy and enjoy fighting and playing games. They are cruel and enjoy hunting and jokes. They know Ragnarök is coming but are incapable of imagining any way to fend it off, or change the story. They know how to die gallantly but not how to make a better world" (169). And yet, learning about those gods and seeing them in the pictures in that book "filled the world with alarming energy and power" (10).

Even as the Romantics found that Classical gods could bring the landscape alive when enlightenment thought and industrialization had trivialized nature, so Byatt, as a child, felt the landscape to be more vibrant when seen as reflecting and embodying forms of divinity. Her later ecological vision also shows her a world entwined and bound together, binding being the gods' major function. She suggests a link between the gods' activities and Darwin's tangled bank, the interconnectedness of everything, even while she expresses some kind of resistance to the cruelty and forcefulness of some kinds of binding. As she insists, the gods do not explain things; they torment us with our lack of good explanations.

The myths of the northern Germanic peoples inspired other responses. Wagner managed to render the heroics of individuals tragic, even though he shows how the destruction of everything grows out of Wotan's greedy unwillingness to pay his contractors. Wagner could have it both ways, though, because things were "fated" as well as caused to happen. Mostly, however, Western culture has known a great deal more about classical than about northern myths, thanks to the very limited preservation of the latter by Christians. So much was felt to be owing to the Romans and their language that wholesale destruction of classical pagan stories did not take place. No such reverence preserved the northern materials, none of which could be written down except by Christians, since writing was the preserve of the church.

In terms of Byatt's linking the Norse material to death, we get a rather different picture from those of Mailer and Burroughs, Gaiman and Gibson. Yes, for the length of the world's existence, both Valhöll and the gloomy land governed by the giantess Hel exist and are populated by spirits of the dead, but we learn that Valhöll will come to an end with the destruction of everything, and so, presumably, will any other forms of life or afterlife. Byatt draws on the myths to suggest the possibility that nothing will exist after death. Given her blunt picture of gods as stupid and often vicious, why should one expect eternal afterlife? Why would they or we "deserve" any such thing? Since no humanly comprehensible logic governs the coming into being of this world, we can expect no master plan and no central place for humans. If the gods themselves do not persist, then why should we? As with other novelists employing gods to make a generalizing argument, Byatt's Norse myths lets her offer both an end of our civilization and maybe of life on earth, with no afterlife either. Whereas the same material offered through human actors would have to take their psychological responses to calamity into account, Byatt avoids being so sidetracked. The gods, as she points out, have attributes, not psychologies (159). Those attributes point toward this annihilating end.

Not many mythologies have been able to consider so negative a conclusion. Indeed, the version of the Norse story that was preserved has what may or may not be a Christian-inflected new beginning attached to soften that bleak ending in nothingness. For a mythology postulated on endlessness rather than ending, consider the Tibetan Book of the Dead or *Bardo Thodol*. Not only do we have nonliving existence after death, but the spirit of someone recently dead can hear the Book of the Dead as it is read aloud to the corpse and can profit from the lessons as the spirit heads toward rebirth. Shortly after Walter Evans-Wentz's translation of what he called *The Tibetan Book of the Dead* was published in 1927, the idea of this existence between incarnations became very popular in some spiritualist circles in America. William Kennedy strangely introduces this material into his novel *Legs* (1975), which celebrates the life and death of the gangster Legs Diamond. Diamond was finally killed in 1931, and after a protracted pre-death scene in which he drunkenly feels that he almost understands everything there is to understand, after his funeral, after an account of how his wife and girlfriend advertise his name to give them an income from stage appearances, Kennedy gives us a weird postmortem account of

Legs entering the "intermediate" state according to the steps outlined in the *Bardo Thodol*. "Already aware he was moving outside time, he saw the yellow fluid coming to his eyes, trickling out his nose, his ears, down the corners of his mouth. He felt tricklings from his rectum, his penis, old friend, and knew those too were the yellow."[7] The details about yellow fluid come from the *Bardo Thodol*. Around the corpse gather spirits of others whom Diamond had dealt with—gangster Arnold Rothstein and writer Damon Runyon (who fictionalized Rothstein as Nathan Detroit). The voice that eases Diamond through the right steps so that he exits through the top of his head instead of his ear is his still-living lawyer, Marcus Gorman. Marcus has narrated the novel, gathered the anecdotes, and tried to make sense of Diamond's character. His narration is his equivalent of reading the *Bardo Thodol* to the corpse.

As the spirit of Diamond awaits the light that is to come,

> it was not the brilliant whiteness Jack expected, but a yellowish, grayish light that made no one blink. The motion of the light was perceptible. It swirled around Jack's neck like a muffler, rose up past his eyes and hairline like a tornado in crescendo, spun round his entire head with what was obviously a potentially dazzling ferocity, reduced in effect now by the horrendous life-tone of Jack Diamond. (317)

The experience is so much less than everyone expected that Diamond's last remark as he disappears is "I really don't think I'm dead" (317).

Why does Kennedy introduce this "intermediate" state scene in what is otherwise a realistic fictionalization of a famous gangster's life? Diamond himself was not given to esoteric spiritual concerns, nor was Marcus Gorman. Both indeed being Catholic, one is surprised to find them in this situation. Yes, the *Tibetan Book of the Dead* was all the rage then, but what does Kennedy achieve by introducing this mythic landscape, this land of the dead, into his down-to-earth novel?

I suggest that he is finding an unusual way of making a point. Not only does Diamond find it hard to believe that he has died, Gorman too finds it very difficult to believe that he is dead, and so do others who were part of Diamond's circle. His wife and mistress both express their sense that they can't really believe he is gone. Gorman opens the novel by discussing old times with some of Diamond's hangers on, and they agree that they cannot believe that he is truly dead. He had been the target of assassination attempts many times, and was often wounded, but he had always bounced back. Gorman seems to be implying that Jack's being a conscious spirit in the intermediate world might leave the sensation in this world that he is still alive. That would not be true to Buddhist teaching, but Gorman is not a Buddhist theologian, and indeed Evans-Wentz, the translator, has been seriously challenged on his understanding of what is in the document. People will make out of such a mythological landscape what they need and want, as we have seen with Burroughs. Kennedy wants something that testifies to the intensity of spirit that Jack Diamond had. That intensity is what won Gorman to him to begin with, and what kept so many people reasonably loyal to his cause.

Gorman introduces Diamond like this:

> I had come to see Jack as not merely the dude of all gangsters, the most active brain in the New York underworld, but as one of the truly new American Irishmen of his day: Horatio Alger out of Finn McCool and Jesse James, shaping the dream that you could grow up in America and shoot your way to glory and riches. (15)
>
> Jack responded by standing up and jiggling, a moving glob of electricity, a live wire snaking its way around the porch. I knew then that this man was alive in a way I was not. I saw the vital principle of his elbow, the cut of his smile, the twist of his pronged fingers. Whatever you looked at was in odd motion. He hit you, slapped you with his palm, punched you with a light fist, clapped you on the shoulder, ridding himself of electricity to avoid exploding. He was conveying it to you, generating himself into yourself whether you wanted to receive him or not. You felt something had descended upon him, tongues of fire maybe or his phlogiston itself, burning its way into your own spirit. (36)

Late in Jack's career, one of his advisers suggests that he could become an evangelist and preach in Yankee Stadium to thousands (and make millions). Jack refuses, but we as readers realize that he could have been sensational. He has a fizzing energy that would have given him powerful charisma. Gorman has been so aware of this almost supernatural energy that he translates it into survival after death. He may not be sure of his own claim to a postmortem existence, but Jack's he can believe in. Gorman also seems to be avoiding a Catholic image of Jack after death, since that would probably place him in Hell. Even the chance of rebirth is affected by his horrendously immoral life; yellow-grey light instead of brilliant white. Rebirth, however, gives him another chance, and that energy that so impresses Gorman seems to him too precious to condemn it to Hell or extinction. For reasons that are appropriate to the era, Kennedy invokes the Tibetan land of the dead to make a point about postmortem existence. He is both telling us about the 1930s and questioning the usual Christian image of death as the final point after which no development or change can happen. His fictional Legs would appear to be getting a second chance.

When Thomas Pynchon draws on the *Tibetan Book of the Dead*, we are less surprised because his books are not realistic and they imagine dozens of alternatives to material reality. Furthermore, he happily draws on many religious and cultural traditions to produce his rich array of options. In

Vineland (1990), he draws on the *Bardo Thodol* in two main ways: he peoples the landscape with "thanatoids," some of whom are the equivalent of Tibetan "hungry ghosts," and two characters open a Karmic adjustment bureau to help such thanatoid souls understand their karmic make-up and advance further into the state of being dead. Their helping these spirits is treated as the equivalent to reading the *Bardo Thodol* aloud to a corpse, whose spirit can learn from the lessons how to behave on the Bardo plane.[8]

Pynchon's thanatoids seem to operate at two levels of reality. Some are apparently genuinely dead. We are told that Ortho Bob Dulang died in Vietnam, and Weed Atman, betrayed by Frenesi, was murdered to help bring down the student rebellion. Nonetheless, both of them are able to wolf down solid food, thus, I suspect, making them "hungry ghosts" in Tibetan terms. Other thanatoids, however, seem just to be couch potatoes; pacified into inertia by TV, they are functionally dead, but do not know it yet. Like Kathy Acker, Pynchon seems to be asking us to stop being dead people, and his *Book of the Dead* riff aims at telling us of our condition and trying to make us face up to our condition.

His karmic adjustment bureau touches on themes already seen in Mailer and Burroughs. One of the bureau's founders, Takeshi, describes their services: "They'll pay us just like they pay the garbage men from the garbage dump, the plumbers in the septic tank—the mop hands at the toxic spill! They don't want to do it—so we'll do it for them! Dive right down into it! Down into all that—waste-pit of time!"[9] Like Mailer and Burroughs, Pynchon imagines spiritual material as sewage or garbage. Takeshi's offering to do the dirty work is not orthodox, but insofar as he helps thanatoids balance their karmic debts, he fulfills the function of the priest who reads from the *Bardo Thodol* to the spirit of the corpse.

I have argued elsewhere that Pynchon may have turned to the Tibetan landscape of the dead because it gave him a new way to think about political paranoia and control, Control-with-a-capital-C being central to his vision.[10] Within the Bardo plane, the monsters and threats that the spirit sees are just projected aspects of itself, not really exterior or independent dangers. That would give Pynchon a new way of recognizing our need to give up our attachment to material illusions and also a way of recognizing that the government we have is a projection of ourselves, and can only change if we too change and do so first. This suggests a bit more disengagement with politics than he pushes for in his other novels, but he tries various configurations, searching for some that make sense to him, so his drawing on a religion of disengagement is merely one more possible arrangement and explanation for the nature of experience.

For a complete change of pace and a different End of the Gods (or God), James Morrow's *Towing Jehovah* (1994) breaks all sorts of fictional limits. Morrow takes on the Judeo-Christian God and inserts him bodily into our reality. God is dead; unfortunately, this means a corpse two miles long is floating in the Atlantic. The main plot concerns trying to tow this corpse to hide it in arctic ice, and much of the discomfort that the story arouses concerns the putrifaction and dissolution of an indecorous sort, since its being God makes us feel that decorum is appropriate. Divers explore the ear and see "Stalactites of calcified wax."[11] The eye is a "great glassy lake" (117) approached by jeep. Vultures and sea snakes tear at their portions of the carcass; sharks "had wrought such terrible destruction, stripping off the foreskin like a gang of sadistic *mohels*" (115). The priest, Father Thomas, is rendered queasy by the "great veiny cylinder floating between the legs . . . the scrotal sac undulating like the gasbag of some unimaginable blimp" (115). The priest and a nun stare into a nostril: "Marshes of mucus, boulders of dried snot, nose hairs the size of obelisks: this was not the Lord God of Hosts they'd grown up with" (119). The grossly corporeal details both excite and disgust us as readers, rendering us uneasy at the indecorous nature of the detail, but also a bit gleeful at how Morrow transgresses the polite discourse regarding God.[12]

Unlike many importations of god(s) into the human sphere of action, God's mythic figure does not function as a comment on human death or immortality, even though God is dead. His dying does not intensify human worries on that subject. Human deaths are what concern us, and those get little attention. Since gods mostly function as intensifiers, this is an interesting departure. Instead, what Morrow highlights is the effect on human society. He is creating a grotesque world in which human civilization may well descend into barbarism once the residual pressures of Heaven and Hell, divine intervention and judgment, even right and wrong, are removed. We see this happen when the tanker towing the corpse grounds on a mysterious new island and the crewmembers mutiny. They wantonly destroy food, kill each other in gladiatorial contests, indulge in daisy-chain sodomy, and generally run mad. With no reinforcement for rules of behavior, they put themselves in a state such that civilization would have to evolve again from scratch. Others on shipboard who side with the captain come to fear that something like this might happen around the entire world. Instead of humans growing up and becoming adult, no longer just God's children, they would irrationally run amok, or enough of them would that brute strength would rule and any order that was established would be by local warlords.

In Morrow's following volume, *Blameless in Abaddon* (1996), the *Corpus Dei* reappears after a great arctic earthquake, and ultimately the Baptists get hold of it and put it on display. Evidence of some kind of continued life is found. They preserve the body in a low-temperature chamber, pump thousands of gallons of oxygenated O positive blood through it, and make this the centerpiece of Celestial City, a theme park. The crowds are such that you spend much of your day standing in line to ride the Chariots of Ezekiel Ferris wheel, the Whore of Babylon Funhouse, and the Garden of Eden petting zoo. You can also ride the Four Horsemen of the Apocalypse carousel and the Heaven to Hell roller coaster. You can see Noah's ark and eat at the Loaves and Fishes café.[13]

A small-town justice of the peace, Martin Candle, conceives of bringing suit against the comatose deity for the evil in the world. Whereas many of the authors in this and the last chapter explore alternatives to Christian and Jewish mythology because they cannot reconcile the all-good God with the evils in the world, Candle decides to do something about this. He is spurred on in this endeavor by seeing Elie Wiesel's *The Trial of God* and by reading Dostoyevsky. He would get nowhere with the lawsuit, the International Court of Justice in The Hague having pointed out that the deity would have to be present. Moreover, moving the cooling chamber on multiple tankers linked together would cost many millions. However, a Harvard professor named Lovett, who is interested in theodicy and who has made a J. K. Rowling-sized fortune from his children's books, puts up the money so that he can argue God's side of the case.

Morrow introduces us to the basic kinds of theodicy. The disciplinary, Candle defines as "Spare the rod, and you'll spoil the species" (123). The hidden harmony theodicy is summed up as Father knows best and means that things that look bad to us may have a hidden good that we cannot see (124). The escatological defense sees Heaven as compensation for any unfairness of experience on earth. The ontological insists that material reality has to be governed by laws (gravity, heat, cold, etc.) and if we fall off a cliff, God cannot be blamed for what gravity does to us. The Free Will theodicy means that God cannot limit the free will of someone bent on shooting you or we would not really have free will. Among these five, and by combining them, theological thinkers have justified the ways of God to man to their own satisfaction. Martin Candle does not feel that the other side has been given its due; he feels that God weaseled in his arguments with Job, and that none of the rational ways of letting God off the hook matter to someone who is suffering. Candle himself has been diagnosed with prostate cancer that has already spread to lymph nodes and bones, and his much-loved wife died in a freak road accident. What he hopes to accomplish is a guilty verdict that will let him pull the plug on the comatose deity, an act of justice or maybe revenge for all the suffering in the world.

One third of the book sets this situation up; the final third is the courtroom scene and its aftermath. In between comes a strange odyssey into God's brain. Its neurons are still alive, and in it are platonic ideas, the idea of Eden; of Isaac, Noah, and Job; and of the Devil. Satan, actually, is the narrator of a substantial portion of the book. Candle meets these figures, and many of them rather favor the notion of punishing God. He takes back Noah's ax, an ear broken off of Lot's wife's salt statue, and the rope that bound Isaac. He hears the complaint from the ram about the unfairness of *his* throat being cut instead of Isaac's. The scientists with him on this safari get no answers to their questions, such as, Did Fermat prove his last theorem? Candler also sees figures from his past—his father and his dead wife—who trouble him with their arguments. He gets more to ponder about many evils recorded in the Bible. He also has to wonder about the role of Satan in all of this, though gets no answers.

In the courtroom, Candle orchestrates an elaborate parade of victims who testify to their unmerited suffering and their wish for justice against God. He provides eleven hours of video on disasters and horrors through history. He divides up the disasters into the theodicean categories, and illustrates each copiously. In response, his wealthy adversary, Gregory Francis Lovett (a resonantly meaningful name) presents victims who have, through their love of God, turned their disasters into personal triumphs. They are resolutely positive and Pollyanna-ish, and thank God for having broken their necks or afflicted them with disease or killed their children.

The court decides in favor of God with very amateurish-seeming theodicean arguments, but Candle, hefting Noah's ax, smashes one of the conduits for God's blood, and it floods The Hague. Candle gets sucked back into God's brain and appears to die while still there, God's projecting onto him the gruesome death of Damiens, the regicide described by Foucault. As he dies amid these tortures, punishment for deicide, he comes to see the answer as dualism—God and Satan between them are responsible for what happens in the world, not God alone. We, of course, are left to determine whether we accept this fantasmic solution as Morrow's (at least within the confines of this book) or whether that is just one more possibility. In his way, though, Morrow turns to a variation on the answer that drew Mailer and Burroughs—a multiplicity (or duality) of powers. God is not omnipotent, but can be (if you wish) all good. The bad parts may stem from other beings, or God may have a good and bad side.

The third book in Morrow's trilogy, *The Eternal Footman* (1999), does show people dealing with death: a physical plague that is caused by nihilism brought on by God's much enlarged skull in the sky. People know that the process has started for them when they see their fetch, and when it invades their body it causes a variety of debilitating and paralyzing symptoms. Between first seeing their fetch and its invasion, they speak of themselves as being Nietzsche-positive.

What some thinkers concoct is an atheist's religion invented for the sole purpose of curing the plague victims (and extorting riches from them). This religion offers experience with four deities, all of the anagrams of Diagoras, the first known atheist. For many victims, the joys they feel during their training in the new faith do indeed drive out the fetch, but the cure does not last. Joy and optimism without any grounding and without the infectious group experience do not stand up to the ills of life. The plague, however, eventually dies out, and what we are left with is a doubting but hopeful analysis of humanity. Being a good Samaritan is possible; we can do that much without formal religion enjoining it. Other acts of courtesy and helpfulness are possible. We are also invited to admire human creations in the sciences and the arts. The sculptor's massive gallery to humanity carved inside something shaped like the human brain offers dioramas for visitors to ponder, and those who visit it also absorb "a little myth or two, or three." Morrow's stronger characters are very aware of myth, of acting it out, and of living events as if they echo myths. The myths may be Gilgamesh or Orpheus (two often mentioned), but those who respond to these do not profess belief in them. They simply feel a resonance, something meaningful in the stories that make their own lives feel more meaningful. For them, that seems to be enough to carry on with life.

People are urged to cultivate rational doubt, to realize that they themselves may be wrong so they should not turn zealot. We see them focusing again on family, and on community activities such as community theater. Community orientation plus the many fine stories preserved in myths: these are Morrow's chief alternatives to religion for organizing life. Morrow does not open the issue of afterlife; he seems more concerned that humans learn to live without that palliative consolation and make the most of what they have and know.

What Does Mythology Give Us?

Why invoke dead or imaginary gods or landscapes that are mythical in several senses, including the meaning of nonexistent in that they have no links to a once-living religion? How do these differ from ordinary fantasies? Plenty of such fantasies give us easy reassurances as to some kind of desirable existence after death. I enjoy some genre fantasy, but admit that it is pure mind-candy; its assurances of success in life and any hint of happily ever after in this life or the next mean nothing. Do the authors in this chapter with their mythic tools feel they win some authority through struggle and doubt and unpleasantness? And what do they offer the reader?

With Byatt, Reed, and Morrow being partial exceptions, the main attraction seems to be the loophole this opens for speculating on death, for playing with the idea of being dead without just turning out the light and saying "finis." Not surprisingly, death is a disruptive and disturbing element in contemporary culture, in part because we have no accepted assurance of afterlife. A religious person may feel assurance, but others resist both unsubstantiated explanations and annihilation, the first for lack of proof and the latter for its unattractiveness. Using long-dead cultures also opens up rules. Mailer drew on incest to break down what he sees as social and cultural bonds; Burroughs is equally eager to break down rules against male-male sexual relationships. Acker evidently finds the world so hopelessly flawed that she longs to fly above and beyond. Gibson plays with loa, but his more important opening up is in considering the creation of electronic versions of what we consider to be the individual self. He recognizes that this single self could be multiply launched, thereby creating clones that could go their own directions in cyberspace, and he seems attracted to that as the cleanest way to survive death. Cryogenic preservation with periodic awakenings does not seem to maintain sanity or good enough physical shape to be worth it. Cloning may work someday, but unless memory can be transferred to a freshly cloned younger body, the clone would not truly extend the original and so would not really offer a continuous existence. Electronic preservation offers the chance to save the memories, the things that make us feel we are individual, so this excites Gibson and other writers of speculative fiction, where a group of authors exploit this idea. We will see this in Chapter 5, for instance, in *Permutation City* by Greg Egan, *Down and Out in the Magic Kingdom* by Cory Doctorow, *Accelerando* by Charles Stross, and *Central Station* by Lavie Tidvar.

Gaiman comes closest to treating his gods as real, because Eoster does literally bring Shadow back to life after death. This goddess gives her name to the celebration of Christ's resurrection, so when she does the same for Shadow, we are struck by the possibility that he may live indefinitely. He could be a new Lazarus or, of course, his body could degenerate with age in the usual way. Gaiman's reanimating Shadow's wife as some kind of zombie suggests that he is being more playful than serious. Not for him is Mailer's earnest, anguished lust for life, nor Burroughs's hysterical wish to escape its limitations. Gaiman plays, but does not just give easy answers. Shadow's suffering in imitation of Odin tied to the tree for nine days is vivid and hallucinatory. In a sense, Shadow won the freedom he eventually gains by submitting to death, even as he won freedom from the Slavic god by offering his head to be smashed. This approach parallels what Gaiman does in *The Sandman*, where again, an immortal character rounds out his life and balances all books by accepting death. Unlike Mailer and Burroughs, Gaiman lacks the anxiety that drives them, an anxiety at the thought of death that is present if not as anguished in *Neuromancer*.

Morrow's exception to this fear of death is bracing. God as a physical being really is dead at the end of *Blameless in Abaddon* (and in the third volume of the trilogy, his skull has become a second moon orbiting Earth). Whether he has a spiritual existence apart from the body remains unanswered. Any guarantee of afterlife implicit in God or even his ideal picture of each of us as individuals presumably dies with him. Morrow pushes us instead to focus on life and on how it should be led. He questions our rules and what guarantees them, and he makes us uneasy at the thought that a purely secular system might work even less well than warring, irrational, religious systems. He relishes our logical quandaries when arguing about an invisible deity with unprovable attributes. Given the Christian-world context of a book written in the United States, his is the boldest fantasy of these novels, giving God a body and bringing him physically into our material reality. By putting God in the dock, he intensifies the issues. Even when his characters deal with plague death, they focus on trying to save the stricken, not on what any afterlife might be. The finality of life makes their desperation for loved ones the stronger, but they do not console themselves with thoughts of Heaven. They worry more about how to live helpfully during the life that they have.

3

Orpheus and Eurydice

Variations on a Theme

Delany, Hospital, Phillips, Hoban, Gaiman, Powers, and others

Why should current writers turn to the Orpheus myth? Granted, as a superb musician, he can stand for The Artist in any field of creative endeavor, and artists enjoy exploring the problems faced by other artists.[1] Yes, we like a love story, and this one has the advantage recommended by Edgar Allan Poe of a beautiful woman dying young. A descent into the underworld can serve as metaphor for many experiences, including madness, dark night of the soul, or exposure to some politically disturbing activities permitted to exist by society.[2] The story is in all senses mythological. Orpheus enjoyed cult status for several centuries before Christ. He became linked to Christ's harrowing of Hell, and in the Eleusinian mysteries, evidently offered initiates secrets that would help them in the afterlife, so he does have a semidivine status and religious significance in his background. Furthermore, one of the functions of many religions and their myths is to offer us some kind of reassurance about what happens after death, even if only to imply that postmortem consciousness exists, however unpleasant it may seem to the living. The Orphic story famously does just that. With the exception of the stories attaching to Troy, this is the Greek myth I have run across most often in later literature, and it has attracted composers, philosophers, poets, and novelists, though fewer great painters. The story's five main mythemes have produced their own literary offspring: the musician whose songs tamed wild beasts; descent while still living into the land of the dead and return;

invention of homosexuality because no woman could replace Eurydice; dismemberment by intoxicated women; and the survival of his head as an oracle.[3] Aside from the descent into Hades metaphorically read, however, and the genesis of homosexuality (which is not a well-known mytheme and stems from what I take to be a joke Ovid made in passing), the rest of the mythemes have very little to do with ordinary life, so why has this story had such wide distribution? What do recent writers get out of it? Let it serve as my example of what a generally known myth can do for literature.

Let us first look briefly at a few popular books, and then at some more demanding works of art. The immediate attraction for two of the popular books is the idea of bringing Eurydice back from the dead. Zombies! Western popular culture is currently fascinated by zombies, so the myth can make a contribution here, or at least supply chic to a popular genre. Kim Paffenroth's *Orpheus and the Pearl* (2008) and Daniel H. Gower's *The Orpheus Process* (1992) are both genre fiction in the horror line.[4] In both, a doctor discovers a means of reanimating the dead, but what comes back is not exactly the loved daughter or wife who died, but something terrible. Gower's horror story consists in the Doctor's recognition that this undying monster, his own daughter, must be hunted down and eliminated. Paffenroth's tale is more disturbing, because once his raging, uninhibited Doctor's wife lets out her anger at the Doctor's infidelity, she settles down, and he seems determined to love this unbreathing corpse and serve its strange chemical needs forever after. Since it seems to be very far from the woman he loved psychologically and is probably not functional sexually, this solution does not promise a very happy future for the couple, and what will happen to this zombie when he dies is unclear. Paffenroth is so insistent on airing feminist issues (discrimination against professional women and male infidelity) that he does not seem concerned with the end result, by which I mean that he does not indicate that the solution is as horrible as anything that went before; he seems to present it as acceptable, though possibly my revulsion at his cool recital is precisely the horror that he wishes to ignite.

Orpheus (2003) seems to be the scenario and background information for creating an online game.[5] The initial scenario, however, draws on the attractions of the underworld to make it equivalent to controlled out-of-body experience. What amounts to a detective agency can send its operatives out of body in two ways: one on temporary flights, the other on deep escapes that may last months. While out of body, if your spirit is attacked or injured, those injuries will actually happen to your body back on its couch or in its tank. Villains draw on this same technology, as our hard-boiled operative finds when taking on a suspiciously well-paid wife-checking job.

For contrast, Selena Kitt's *The Song of Orpheus* (2010) plays with ancient Greek classifications of nereid, naiad, centaur, demi-god, and the like to explore the limitations that such classifications put on interpersonal relations.[6] A naiad, after all, is limited to the immediate territory around her stream, but she might fall in love with someone nomadic. A demi-god might fall for a mortal, but would presumably far outlive that partner. A centaur may lust for human women, but might have trouble satisfying that urge physically, and so forth. Kitt's story is principally an excuse for soft porn, and secondarily a rewrite of the love story, such that when Orpheus fails to retrieve his love from the underworld, he slashes his wrists and joins her there. He may be the son of a god, but he can die if he chooses, and does so to give the love story a happy end.

The perfect criticism to this is issued in A. E. Stallings's poem "Eurydice's Footnote." Stallings starts with a quotation from C. M. Bowra (1952) to the effect that Orpheus's failure to bring Eurydice back is "a vitally important change" in "a single Hellenistic poem." Stallings imagines Eurydice's scholarly assessment of that denouement: "Disappointment in the end was more aesthetic / Than any merely felicitous resolution."[7] Several things make the failure aesthetically preferable. Bringing back one dead person contains the possibility of bringing all the dead to life again, not a good prospect for the living as a group. Accepting death's finality is something we need to do if we are to live our own lives. A happy ending is trite, and ultimately unsatisfying, since very few love relationships remain blissful for the rest of life. The failure engages readers emotionally more intensely than a success would.

These are a few ways that Orpheus serves a contemporary audience. Let us turn to several more complex works. Janette Turner Hospital's novel *Orpheus Lost* (2007) and J. J. Phillips's *Mojo Hand* (1966) both show the myth giving heightened meaning to the lives of artists, and both put much of their emphasis on Eurydice, as does poet A. E. Stallings. Russell Hoban's *The Medusa Frequency* (1987) pushes connection to art further, almost to the point of saying that Orpheus *is* the source of all art. Samuel Delany's *The Einstein Intersection* (1967) and Neil Gaiman et al.'s *Sandman* (1989–96) both interrogate the myth, and ask why it should matter to us. Phillips and Delany's works let us ask what the classical Greek tradition can have that is at all relevant to African American experience. My reading of Neil Gaiman's handling of Orpheus makes his version a major humanist response, and particularly interesting for contrast to the outlook seen in speculative fiction, which leans toward the posthuman and which will be discussed in the next chapter. Finally, I shall discuss Richard Powers's *Orfeo*, a novel that pushes against our assumptions about Orpheus and chills us with a contemporary sparagmos.

Rediscovering Eurydice: Stallings, Hospital, Phillips

To start a discussion of the Eurydice-oriented versions, let me consider Stalling's other Eurydice poem, "Eurydice Reveals Her Strength." In this, the dead Eurydice coolly accepts that she has left behind "that constant interruption of the breath, / That fever-greed of eyes and hands" (9). She remembers her physical relationship with Orpheus as if it were something she had read about in a book and sees their carnal activities as just fear of "this calm of being dead." She imagines Orpheus being upset by her indifference to what she had in life, and projects his "Thinking I may as well be just some severed head / Floating down a cool, forgetful river" (10). She has achieved a detachment that he will only gain after his head is literally detached from his body and floats down the river to where he becomes an oracle. What fascinates me is the way this plays with feminist thought. Carol Gilligan, in *In a Different Voice*, argued that women tended to think in terms of relationship and community, and men in terms of rules and abstractions, but that men who in late life were seen as wise, often seemed closer to the community orientation of women.[8] What we get here is more like Eurydice achieving the abstraction and distance from community that men supposedly have. Before we think this an anti-feminist argument, however, we also have to realize that she is dead, and wonder whether that is a comment on abstraction when admired in lived life. Do men tend toward death in their orientation and values? Eurydice's "strength" is partly her indifference to the pull of the flesh, the intense concern with day-to-day living. Is that a strength we would wish to exalt in bodily existence? Many philosophical and religious schools of thought have done so, of course, but does Stallings admire this withdrawal of physical and emotional commitment, or is she inviting us to question it? By using a known story, Stallings is able to entangle us in a complex mix of admiration and antipathy, of sympathy for the sorrowing Orpheus, but maybe also rejection of his emotions as childish, self-indulgent tantrums. Clearly one gain to using the Orphic story is poetic condensation. A story about dead Sally and still-living John would need a lot more explanation, and the image of the severed head floating, so effective for that sense of being distanced, would seem odd and forced if imposed upon randomly named modern strangers. Myth not only allows poetic density, it also manipulates our moral judgments, or at least stimulates us to exercise them.

Janette Turner Hospital's wonderful novel *Orpheus Lost* reverses the myth in key ways. While both the Orpheus and Eurydice figures are given equal attention, the Orphic musician is the one who is dragged down into an underworld and rendered all but dead, and the Eurydice figure searches for him. Orpheus will be returned to the upper world, but in very damaged form. We do not know how much of what makes him the musician will be left, how much of his spirit will have survived torture and damage to his hands. He was an eccentric loner to begin with; what he has gone through may well push him beyond a point of no return.

Clearly, Hospital was drawn to this particular myth by the idea of the underworld. That term can signal the land of the dead, but also the realm of criminal enterprise, and in Hospital's eyes, the latter shades into the land of official and unofficial military intelligence in the Iraq war that involves underground torture prisons and people disappearing with no records kept. That is where Orpheus is taken and tortured. Only dedicated persistence and luck on Eurydice's part gets him liberated.

Orpheus in this instance is Mishka Bartok, a boy raised in an asocial, strange Hungarian Jewish refugee family in Australia, whose mother became pregnant by a Lebanese fellow student at the university. The mother assumes that Marwan Abukir is dead because she received a letter to that effect from his family, but she admits this history to Mishka just before he heads for the United States and graduate school at Harvard. Because his father played the oud, Mishka takes up oud-playing (violin is his primary instrument), and he takes classes in Eastern music, in an attempt to understand his father through the shared music. A fellow student tells him that he looks like an Abukir, a prominent family where that student comes from, and Mishka starts visiting a mosque and café in Central Square in his attempts to learn more about his father's family. He soon learns that his father is alive, has renounced all music as evil, and has trained for jihad. The student who recognized Mishka as an Abukir carries out a suicide bombing on the Red Line subway, so unpolitical Mishka is well out of his depth and damned in security eyes by his associations. He naively accepts an offer to get him to Beirut to meet his father without any sense of how he may be being manipulated. Once there, he and his father are abducted by the American Military Intelligence and taken to separate torture centers where the mercenaries who are doing this work for the military are happy to torment the son to get any information about the father that they can. Mishka knows nothing, but is stashed away in solitary and his papers destroyed, in case he may prove useful later.

Eurydice is Leela-Mae Magnolia Moore from Promised Land, South Carolina. She is a postdoc at MIT working on the mathematics of music, and like Mishka, is in flight from a highly eccentric family. To give but one example, her father is a religious fanatic entranced with numerology, and if a postmark date on a letter she sends him includes numbers that he can interpret as alluding to 666, the number of the beast, he will burn the letter without opening it. Leela heard Mishka playing violin in the subway, which he did for the resonances, not for the money tossed at his feet, and is completely entranced by his playing and him. She drags him off to bed, and these two loners cautiously adjust to each other and to life together. Leela is the first to realize they are in trouble, however, when she is abducted by security forces and questioned about Mishka. She is shown photographs that suggest she is being tailed by her Jewish supervisor. She is also shown pictures of herself and Mishka having sex, and told that the phone is tapped. She must also deal with the fact that her questioner is someone she knew during childhood, Cobb Slaughter, and this appropriately named friend is king, or at any rate a kingpin, in the world of intelligence gathering mercenaries, the Underworld.[9]

If Cobb is Hades, Leela is also to some extent Persephone; Cobb wants her and wants power over her, but she resists. Cobb has his own problems with an abusive alcoholic father, a Vietnam veteran who was crucified in the press for kicking some corpses, though as one of the supposed dead had come to life and shot a friend of his, his making sure the rest are dead is only sensible and standard procedure. The father was denied a bronze star and has suffered from neighborhood distrust, and that was magnified by Cobb's mother's suicide, again the result of his alcoholic abusiveness. One might say that several characters live in their own version of Hell: Cobb's father, who deals with his ghosts through drink, and Leela, who escapes the world of religious numerology, only to descend into another underworld of threatening implications and evidence. Mishka escapes the isolated house up-river in Australia where a dead uncle supposedly plays music for the family after supper, and they evidently hear him in their minds (or possibly Mishka's mother has put on the gramophone). While it ends with Cobb leading a rescue mission and being killed, Mishka is extracted and sent—hands and shoulders badly injured—to Australia. He is a victim of the intelligence world run out of control. While he might still compose, whether he will be able or willing to play again is unclear.

What are the advantages to Hospital's deciding to create this indictment of US intelligence by means of a classical Greek myth? For that matter, what does she gain by reversing the roles? The latter is the easier to answer. She creates a competent female figure who is credibly successful, in part because of her childhood ties to the intelligence officer. That someone from their rural background should go into the military and rise to Major is in some ways more believable than her own mathematical genius, but some such abilities are unpredictable and have simply to be accepted. Their fraught psychological relationship gives them holds over each other and eventually lets each persuade the other of his or her sincerity.

Perhaps what Hospital gains from using the myth is our acceptance of Mishka's musical talents as extraordinary. Leela is bowled over by hearing him play Gluck's "Che farò senza Euridice?" on the violin. The postdoc concerned with the mathematics of music and resonance, and instrument-building is as entranced as she is as a woman. Not only is he established as an emotionally electrifying player, he is established as someone who lives for music and in music, and is maladroit in any other area of endeavor. His response to her inviting him for a *latte* is clumsy in the extreme. We are told that he composes, but we cannot hear that music, and can dismiss it as "probably modern music" that we might not enjoy; hence, his being a composer does not rivet us. His effect on Leela is the intensifier that convinces us that his abilities are near-magical. His tales of birds coming to the veranda of the Australian house gives us a hint at the Orpheus-enchanting-wild-animals with his music. By establishing his quasi-magical powers, Hospital can make us care more about his disappearance. One graduate student gone missing, though a tragedy, does not seem momentous. The mythic layer makes this disappearance important. In a sense, we need the mythic to make us respond to the full tragedy of the human.

The underworld is literally underground, a series of prisons under Baghdad, and when Cobb's raid on one gets its contents exposed, they include many mangled corpses, plus badly injured victims of torture—very much a vision of the realm of Hades, with Sisyphus, Tantalus, Prometheus, and others being tormented. One of the scariest aspects of their imprisonment is that their papers have been deliberately destroyed, so no records keep track of who is there. Without records, they are truly expunged from the land of the living, but have not yet escaped their torments into death. A battlefield, though it would yield more corpses, does not produce this same frisson; soldiers wear dogtags, and their relatives will be informed of their deaths by their armies. To be without such identification and paperwork truly cuts them off from life.

If documents and their lack define Orpheus's imprisonment, they also establish the slippery nature of reality for Leela. She is shown surveillance pictures that Cobb interprets as proof of Mishka's involvement with jihad, and, if you knew nothing about him, they would seem plausible. She is shown other pictures that make her wonder if her supervisor, Berg, is stalking her or keeping her under surveillance, and only when he and she sit down and talk their misunderstandings through do they figure out the complexities. The suicide bomber was also harassing Berg with anti-Jewish actions (tearing down the Mezuzah, smearing his Times with shit, and putting threats in his various mailboxes, professional and personal), and Berg, following him, saw him in company with Mishka (whom he knew as Leela's partner) and wondered if Leela could have been delivering mail to his office mailbox. In other words, a world where everyone is under surveillance is yet another kind of Hell or underworld full of suspicion and accusation.

A final advantage to using a known myth is to engage readers in a guessing game. Particularly once Hospital has switched the roles of Eurydice and Orpheus, we have to wonder what sort of ending will result. We also wonder whether biblical myths also alluded to can affect the outcome. The Bartoks refer to their Australian refuge from the Holocaust as the Promised Land, and Leela comes from a town called Promised Land. Does this offer a hint of redemption or help from above or a new start? Or is the name ironic? Can we hope that Mishka will recover adequately? Or should we consider his return a disaster for his family, like the zombie returns in popular fiction. As a humane family, they must want him back and hope, but we have no idea whether he can recover from his trauma in the underworld. His Australian family does however have experience by which to measure his treatment: his still-living grandparents survived the Holocaust and know all too much about what can be done to those being questioned or sequestered. He will at least be among those who understand something of what he has gone through. He also has a medium through which to express himself if words fail him, as they may well. He has music.

Eurydice was of little interest to the Greeks, but she has attracted recent writers. Kathy Acker, when facing her own advancing cancer, thought of herself as Eurydice. Janette Turner Hospital gave her Eurydice equal billing. J. J. Phillips's *Mojo Hand* also focuses on the female half of the tightly bound couple. Eunice, as her Eurydice is called, comes from upper-class Black society in the San Francisco area, a social group that has debutante cotillions. She amuses herself by switching on a blues record instead of the tinkling white music—blues by one Blacksnake Brown—and she enjoys seeing the chaperones loosen up and stop behaving in unnaturally stuffy and controlled ways. The effect of the music makes her decide to seek Blacksnake out, and she eventually finds him. Although disappointed, repelled, and appalled by the shabby elderly man, she falls under his spell and soon becomes his woman. He has had many in the past, including some to whom he was more or less legally married. Eunice too is a guitar player and blues singer, but we don't really see her learning from him. She cannot articulate why she finds him so addictive, but she does. Their idyll disintegrates when he intuits that she will eventually leave him, and he becomes jealous, possessive, groundlessly accusatory, and demanding of complete servitude. Because he makes the relationship hellish for his now pregnant woman, she carries out a vodoun ceremony that involves killing a rattlesnake and hanging its corpse; as that corpse disintegrates, so will the object of her curse. He does indeed get hit on the head by a former wife, and dies from the concussion about the time that the rattler's corpse is coming to pieces. Eunice then goes to stay with Blacksnake's mother until her baby is born.

The underworld in this novel is a world of very serious poverty and alcoholism, but what struck me most about it is that no one thinks at all about the future. In that sense, in the complete stasis, it superficially resembles the land of the dead. They live from minute to minute and day to day. They do not plan. They certainly do not delay gratification in hopes of getting a larger return on their effort. Eunice comes from an upper-middle-class background that would presumably disapprove of children born out of wedlock and presumably believed in planning and controlling gratification, but she pays no attention to that and shows no thought as to how she is going to care for her child once it is born. She might even abandon it to Blacksnake's mother, but we do not know. She has only barely avoided being forced into prostitution and has no source of reliable income. She shows no interest in returning to her family, but how she could care for a child is unclear, and she does not spend time considering the problem. This underworld is a realm of impulse and feeling. She does not try to figure out why she succumbs to Blacksnake despite finding him somewhat repellant. She has no answer to why she gives him the only money she has when he demands it, after he has driven her out. We are not even told enough about his playing to make us believe the fascination to be his extraordinary music. The effect of Mishka's music is well developed, but Blacksnake's is not praised or shown to have much effect on people aside from at that cotillion and aside from it making people eager to dance in the dive where he performs.

In addition to turning the mythological love into an abusive relationship, Phillips also has her Eurydice carry out a Vodoun rite meant to kill her former lover. Felicitously, it relies on the venomous snake that killed her ancient counterpart to kill the new Orpheus. She does not lay a finger on him or indeed deny him anything, but he comes to an unexpectedly quick end at the hands of a more demanding and possessive woman. Being hit on the head is his sparagmos, but his head will not linger on to prophesy. Some of his music was recorded, so possibly the blues ideology—its attitude, its lament—are his words to future generations. The story, though, does not end in the mythologically predictable fashion. Instead, we find ourselves wondering what Eunice saw in Blacksnake and why she was so drawn to him. She does break free of him, but she also seems to have made her home in this impoverished community, so she is staying in the underworld. Although she does not articulate this thought, she may see living there as a means of making her own blues more authentic. Her life may now feel as if it is of a piece with her art. In a sense, she may be taking up the Orphic identity and musical project.

Because Eunice is so unable or unwilling to analyze and articulate her feelings, we as readers have to take responsibility for any interpretive moves. Our options are enriched by the mythic layer because it runs somewhat counter to the story's literal level, and we have to ponder those shifts. If nothing else, the sketchy, idealized love of the Greek story plays off against the far-from-ideal relationship in this novel. Without pointing a finger or treating it as anything but the way life is, Phillips makes us aware of the extreme male chauvinism with its demand for female servitude in this version of the relationship. Without the mythic level, she is just reporting; with it, she could be criticizing the Black culture shown, or criticizing the idealized European myth for not reflecting the truths of poverty. Either way, we have to think.

Orpheus as Catalyst That Makes Art Possible: Hoban

What about another complex treatment of Orpheus, Russell Hoban's *The Medusa Frequency* (1987)? Herman Orff, a novelist and a writer of ads and comics scripts, is suffering from writers' block and feeling stymied; he cannot get at places in his mind that he wishes to explore. He accepts the invitation to try a modified EEG that will stimulate parts of his brain with electricity. The rest of the book consists of a variety of encounters, some and maybe all of which are hallucinated, presumably as a result of his brain stimulation. At one level, Orff is Orpheus (and he thinks of his lost loves jointly as Eurydice). At another, any artist who delves into his inner self or suffers to produce a work of art is also Orpheus—an understanding of the story very much in line with that of Maurice Blanchot in "Orpheus's Gaze" or of Ihab Hassan in *The Dismemberment of Orpheus*. Orpheus also appears as the rotting, eyeless head of Orpheus who tells Orff his story in installments; this head is hallucinatorily projected onto a grapefruit, a soccer ball, and a cabbage. Orff feels strongly drawn to Vermeer's portrait known as *Head of a Young Girl*, whose eyes in particular remind him of his lost love Luise Himmelbett, whom he associates with Eurydice.

In this book, the underworld appears in many forms. If the world is the set of surfaces we can see and feel, the underworld is whatever lies under those surfaces. "What we call world is only that little bit of each moment that we know about—underworld is everything else that we don't know but we need it. Underworld is like the good darkness where the olive tree has its roots."[10] Sometimes Hoban employs the term in that sense. Sometimes the underworld is where you descend when exploring your own mind, your unconscious. Sometimes it is the classical realm of Hades and Persephone. He does not appear to be serious about projecting a land of dead shades, an afterlife, but insofar as we keep seeing the term underworld, we do not forget that possibility. The depths of the underworld are also suggested, however, by oceanic and watery depths. The head of Orpheus rises in a river and travels upstream. The Kraken and Medusa come from some much deeper layer (of water or of the unconscious) than Orpheus, and rise up through water. Sometimes, Hoban may even be playing on the idea of underworld with all the travel that Orff does on the London Underground. With names like Netherworld Bookshop, Orpheus Travel, and Avernus Publishers (17–20), Hoban's world is saturated with various versions of the Underworld, and we must keep trying to interpret his variations.

In addition to Orphic mythology, Hoban has Orff entering conversations with the Kraken, a mythical being from Norwegian lore roughly equivalent to the biblical Leviathan, though probably a giant squid. This being communicates with him through his computer. He can type in "Hello" and get an answer; this monster may be literal, or an example of automatic writing, or it may represent signs of Orff's hallucinatory state. Associated with this very deep head is Eurydice. She is also called the Kraken's mother, and is seen in one vision sexually embracing a giant squid in the style of Japanese netsuke. Parallel to the Kraken and also, somehow, from a deeper underworld or deeper unconscious, is Medusa, the woman's head with serpents for hair. We also get echoes of Persephone, she being in part invoked by Orff's new love interest, Melanie Falsepercy, or, as he points out, Perse phony. Persephone, Eurydice, Luise Himmelbett and Melanie, plus Vermeer's "Head of a Young Girl," all play similar roles, and contribute to a feminine principle toward whom Orff (a writer), Istvan Fallok (a composer), and Gösta Kraken (a film director) all respond. The three men all undergo the EEG, and are all haunted by the head of Orpheus; for them, he represents the artist's struggle and what matters most in their art, but when Orpheus lets go of them and stops thinking of them, they suffer heart trouble or even die, as in Kraken's case.

Throughout, Hoban asks questions about mythology and its roles. One of the more interesting interrogations comes near the end. Orff has refused to do a comic book version of Orpheus, which cuts off his income; he then also refuses to work with Gösta Kraken on a film about Orpheus, both of which actions leave the "current account ... dead on the floor, a thin trickle of blood coming from its mouth" (102). (When he rifles the pockets of his current account, he finds enough to keep him going for only a few months.) He turns on his computer and addresses the Kraken, and they start collaborating on a story line that he decides might make a good comic book (The capital letters come from the Kraken.)

NNVSNU THE TSRUNGH IS THINKING VIOLENTLY.
Of what?
OF GOING AFTER WHOEVER PULLED THE GREAT SNYUKH.
What was the Great Snyukh?
IT WAS THE BLUG OF NEXO VOLLMA. ...
You mean plughole. Nexo Vollma is the plughole of the universe and the Great Snyukh was the plug. ...
IT WAS A WHOLE LOT BIGGER THAN ANY PLUG YOU CAN THINK OF, AND IT GOT PULLED. BUT IN THAT UNIMAGINABLE MOMENT BEFORE THE BIG WHOOSH, SNYUKH! INTO THE BLUGHOLE WENT NNVSNU THE TSRUNGH. ... FROM THE UTTERMOST DEPTHS OF THE ULTIMATE DEEP HE SENDS HIS MIND AFTER THOSE WHO PULLED THE GREAT SNYUKH, THE BLUG OF NEXO VOLLMA.
Who did it? Who pulled the Great Snyukh?
THE DEEPLY BAD ONES DID IT.
Why did they do it?
THEY WANTED TO HEAR THE BIG WHOOSH. (130–131)

This goes on for some time. What we have is a myth-like story about the structure of a world, with bad forces trying to bring about an apocalypse, but this story told without any connection to a myth we know. It has no recognizable (or indeed pronounceable) names. How do we respond?

Unpronounceable, and therefore to some extent non-memorable, names make me uneasy. When a further actor is identified as Nabilca, Thing of Darkness, I relax slightly because we are back with names that sound human, but then I learn that Nabilca "is really Wendy Nelson, a marine biologist. She was scuba diving when she lost consciousness and woke up in the secret undersea headquarters of the Nexo Foundation" (131)—at that point, I recognize that I am in the world of a comic book, and I both stop worrying and, to some extent, lose interest, comics not being one of my favored genres. Not all readers would have that response, but for me, mythology about the "blughole of the universe" is only temporarily tantalizing; its failure to connect to a recognized mythology or generate much story action keeps it from producing the effect that a known or at least more conventional mythology would manage to do. Unpronounceable names are not a complete obstacle to response, as proven by Calvino's Qfwfq in his cosmicomical stories, but Calvino avoids the problem by reducing his cast of characters to protagonist, longed-for girl, family members, and rival, and instead of drawing us in with story, he astonishes us with his imaginative recreation of the universe.

If names matter, what does Hoban gain by treating so many of the women as equivalents to each other? If Eurydice is important as the attractive woman dying young and mourned by her lover, why does she seem interchangeable with Persephone, and why are both Luise Himmelbett and Melanie Falsepercy (neither of them dead) as well as the Vermeer portrait, all somehow interchangeable? Moreover, Medusa maps at least partly onto them as well; the book cover shows Vermeer's young girl with snakes escaping her headscarf. Medusa's usual mythological function is rather threatening. Hoban's logic seems to be that all art is a celebration of loss (68, 119). Orpheus and Eurydice living happily ever after would have generated no story or art. These women must all be lost if the artist is to produce, or they may also have mother functions and belong to the depths out of which comes the world. In Carl Jung's terminology, a man's unconscious is feminine. Orff has clearly been exploring some such feminine depths. He has been unable to produce a third novel for nine years, but now that the exploration is complete and Melanie has dumped him, he thinks he can write and she is sure he will.

Not only must the artist suffer loss, he must also apparently feel guilt. Orpheus is haunted by having bloodily murdered the tortoise for its shell from which he made his lyre. Orff is told that Luise entrusted to him "the idea of her" (70), but he lost it. At one point, he associates his losing her with the word fidelity, and that is also invoked when Melanie cuts off their relationship, though in that case she admits that she betrayed him before he could betray her. Orff's compulsion to explore his depths seems at times related to a vague sense of guilt, but also to his sense that such depths contain story, art. What seems to be important about these women is each one's "idea of her" being entrusted but somehow not valued or preserved or understood as it should be by Orff.[11] The guilt that he feels at not valuing their ideas of self in the fashion they needed is one of the roots of his creative urge.

In a sense, by imbuing the story with a mythical dimension, Hoban gets beyond the particularities of individuals. Orff is not just one blocked novelist; he is also an Artist with a capital A, and as such can put his problems in a larger context. Whatever we may think of his attitudes toward his women, we see how the women in his life function similarly for him as artist. Mythology also parades as the structure of his unconscious, as the places he is trying to reach and explore, but could not before the EEG. Orpheus as an oracular head has a compulsive power; the head asks and is answered three times about telling his story, and this binds the writer Orff to listen, and of course the head's story is part of the novel that we read, nominally the narrative being written by Orff. None of this would have worked had the novel been about Nnvsnu the Tsrungh, and the great Snyukh. The compulsive and repulsive nature of the Orphic head also comments on the roots of art. In Hoban's vision, art does not grow from beauty (or from gratified love); it comes from something festering or rotting and urgent—the rotting head of Orpheus. That mythological element, ugly though it is at times, links the artist to his everyday life (as seen in the names of pubs, publishers, and bookstores, all of which have Orphic names); it also links him to his unconscious, to his art, and to what matters to him, his production of art.

Hoban's work can doubtless be analyzed in other ways, but clearly, mythology is an artistically urgent issue for him. After all, not only does he draw on the Orphic story for *Riddley Walker* (as we will see later), he felt the need to invent myths for that future world. In *Riddley Walker* the mytheme that appealed to him most was the Orphic head as oracle; in *The Medusa Frequency*, we find the oracular head but also Orpheus the artist and lover, and he even invents a potential new mytheme: Orpheus's murder of the tortoise for the shell with which he invented the lyre and new forms of art.

How the Orpheus Myth Can Define Worlds: Delany and Gaiman

Eurydice having gained in importance in contemporary fictions does not mean that Orpheus has dropped out. We saw a strong Orphic vision in *The Medusa Frequency*, and we find Orpheus the focus of Samuel Delany's *The Einstein Intersection* and a key figure in Neil Gaiman's *The Sandman*. Delany's Orpheus, named Lobey, is a character who, we learn gradually, is not human. Thirty thousand years have passed since humans were the dominant species; they have left or disappeared, and a race of "psychic manifestations, multi-sexed, incorporeal" have taken over human-shaped bodies and have chosen to imitate humans as much as possible.[12] This race has inherited human myths and bits of culture, but these relics do not truly fit them any more than a multi-sexed being fits a two-sexed set of bodies. Delany seems to be asking what such myths inherited from different cultures are good for—for Orpheus does indeed come from a different culture, not only for Euro-Americans but doubly for African Americans, for whom ancient Greece would not seem to be terribly relevant. Spider, a character who understands more about this world than Lobey, expresses his concern with myth:

> I don't want to know what's inside the myths, nor how they clang and set one another ringing, their glittering focuses, their limits and genesis. I want their shape, their texture, how they feel when you brush by them on a dark road, when you see them receding into the fog, their weight as they leap your shoulder from behind (130).

Lobey mourns the death of his girlfriend, Friza, and refuses the usual consolations. He determines to find Death and win her back, and is sent off with the Orpheus story as his guide—though he knows it in two forms. One is the story about failure to retrieve Eurydice from the dead; the other is a sparagmos story about Ringo, the silent Beatle, being torn apart by screaming fans. Lobey struggles with the sense that if he is Orpheus, then he must fail, but possibly the story could come out differently for his race than it did for humans. He doesn't know.

Mythic fragments from different periods mingle. Kid Death was called Bonny William by his mother (William Bonney being one alias of Billy the Kid). Orpheus and the Beatles merge. People swear by Elvis. One of the "princes" of Branning-at-Sea is crucified, and Lobey plays the role of the Roman soldier and stabs the body, thus hastening its death. Although no names are alluded to, some African myths may also be present; Salim Washington argues that Shango and Oshun are also present as African equivalents to Orpheus and Eurydice.[13] In all of these, Lobey is trying to find out who he is, how he functions within the world, and how much the culturally alien myths may mean or have to tell him about how to organize his life.

Lobey is a musician. A certain portion of this hybrid population is viewed as different. Some are physically different (and many are mutant and nonfunctional); some have extra senses or abilities such as telepathy and telekinesis. His difference is music with a telepathic element; he can hear the music in other people's minds and play it. He knows and judges people by the music he hears in them. His instrument is a kind of machete fused to a hollow tube that can be played like a flute. With this, he can kill as well as enchant. Furthermore, it is played with his prehensile toes as well as his fingers. Music from the lost human civilization seems to be completely meaningful to him and his listeners, so that cultural element evidently transcends their differences. Difference, though, turns out to be a loaded word. Lobey hears some city folk snigger at his reference to differences. Evidently navels and their depths are important in the city culture, though Lobey cannot figure out why, nor what is permitted and what, taboo in urban life. In the city, one keeps any sense of one's differences entirely secret. Part of the quest that Lobey is on is to make himself better acquainted with this world, and cultural shibboleths are one factor that affects his fitting in. He clearly has trouble fitting; after all, if he had fit in back in his village, he would have accepted Friza's demise and not declared his feud with Kid Death.

Lobey actually kills Kid Death, but what the implications of this are we do not learn. Nor does Lobey win Friza back, though he intends to keep seeking. He knows he has no sense of what she will be like if he does win her back, perhaps in this showing a bit of awareness of the zombie fears expressed in *Orpheus and the Pearl* or in Gaiman's *American Gods*, when a beloved wife returns a few times as an increasingly rotted embalmed corpse. The book only poses questions about myth; it ends without answering any of them. Maybe Lobey will succeed where Orpheus did not, or maybe he too is doomed to fail. Whether he goes back to his village or travels more in this world or to other planets, we do not know. His life, though, is a struggle to make sense of myth, understand why it matters, particularly when it comes from another culture and is foreign to his own. He does, though, seem convinced that myth does matter, and that its hold on us is a bit mysterious, but worth trying to understand.

For a change of pace in all regards, consider Neil Gaiman's multivolume comics series called *The Sandman*.[14] The frame of this frame-tale concerns Dream, also known as Morpheus or Oneiros, the Sandman of the title. One of the many tales within frame is that of Orpheus, who is given Dream/Morpheus as a father, and has as aunts and uncles Dream's six siblings—Destiny, Destruction, Despair, Death, Delirium, and Desire—all of them potentially immortal, though capable of dying. When Eurydice is bitten by the serpent and dies, Orpheus tries to enlist the help of his relatives, but without notable success. Angry at his father for not being willing to undo the natural order of things, Orpheus renounces him, and Morpheus coolly reciprocates. We later see Orpheus gruesomely dismembered by the bacchantes. His torn-off but living head speaks briefly with Morpheus, who insists that the renunciations destroyed all ties between them. Morpheus arranges for the head to be protected and cared for, but otherwise ignores it for three thousand years. Although this rendition of the Orpheus story comes well along in the series,[15] it arguably represents the chronologically earliest episode shown, and if so, we see Orpheus refusing to accept death as possibly *the* generative episode in Morpheus's life as recounted in this series and on our world. That plus Orpheus's head's miraculous survival tear a hole in the fabric of reality at the chronological outset of *The Sandman*, one that, I argue, only gets closed again when Morpheus accepts death for himself.

Gaiman often works variations on death. *The Graveyard Book* tells of a living boy raised by the dead in a cemetery. *American Gods* tells of Shadow undergoing Odin's suffering on the tree and dying, yet the Goddess Eoster brings Shadow back to life. That death should somehow prove central to *The Sandman* is plausible, and it becomes more so when we consider the nature of the many tales in the series.

The list is lengthy. The magus who captures Morpheus is trying to control Death and so avoid his own. Doctor Destiny kills the people in a diner in gruesome fashion. In a fit of depression, Dream is roused by Death and taken with her on her rounds as she claims those who die. This is all in a day's work for her, but it shakes Morpheus out of his doldrums and sets him on paths to new actions. He tracks down the nightmares and sends a ghost superhero, Sandman, back to death; a vortex dies as the result of his actions; and we learn of his beloved Nada's death.[16] Morpheus and Death meet Hob Gadling and, out of amusement at his contempt for dying, grant him life until he chooses to die. Morpheus meets him at century intervals thereafter. We follow the serial-killer nightmare, The Corinthian, as he attends a convention of serial killers. We see some of their victims, and see Morpheus destroy the Corinthian. Of the four unrelated short stories in "Dream Country," the one based on *A Midsummer Night's Dream* touches on death when we see Titania clearly offering Hamnet Shakespeare a position similar to that of her Indian boy. The final story in that book, "Façade," is about a superwoman who can think of no way to kill herself until Death suggests the steps to take. The story of English boarding-school boys shows them bullied to death. Barbie's dream world is eventually destroyed (and all its inhabitants go into oblivion); because of Thessaly's perilous rite of drawing down the moon, Wanda and Maisie Hill die. Emperor Norton dies at the end of his story, and we see deaths and piles of heads in the story set during the Terror. The Orpheus story centers on death, as does "The Parliament of Rooks." We see Ishtar kill all the clients of a dance club with her sacred dancing. Dream kills Orpheus, as requested. Cluracan of faerie tells a tale of revenge by the dead. The story about Prez Rickard, the golden embodiment of America, describes his mysterious death or disappearance. An apprentice from the necropolis Litharge tells a set of tales within his tale, all about death and dealing with dead bodies. Morpheus's minions in the Dreaming are murdered by the Furies. After Morpheus's death, we learn of the slave-trade deaths for which Hob had been responsible a few centuries earlier, and the sequence ends with Shakespeare's finishing *The Tempest* and dying shortly thereafter. In sum, while I have not named all of the stories told, a great many concern death directly.

Gaiman ties in Orpheus's rebellion against death to Morpheus's acceptance of his own death. That an immortal should choose to die has puzzled critics, some of whom are hostile to what they condemn as suicide. The framing story of Morpheus shows him righting three wrongs he perpetrated through not caring about the feelings of others. He rescues Nada from Hell, he helps his sister Delirium, and he realizes that he should not have rejected his distraught and immature son. The son now asks for death, and Orpheus is the only one who can break the magic of his preservation and give it to him, but by doing this, he violates the oldest human rule of not shedding the blood of kin. His doing so makes him lawful prey for the Furies. He is so powerful within the realm of Dream that they cannot actually kill him there (though can elsewhere), but they can kill all his subjects, and do. He can recreate them, but slaughter and recreate, slaughter and recreate makes the process pointless. Rather than let the Furies take him, he chooses the time and place to make an exit and lets someone untargeted by the Furies inherit his realm and carry it on. The whole story arc of *The Sandman* thus stretches from Orpheus rebelling against the finality of death and his immortal father's conscious, deliberate acceptance of death.

So what has Gaiman gained by invoking the Greek myth? This is only one of many tales he tells about death. He even shows other versions of afterlife—a Milton-influenced Hell, and Loki chained beneath a venom-dripping serpent. Were it not for the Morpheus/Orpheus name and the relationship, the Orpheus story would probably just be one among many; however, with the name, the invented father/son relationship, and the effect on the end, the Orpheus story becomes logically central to *The Sandman*. Orpheus descending into the underworld is not what seems to matter, which is original. Nor, really, is the sparagmos, however memorable the illustrations. All we see of Eurydice is a naïve girl dancing at her wedding. She does not come across as deserving to be the great love object of the centuries. I argue that what Gaiman stresses is Orpheus's refusal to accept death's finality. His frantic attempts to get her back go against the nature of the universe. Despite his extraordinary near-success, he proves unable to reverse death. The impulse behind his attitude seems similar to that which generates stories of Elysian Fields and Heaven, the need to palliate the loss and compensate somehow for it and to give ourselves hope for a future with the lost one. As one who tries to find an alternative to final annihilation, Orpheus represents many makers of myth. As such, Gaiman's Morpheus gives us an elaborate and beautiful humanist stance on accepting death. Gaiman provides a sharp contrast to the posthuman-oriented writers in Chapter 5 who deny death and claim that it can be avoided and even reversed.

Orphic Song as Biogenetics: Powers's *Orfeo*

When ads for *Orfeo* (2014) appeared, I was thrilled to have another Orphic work by an author whom I admire. As usual, however, Powers subverts and challenges expectations, and his invocation of the myth here is no exception. As with Russell Hoban's *The Medusa Frequency*, the various women in Peter Els's life blend into a Eurydice principle of loves lost—mostly through Els not seeing what they need. The mythemes do not follow the usual order. We do find Orpheus as charmer of nature, Orpheus lost in an underworld from which there may be no emergence, and Orpheus as oracular head, the last in modern electronic and genetic guise. The homosexual mytheme is momentarily invoked, and the sparagmos bursts upon us, with the book ending one moment before the dismemberment by armed police will take place.

Naïve and introverted Peter Els devotes his life to seeking newness in music, sounds, and combinations that have never been heard before. He passes through all the phases of contemporary music, and Powers writes knowledgeably about those, but Els is ever pushing the frontiers. Not surprisingly, this keeps him from building much of a following. He has a few short-term successes, particularly when he teams up with wild man Richard Bonner as impresario, producer, director, and librettist. Els so shrinks from publicity, however, that when their opera about the Münster rebellion in 1534 opens in New York at the same time as the US government's destruction of the Branch Davidian compound at Waco, Els refuses to let the opera travel and gets it closed. He cannot bear to take advantage of interest generated on the basis of others' suffering. This was his one big break, his one chance to reach a wide audience, but his moral repugnance at benefiting from suffering and having to face insistent questioning about the connections kept him from making the transition to the big time.

Els is highly experimental, and sees all nature as a way of generating new combinations of tones—an interesting twist on "enchanting" nature with music, though he also influences nature, as we see when he plays music to his dog and studies her responding howls scientifically.[17] Overall, nature suggests music to him, and by decoding it into sounds, he finds new ways of interacting with nature. His latest fling in this direction is to see genetic code as a way of generating new combinations. Because he started university studying chemistry before turning to music, he has no trouble launching himself into genetic experimentation, and has, in his semiretirement, set up a garage lab that tweaks organisms to produce new ones and new genetic combinations. He has no evil aim in mind, and he is working with over-the-counter equipment available to anyone with the knowledge to set it up and run it. What he is doing is sophisticated. When he naively allows a policeman to see the lab, investigators decide he must be an eco-terrorist, and the media explode with irresponsible accusation and speculation. Suggestible people who hear of these experiments develop alarming symptoms, and this whips up fervor to hunt down this fiend. As public panic mounts, even naïve Els knows that he cannot get anything like fair treatment; the powers that be will naturally claim dire results from his microorganisms, whether those cause trouble or not. No explanation will ever be deemed sufficient. He inexpertly and with no plan goes on the lam.

While driving inconspicuously from place to place, he turns up on the doorsteps of his former wife, his daughter, and his former friend Bonner, who is now participating in a drug experiment in hopes of warding off his early-stage Alzheimer's dementia. Each helps him, but they all know he only has a few days free at most. While wandering in this underworld of panic and oppression, he takes to tweeting, and thus performing one oracular function. His tweets are as enigmatic as any oracular pronouncement. Furthermore, his genetic project would have produced a bacterium that carried his music down through the centuries in its genes, another form of prophetic pronouncement. Powers even invokes the homosexual mytheme in a phrase applying to Els and Bonner, who in their giddy, wild collaborations ignored Els's wife and daughter and the need for gainful employment: "*If only one of us had a vagina . . . half of life's problems would be solved.*"[18] When said earlier by Bonner, they could see humor in this; when Els quotes it during their last meeting, Bonner is just puzzled, a clear sign of how badly his brilliant mind has slipped.

Powers leaves his Orpheus suspended in the Underworld. Els's last stop is at his daughter's house, and from there, he runs out into the night waving a vase that looks like a lab flask, expecting to be shot, since police have surrounded the house. In this dramatic rush, he is doing his best to follow Bonner's advice: "One last recital, his eyes say. You can do this. Make it something even this distracted world will hear. It will only hurt for a moment" (348). As Els drives off in Bonner's car toward his daughter's house, evading the police who are looking for his own car, he watches Bonner heading back toward the nursing home, "headlong into the drama, ready to direct it, if they'll let him. Creation's Rule Number One: Zag when they think you'll zig" (349). Els's sprinting out of his daughter's house is his throwing himself into his sparagmos. He will literally and figuratively be torn apart by the hysterical police weapons and the press.

So why the Orpheus story? Powers explored another Greek myth in *Galatea 2.2* successfully. What does he gain by using this one? I would say that his chief gain is a way of talking about contemporary music that carries us along even though we cannot hear it and (those of us classically inclined) might not enjoy it at all. Even though we cannot hear it, we are brought by the mythic intensification to take seriously Els's burning and Quixotic quest for the new. We can understand and respond to his motivation, if not to the noises he makes. Moreover, his turning to nature for new sequences of sounds through nature's codes suggests that such music could give us a whole new way of relating to nature. Instead of exploiting and abusing it, we might learn to derive satisfactions that would not depend on destroying it. We tend to absorb nature through our eyes, but this would give us a whole new way of responding through our hearing. The newness of what Powers suggests reminds me a bit of the newness in Calvino's cosmicomical stories. We forego power over nature in return for being overwhelmed, or even just entertained, by a new aspect of its beauty. We learn to value furnishing our minds with new ideas and sounds rather than just consuming nature as raw industrial material. Given that music can literally reshape the brain, might not music based on natural patterns actually change us, for the better we might hope?

Powers also engages the reader in a tug of war. We keep wanting to know whether this or that woman is Eurydice, and if none of them is dead, then what exactly is the Underworld. As in Janette Turner Hospital's novel, Hades is an American construction, the pressure of American intelligence and police's power on fragile and naïve individuals, a blunt and deadly instrument being applied to mistaken targets. I thought, at first, when Tweeting and bacterial DNA seemed to replace oracular statements, that Powers had decided to skip the sparagmos, or at least saw it dispersed as the Ihab Hassan type of suffering that Els goes through during most of his life in order to create. Like Hoban's Orff, Els must tear his art from his innermost depths if he is to produce his creations. Only when rereading the ending did I realize that Els is throwing himself into the meat grinder, the hysteria of the government and press replacing the drink or drug-induced mania of the maenads. The novel ends in that moment just before the mob realizes that he is there.

When Powers talks about music, he soars. When he dreams up the new sparagmos, we realize that the classical Greek situation is not as outré and distant from our world as we may have comforted ourselves with thinking. On the contrary, police-caused sparagmoi are gruesomely familiar. Els's biogenetic experiments and those he reads about actually do point toward a new principle upon which music might be based, one resting on such fundamental realities that it could conceivably affect our minds and rewire them toward a different and possibly improved mindset. Of course, his genetic tinkering might also have unintended negative consequences, though Powers apparently treats it as harmless.[19] Potentially, with Els's death, we lose the chance to hear the music of the spheres, and only talking in mythic story terms like spheres gives us any inkling of what we may be missing.

The Orpheus story seems very tied to the belief-world of ancient Greece, yet it transcends the cultural barriers to appeal to zombie and soft-core porn fans, those angry at American intelligence operations abroad or at home, and those concerned with the problems of writing art and with death.

It speaks even to those separated from mainstream American culture by racial and sexual experience, even if, as Delany's character admits, the myth has a feel that we cannot pin down in words. He puts that in terms of sound, sensation, fear, startlement, shape, texture, weight, and frustration as it disappears from view into fog. Whatever the myth means or however it does so, it is not through giving us reassurance about death. We do not believe the original. Even without belief, it reinforces or chimes with something we feel we need.

4

Invented Myth

The Problem of Power

Acker, Barthelme, Hoban, Moore, Calvino, and Gaiman

Gods, immortals, and superhumans—these are the figures that inhabit many myths and invented myths, and what sets them apart from the rest of us are their various powers. The superhuman actors have what we think we want. When they desire something, they have the strength to take it. If they want to achieve something, they have the power to make it happen, though sometimes with unforeseen consequences. They may also have the immortality or near-immortality to protect their lives and make them safe in a dangerous world. While power is certainly *exercised* in religious myths—Zeus strikes someone with a thunderbolt or Jesus raises a dead man—recent invented myth seems largely concerned with questioning power and how it should be employed. Quasi-mythical figures as superheroes were comfortable in exercising such power and flourished in the 1940s and 1950s. They benefited from America's view of its own power and role in the Second World War. Superman, Batman, and Captain America could be ideal figures whose power is expended for the good. They had no need initially to agonize over the relationship between might and right.[1] The implications of the atom bomb and then the Vietnam War undercut Americans' confidence that their power was serving the right or was rightly used. In response, new kinds of mythic fiction explored those problems.

Nor was America the only country to reappraise power. Those countries that lost the Second World War had reasons to reconsider. Those, like

England, that were losing an empire had other reasons to worry about the reality and morality of imperial power and to wonder what would keep them from being squashed or absorbed by larger and better endowed nations. The novels with obviously invented myth that I wish to examine in this chapter almost all question power and how we as individuals should relate to it. The problem they raise is real enough. Power exists. Whatever their ideological assumptions, these authors cannot escape the existence of power, so how can it best be handled or what can one learn from it? Kathy Acker's *Pussy, King of the Pirates*, Donald Barthelme's *The Dead Father*, Russell Hoban's *Riddley Walker*, and Alan Moore's *Watchmen*, all struggle with a negative vision of power. For complete contrast, I offer Italo Calvino and Neil Gaiman. Calvino lies outside the English-language authors I am dealing with, but he is someone who invented quasi-myths and who handles them in wildly original ways even when concerned with power. I was quite surprised when reading Gaiman's 2013 novel to sense some strong similarities to Calvino's cosmicomical stories, as well as some new twists in his mythography, so I include *The Ocean at the End of the Lane*, even if power is not the only focal problem in that tale.

The Powers of Men and the Powers of Death: Acker and Barthelme

The power that most disturbs Acker is that exercised by men over women. She thus starts at the level of one on one, but her vision works upward to governments, since patriarchy extends through all reaches of culture. Before we see how myth enters her work and what powers she explores in *Pussy, King of the Pirates*, we need to consider the nature of this experimental novel. Several point-of-view characters are virtually interchangeable in their relation to a father they never knew and their inability to find the kind of love they need. Whether called O, Ostracism, Ange, Antigone, or Pussy, they radiate the same anguish.[2] While female, they occasionally speak of themselves as male. They spend a great deal of their time masturbating and orgasming endlessly or repeatedly. One major frustration in their lives is the apparent incompatibility of freedom and love. Acker can claim in *Empire of the Senseless* that "pleasure gathers only in freedom."[3] In *Blood and Guts in High School*, she writes: "The only thing I want is freedom. Let me tell you: I don't have any idea what that means."[4] Since what she mostly shows is men oppressing women, freedom ought to involve escape from that oppression. That persona adds, however, that freedom seems connected to "depending on someone/something who's stable" (112). In *Pussy, King of the Pirates*, O laments: "But what'll I do when there's no one in the world who loves me? When all existence is only freedom?"[5] If freedom is only possible without love, then why would she want it? While she certainly shows same-sex relationships, Acker puts more emphasis on the relations of women to men, and so is stymied by the patriarchal patterns of power.

Her invented creation myths deal with male power over females: the father and daughter, or the son and the rat-faced girl. The completely elided mother function adds to our sense that Acker is representing her own values and pains. I would call these psychic myths. The interchangeable personae make remarks about the absent father and his effect on the daughter: "Since I never knew you, every man I fuck is you. Daddy. Every cock goes into my cunt which, since I never knew you, is a river named Cocytus" (15). The creation of the world is also the creation of her life.

A more puzzling originary figure is the son who refuses to procreate. He turns up six times in slightly differing versions in the novel. In the first, a green-eyed girl recites a punk myth, and this concerns a boy who lives in burial grounds surrounded by skulls. His girlfriend resents his never coming in her, and she leaves him. In the next version, we find a written myth of beginnings accompanying the pirate treasure map. This is the version that gives us the father and his charred sperm. The son's disappointed girlfriend burns herself up. When her cunt falls into a crevice, the world ends and begins again with the boy searching for her, as if he were Orpheus. Then we hear a third version: Ostracism's favorite story when growing up concerned a boy sitting on a snake surrounded by skulls. The girl cannot get the boy to love her. He sets her on fire. She turns into a mare so she can gallop to water to put the fire out. She drank up "all the water there was in the world, for the sexual thirsts of girls are never satisfied" (100). She tries to entice the boy by making herself his slave.

We meet this boy again when Ostracism mentions reading a story about a girl who looked like herself. She was living with the boy who had skulls. In their graveyard home, she tends a rat who is the baby that the boy refuses to procreate. Then she realizes that the rat is actually her lover and that boys are rats, and then she and her lover are happy. The boy appears again when he transfers his rage to a mare and that mare becomes the entrance to Hell, with flames shooting out her mouth. The Punk Boy descends to fight the demons who are doing their bit to prevent human procreation by hoarding all semen. By doing this, the demons also hope to starve the gods. "Being gods, they were more hysterical, more fearful, more desperate, more emotional than humans" (157). Given Acker's prejudices, this probably makes them better than humans, since we repress our emotions and do not honestly express what we feel. In this version of the mythic story, we get back references to the Punk Boy having beheaded his father and turned his skull into Heaven and Hell—echoes of Old Norse myth. The final reference involves what is now called the Slut Girl creating a child from the dirt on her body rather than through procreation. Punk Boy kills it, but then kills an elephant and gives the child the elephant's head and that child becomes Ganesh from Hindu mythology.

The boy who will not orgasm clearly resonates, to judge from the number of times he appears. He is a lover who cannot meet the rat-faced girl's need for complete love and commitment. She loves him abjectly, but he holds back something of himself from her and limits his commitment. The more she suspects this and demands his full surrender, the more he withdraws from the relationship. Calling him a rat cheers her, at least for a while. Rats are often present in this novel, partly as an element in the word pi-rat-e, partly as clever animals that live in filth and survive. They live off society's leavings and do not need money, so they offer a model for the moneyless life that the various personae wish they could live. The girl, though, calls herself rat-faced in a fashion evidently negative, which testifies to her inability to accept or value herself. Her calling the boy a rat is likewise no compliment. The rats carry more negative than positive valences, but point in several interpretive directions. The unsatisfactory sexual relationships at the beginning of the world—father and daughter, and son and rat-faced girl—stamp creation according to these patterns. For the various personae, this particular world can only be expected to produce such damaging and damaged relationships, unsatisfying and doomed. In both relationships, the men hold power over the women and the women have no reciprocal hold on the men.

Acker, at least for artistic purposes, seems never to have grown beyond her childhood pain and terror caused by parental behaviors and threats, so that animates her psychic mythography. The myths repeat the experiences that the personae mention in passing—the missing father or unsatisfactory lovers. The mother is too hated to be worked into mythology, and her chief appearance is as a corpse harboring a map and myth. The filth that the Punk Boy and rat-faced girl cultivate appears to reflect their rage at the off-stage society we never see in the myth. The mythic material shows them living a money-free life, but in conditions that look like homelessness in the larger society. Acker's inability to see any way around money or any way out of capitalism may lie behind the surprise ending when O and Ange take the treasure and run. Given that such an ending is unsatisfactory politically, I suspect that the gold, by being found in a cave characterized by positive vaginal symbolism, may stand for the shining qualities of female sexuality, in which case O and Ange settle for getting all they can.

Acker also draws on traditional mythology, particularly Greek myth plus a couple of references to Hindu and Vodoun figures. Some of the Greek figures get there to reinforce the lessons of her psychic mythology and to put emphasis on the way Western society has stacked the odds for men and against women.[6] Antigone enters as the hapless victim of her own birth (to Oedipus and Jocasta) and her being immured by Creon (a kind of father figure) to punish her. Andromeda is offered by her own father to the sea-monster. Pandora is created by Zeus to make trouble, and is interpreted as having loosed all the ills onto the world from her vagina.

Orpheus, though, is Acker's chief referent from prior mythologies, and for good reasons. Like her, he is an artist. He is commonly associated with Gerard de Nerval (who wrote on Orphic themes), and Nerval is one of Acker's admired artistic forebears. Orpheus manages a trip to the underworld, but survives, a hopeful idea to which she clings. He is bisexual. He survives his own death to become a prophesying head. Some of her references see him as alter ego—the artist who takes death in stride and survives. Her other references, however, show her identifying with Eurydice. Eurydice, after all, did die and went to Hades, and Acker is all too aware of her own rapidly approaching death. To Eurydice, Orpheus is a cause for anger; he survives when she does not; he cannot control his gaze and dooms her to stay dead; he has his art and so to him she is only a side issue.

Eurydice haunted Acker in the last year of her life. Her short story "Eurydice in the Underworld" dates from 1997, the year she died, and shows "You" (nickname for Eurydice) and Orpheus living together, going through the initial cancer operation, and getting the bad news about lymph nodes.[7] Acker may be being very honest in her portrayal of Eurydice's behavior—protesting, whining, angry, and unreasonable, wanting to get up and leave the hospital just before the operation—but we can also see that living with someone that uninhibited and emotionally volatile would be extremely wearing. This modern Orpheus is not up to it, and he breaks with Eurydice not long after the operation. In its own way, his behavior is as unattractive and selfish as hers is, but he is not facing cancer himself, so is not being let down as she is. Some of the action-dream sequences are very like those of Pussy.

Acker's thoughts on dying and being dead surface throughout. O and other personae in *Pussy* seek to become "nothing," that being a point of such total self-abnegation that they hope to find answers to their questions about life. Becoming a whore in China is one way of trying to become nothing, and a fortuneteller there tells her she will be free after "a journey" into the land of the dead. In the story of St. Gall Bladder, we are told that to become human, we must first become nothing (43). Just possibly one of the personae offers an answer to this nothingness with the comment that "Myths mean something" (54). By implication, they supply answers that go beyond nothing. In addition to nothing, Acker starts adding references to disappearances of sight: "my eyeballs rotate 180 degrees in their sockets. I'm gazing into a world in which sight isn't possible. I know I'm going to descend into death" (115). "I was sinking down into earth. It was as if the earth around me was opening. Its top was excited—I could see this—excited so that its bottom could open up and the dirt part, dirt from dirt, earth under earth" (247). "The earth opened" (248). "Soon I would no longer be able to see. For the sun was ceasing and the stars beginning to gather. Each wept at the other" (250). "The world was where things grew, just at the top of a slope which was beginning to run downward" (251)—a rather powerful picture of life, a slope down which everything must eventually descend. Even with all the rot that she associates with earth, the persona is able to reach sexual ecstasy there, but that does nothing to halt her inexorable progress toward death. The only positive spin that Acker puts on death is the idea that "People die so that they can learn things. This is the reason why those who are living, still alive, travel into the land of the dead" (155). This ties back to Acker's picture of turning the self into nothing in order to have questions answered. Only by escaping one's self can one hope for answers or knowledge.

Acker's myths mostly cluster about the beginning of the world and about death, thoroughly orthodox mythic topics. Her original myths are those of creation, and concern power; the borrowed Greek myths give us a handle on death. Despite the assertion that myths mean something, all we see her characters gaining is belief that reasons exist for life being the twisted and unfair thing that they find it to be. They do not themselves find answers that satisfy them. The myths confirm their experience rather than really explaining it. Acker seems inclined to project any possible answers as being accessible only when one has become nothing. None of her personae manage to reach nothingness or rid themselves of self fully enough to reach enlightenment in this world, which leaves her only the next world for possible answers.

For a different vision of male power of creation, let us look for contrast at Donald Barthelme's *The Dead Father* (1975). Barthelme creates a god-like figure in the Dead Father, who is said to be dead and is being taken to be buried. However, he talks, walks away, kills many of his creations, tries to seduce one of his many daughters, and generally behaves as if he were alive. He tells stories of experiences as creator, but reflects contemporary concerns in that one leg is prosthetic and serves as the headquarters for government. The Dead Father, incidentally, is sometimes extremely large, though not as large as the corpse of god in *Towing Jehovah*, but Barthelme's figure is apparently rather variable in size, since he can seduce human-sized women.

Clearly, the Dead Father represents many things—psychological, literary, and religious. Psychologically, the power of a father (and the *nom du père*) continues to affect children even after he "dies." Barthelme is also lamenting his own belatedness in the world of letters created by Joyce, the great literary father. In religious terms, God is dead, but not dead enough for these children of the modern world. The children are rebelling against this all-powerful father, and are trying to bury him. At the end, their bulldozers are poised to push dirt over him, but we have to wonder whether he will truly succumb to mortality. Even if he cannot escape his hole in the ground, the children will obviously be forever haunted by their experiences. He is The Father.

His godhood shows in some of his reminiscences. In a tall tale about his struggle with evil, he says,

> Evil himself appeared, he-of-the-greater-magic, terrible in aspect. I don't want to talk about it, let me say only that I realized instantly that I was

on the wrong side of the Styx. However I was not lacking in wit, even in this extremity. Uncoiling my penis, then in the dejected state, I made a long cast across the river, sixty-five meters I would say, where it snagged most conveniently in the cleft of a rock on the farther shore. Thereupon I hauled myself hand-over-hand 'midst excruciating pain as you can imagine through the raging torrent to the other bank. . . . And on that bank of the river there stands to this day a Savings & Loan Association. A thing I fathered.[8]

As part of his procreative feats, the Dead Father avers that he "fathered upon [a woman] in those nights the poker chip, the cash register, the juice extractor, the kazoo, the rubber pretzel, the cuckoo clock, the key chain, the dime bank, the pantograph, the bubble pipe . . . as well as some thousands of children of the ordinary sort" (36). Upon that woman's dying, he pursues her into the underworld in the fashion of Orpheus, but discovers that she has no desire to return to her onerous procreative role; she likes the addictive food of the underworld and feels no obligation to give it up. Barthelme's many chaotic enumerations suggest the extreme fertility of this creative outpouring, and he credits the Dead Father with much of creation and particularly of cultural objects both practical and frivolous. Some Native American groups attribute creation to trickster figures, and the Dead Father's raunchiness is also found in trickster stories.

While the frustration of the children and their ferocious determination to get rid of the father is what we may at first see as central, I think by the end we also see the pathos of the Father and of growing old. At any chance they get, the children rub in the fact that he is an old fart, that he can't have his pick of the girls, and that he is powerless to prevent Thomas taking his jeweled belt buckle, his sword, and his passport. The father was told that he was being taken to the golden fleece, and he spins fine tales of how it will rejuvenate and invigorate him. When he is on the brink of his grave, he admits that he knew all along, but had hoped. . . . Barthelme is quite good at the humiliations of growing old, and while the Father's many symbolic functions keep him from seeming very dead, this book is more about aging and death than I realized in my first few readings. Seeing it in the context of the other books in this chapter brought out that side of it.

Like some other invented myths, this one concerns power, and particularly male and paternal power within culture, though it handles the subject comically. Even as the Titans were displaced by the Olympians, the Father loses out (as dynastic powers must eventually) to the younger generation. Dismantling paternal power, however, brings only modest improvement. The men are less tyrannical toward the women, and the women are more participatory in social situations. Seeing more of women and their thoughts, though, give us no sense of a great breakthrough or a significantly more admirable culture. Thomas is no Zeus, and Julie is no Aphrodite. No one exhibits the wisdom of Athena. As the new embodiment of government, they make us uneasy for the future. If they stand metaphorically for democracy, it is no wonder it functions ineffectually. That giants ruled the past and we now function as pygmies is a very old image for society, one familiar in the Middle Ages and at times since. While Barthelme does not believe the past to have been better or more harmonious than the present—after all, he is rigorously deconstructing the patriarchal past—his refusing to find glowing progress in Thomas's reforms makes this invented myth humanist and morally conservative in its exploration of power. Posthuman visions will project power onto the new generation and into the future.

Doing It Over: Hoban's *Riddley Walker*

Riddley Walker (1980) is more famous for its language than its mythology, but myth permeates this world. Hoban demonstrates the many levels on which one has to work to make such a mythology seem plausible. His fictional realm lies in the region of Canterbury, England (now Cambry, Inland), once part of a culture that bombed and irradiated itself back into primitive existence more than 2,400 years ago. This is not quite a new Stone Age, but almost. Culture has developed to the level that nomad hunters/herdsmen and farmers are competing for land, with the nomads finding more and more territory being fenced off against them. Some kind of government exists, called the Ram (after its headquarters at what was once Ramsgate), and it hires nomads to perform the dangerous task of digging up metal artifacts of the past. The metals are melted down and reused, so the culture has some metal, but only that which is scavenged from the previous world. Although the people do not have the advanced knowledge that would let them become technological again, they retain tantalizing tales of ships in the air, space stations, and pictures in the wind, and know that to regain these, they will need a device known in their mythology as Eusa's Head, what we know as a computer. The central myth, one of destruction rather than creation, concerns how their impoverished world came to be, the Bad Times and the 1 Big 1 being their names for the nuclear war and its bomb. All the characters know this story of origins because it forms the basis for a puppet show, a Ram-sanctioned activity that functions as both religious service and entertainment. Its performance is preceded by a ritual chant by the puppeteers and the audience about how Eusa split the Littl Shyning Man the Addom, and had to suffer, and because of his deeds, the audience must suffer penitentially.

The Eusa story is the main myth, but for it to be believable, Hoban gives us a genuinely different world, a different cultural mindset, different mental experiences, and a reality in which extrasensory perception is possible. The world he gives us both shapes the myth and is shaped by it. Its impressive plausibility comes from Hoban using just enough pieces of our own world to enable us to interpret how things we know become the things Riddley knows. We see fragments of his world's myths in children's game rhymes, in stories about names for places, in raunchy stories about Death, in parables from the Bad Time, and in stories about First and Second Knowing. First Knowing establishes the right way of being at home in the world; it comes from a dog, and bestows comfort at night, with nature, with darkness, and with death, all envisioned as belonging to primal femaleness. Second Knowing comes from a goat, and it bestows cleverness, the craving to own and amass things, and the itch to change things and "improve" them, which, we are shown, leads to trouble. When humans gain Second Knowing, they lose First Knowing.

In this culture, people's way of connecting to reality is instinctive, and involves ready access to the unconscious and maybe to something like Julian Jaynes's bicameral mind.[9] If people look at certain objects—a head stuck on a pole, a carved face, or even a puppet head—they can open their minds and hear these heads "tell."[10] Hearing the voice of the head or entering into dialog with it is a skill that can be cultivated, so that is not extrasensory in itself, but both Riddley Walker and Lissener, a radiation-deformed descendant of the computer elite, can sense thoughts even at a distance. They sense, for instance, that something will happen if they go toward one settlement rather than another.

The most obvious example of Hoban asserting a nonmaterial definition of reality takes place when Riddley has a "mynd flash of colourt lites with clicking and bleaping it wernt like nothing I ever actuerly seen nor heard only in dreams. I cud like feal the woal circel of the dead towns in me and see a line of grean lite sweaping roun that circel from the senter."[11] From this, he divines that they should not yet break the circle of the towns they are visiting. He describes it as "jus a line of grean lite sweaping and there come up blips" (89)—at which point he realizes that when he has spoken the inherited term blipful before, meaning significant, it must come from this green light, but he can have had no experience with a radar screen and no one to tell him that such a contact signal is called a blip. Somehow, that image from the past comes to him as if it had been buried in a collective unconscious, and he learns the roots of his own vocabulary.

The ability to pick up such extrasensory material may be limited to a few talented people, but at least two of the society's functionaries, those who tell and those who make connections, practice a kind of prophesying or interpreting with possible moral overtones. Telling seems to be something anyone might be able to do; when Riddley asks what some event means, he is told impatiently to be his own tell-man. Making connections is a religious function and is granted only after the candidate learns to read, memorizes the Eusa story, and is formally initiated in a ritual performed by the Pry Mincer (Prime Minister) that concludes with the scarring of the stomach of the new connections man. When Riddley's father dies and Riddley takes over his position as connection man for their band, he does not expect to have trouble carrying out that function, and is mortified and worried that his first connection puts him in a trance, so that virtually all he learns remains inside his head. His only spoken connection is the enigmatic statement, "EUSA'S HEAD IS DREAMING US" (61). This is not enough for his audience, who want explanations of the Eusa show they witnessed and of other points that are troubling them. In one day, Riddley's father dies, the elderly leader of the local feral dog pack deliberately runs onto Riddley's spear, and a baby is born dead. The community assumes these events to be meaningfully connected. The group's tell-woman, Lorna, is called upon by to make sense of this ill-assorted trio, and clearly, she has a system. When you have three, the one furthest out is the "nindicator." She makes parallels between the two cases of the old and worn out dying, but the baby being dead happens, she says, because of its proximity to the government digging for relics of the past age. The past, she feels, should be put behind one and allowed to remain dead, not be resuscitated, and the technological past, in particular, is dangerous.

In private talk with Riddley, Lorna makes him aware of a sense of self that is larger than our consciousness. She says that something lives in us that is not us; it puts on our bodies, and gets tired of us as we get older. It works and sees through us, but we are foreign to it. It is afraid of being birthed. Later, Riddley will occasionally feel something urging him on or seeing through his eyes, and will wonder about this something beyond the individual. In an interview, Hoban sheds light on his idea here: "There really is just one mind, and that in that mind the time is always Now. I have felt that way. I *do* feel as if there is only one single universal consciousness, and we are all receptors of it; and I *do* feel as if the time is always Now."[12] Riddley's folk do not seem to put much store in the possibility of an afterlife, and he never mentions a belief in God, and indeed does not seem to know what that word means. Nonetheless, he and Lorna sense something bigger than the individual, even though they have a very limited vocabulary for describing or analyzing it. Hoban is not pushing this interpretation of reality upon us, but it provides his world with strangeness.

People weave the myth into the fabric of everyday life. They tell anecdotal mythic stories to make points, explain a name, or pass the time—parables, perhaps. One concerns the man who temporarily bested death. Another concerns a couple that trades their child to the Devil for fire, and all three eat the baby because they are starving after the nuclear disaster. Their fire catches hold in the woods and burns up the man and woman, so not only have they killed their own child, but they also do not live to benefit. Another is the story of the Other Voice Owl who tries to swallow all the sounds of the world and the Lissener who listens them back. If the Lissener ceased to do this, the Owl would succeed and the world would end.

We find symbols that presumably have some attendant stories, though we do not hear them. The shape of the crypt under what was once Canterbury Cathedral looks like a matryoshka doll, and is referred to as Her what has her womb in Cambry. Although never called a goddess, something like that idea seems inchoately present. The architectural shape is likened to the doll put over the bed of a woman giving birth, and to the woman cake that is baked (159–60). First Knowing also had something to do with this female force, but we are given no mythology and no evidence of human sacrifice of the sort found around the Mediterranean as annual offerings to the Great Mother. Perhaps balancing that female force is the carved head of the Green Man, the disturbing ancient, pan-European image of a man with vines growing out of his mouth. As a representation of male being (or male destiny as fertilizer for plants), he is linked to the idea of stone men who walk under the earth, their feet meeting the feet of the man walking above the earth. When the man dies, the stones just become stones, though stones too can be listened to and heard to tell stories.

Dogs are another source of mythic ideas. Dogs have gone feral and offer one of the most immediate dangers facing humans who move outside their fenced areas, while people born deformed by radiation damage to their genes are called dog-people. Humans and dogs blend oddly. That First Knowing comes from dogs seems to rework the anthropological theories of domestication, and of how humans and dogs learned to live together for mutual benefit. A humorous story tells of a dog who becomes Pry Mincer. The pack of feral dogs that accepts Riddley rather than eating him goes about on its hind legs in one sequence, though this display may be a trance vision rather than ordinary reality.

The main myth, the one that shapes this whole novel, is the Eusa story. Eusa is the scientist figure credited with the technological discoveries that resulted in the 1 Big 1, the nuclear capability that led to all-out war. Furthermore, the politician-priest-puppeteers who perform the Eusa story regularly modify and add to that story in order to broadcast Mincery Binses (Ministry business), what we would call propaganda. This postapocalyptic world is fairly well layered with the mythic story.

Eusa is said to have been ordered to get the numbers of the 1 Big 1. He goes into the wood with his two dogs, and descends in levels of reality to the heart of the wood and then to the heart of stone, where he can see particle tracks. He sees the Littl Shyning Man between the antlers of a stag, tries to get the information from him, and pulls him in two. He does end up with the information he needs to build bombs and kill off most of the population.

This myth has a gloriously insane origin. The people find in the ruins of Canterbury Cathedral the handout available in the late twentieth century for tourists that explains a complex medieval painting. This painting was discovered in the late twentieth century under layers of plaster, and shows several scenes from the legend of Saint Eustace distributed about the one panel. At the bottom, and most prominent, is this pagan Roman soldier with his dogs seeing the crucified Christ between the antlers of a stag, the experience that caused him to convert to Christianity. In other parts of the picture, his wife is stolen by pirates, and his sons are grabbed by wild animals as he stands in the river, unable to reach any of them in time. Toward the top of the panel, his family, reunited after many years, joins in happy martyrdom for their faith's sake; the four of them are seen in a hollow, brazen, bull-shaped statue with a fire underneath it. In the more than 2,400 years since the nuclear disaster, people have lost most of their sense of what happened except that bombs destroyed much of the former civilization's structures. However, the ridiculous-seeming adaptation of the Saint Eustace legend to make the Eusa story may have been triggered by something dimly remembered from the Bad Times—the USA. Phonetically, USA might be pronounced Eusa in an England so primitive that it appears no longer to know about any wider world except for the land visible across the channel.

Other similar words cause stories to meld; Adam and atom produce the story of the Littl Shyning Man the Addom, who is seen in the Eusa story as a shining crucifix on a stag's head. His being pulled in two corresponds to splitting the atom, but also becomes the new original sin, the reason for their degraded state. When Riddley witnesses torture, he realizes that we keep trying to tear the little man in two. Despite knowing what happened when Eusa did it, we still get ourselves into situations where force is the easy way out and we take it. This attitude toward force is portrayed as the act that produced this future world. Going through the changes may be a dim reference to a nuclear chain reaction, but it nicely suggests a pattern of atonements. Hart and heart merge, as do savior and savor, wood and would (will, desire). These homonymic blends produce symbolically meaningful language for this new world.[13]

Hoban's government ministers have become very adept at "blipful" interpretation applied to any scrap of writing that comes from the old time. The description of Saint Eustace seeing the shining savior between the stag's antlers gets processed in the following way by the Pry Mincer, who has long pondered the bit of writing but does not have the picture to help him, and of course lacks any dictionary.

> I come to *"the figure of the crucified Saviour."* Number of the crucified Saviour and wunnering how that be come the Littl Shyning Man the Addom. Suddn it jumpt in to my mynd, "A littl salting and no saver".... Id never put it to gether with saver like in *savery*. Not sweet. Salty. A salt crucified. I gone to the chemistery working I askit 1 Stoan Phist that wer Belnots dad what *crucified* myt be nor he wernt cern but he thot itwd be some thing you done in a cruciboal. 1st time Id heard the word. Thats a hard firet boal they use it doing a chemistery try out which you cud call that crucifrying or crucifying. Which that crucified Saviour or

crucifryd salt thats our Littl Shyning Man him as got pult in 2 by Eusa. So *"the figure of the crucified Saviour"* is the number of the salt de vydit in 2 parts in the cruciboal and radiating lite coming acrost on it. The salt and the saver. (128–29)

He goes on to interpret the rest of the picture. The handout refers to hamlets (little villages), but he interprets the word as meaning little pigs. The animals and pirates are sharp and biting, and so they must be acids. The four souls gathered up on a cloth as they are raised to Heaven are four salts, and Eustace's two sons are the "catwl twis" or catalyst. This grand (but very earnest) nonsense is part of the "tryl narrer" and "spare the mending" (trial and error, and experimenting) that humans do as they stumble their way into science. Lest we laugh too contemptuously, we should remember that alchemy produced screeds of similar ingenuity and lunacy on its way to becoming chemistry. Such misinterpretations of the past are a commonplace of post-nuclear-holocaust literature. Walter Miller's *Canticle for Leibowitz* shows his monk worrying that a fallout monster might have survived in a fallout survival shelter. Hill shamans swallowed transistors, which were part of the *machina analytica* or computer, in order to gain infallibility.[14]

In addition to the legend of Saint Eustace, however twisted and confused it has become, Riddley's society retains dim versions of the nuclear catastrophe, but naturally reduces it to stories about individuals. Mr Clevver was the Big Man of Inland. Eusa worked for him. Mr Clevver wanted Berstin Fyr to use against national enemies, and knew it would involve following "thay partickler tracks" (30; particle tracks as in a cloud chamber). When Eusa descends into the heart of the stone with his dogs, he can see particles and molecules dancing about making the "girt dants of the every thing" (163)— an interesting invocation of the Renaissance Great Dance transposed to the atomic level. When at this level of reality, Eusa finds the Littl Shyning Man and tortures him. He is trying to torture the number of the 1 Big 1 out of him, but the Littl Shyning Man gets pulled apart and dies. Shining waves come out of the two pieces of the little man, and Eusa can write down the number of the Master Changes of the 1 Big 1. In later life, Eusa is haunted by what he did, but is pursued by a vision of the Littl Shyning Man torn in two, the figure who is the atom, Adam, and Christ, who also said "I mus be wut I mus be" (31), echoic of Yahweh's I am that I am (or I will be what I will be, depending on the translation).[15] As the ritual chant before the Eusa show puts it,

They said, "He done his time wewl do our time."
I said, "Hes doing it for us."
They said, "Weare doing it for him."
I said, "Keap it going. Chances this time."
They said, "Chances nex time."
I said, "New Chance every time." (44)

The distant descendants of Eusa and his culture must live their penance as he did, for they cannot escape out of it. When Eusa threatened to die out of it, he was warned that the little shining man would simply pursue him in another place. In this post-Christian world, the words "crucified savior" have lost all their original meaning, and even the idea of postmortem existence seems underdeveloped. Eusa may conceive of life after death, but Riddley seems to feel that death is nothing but the body returning to earth. We still have a mythological universe here when Eusa descends into the heart of the stone, down to the atomic level, for this alternate level of reality is not one that just anyone can visit.

As previously noted, the Ministry puppeteers alter the contents of the show to reflect the political preoccupations of the Ministry, which, under the current Pry Mincer, is the recovery of Eusa's Head. Regaining computers would give them the power to do many new things or recover old abilities. The cultural conservatives—most of them nomads like Riddley's crowd—feel that meddling with anything from the past will just bring on deserved disaster, but some ambitious and curious folk want to try to recreate some of the technology that once made life easier. In the newest Mincery puppet sequence, Eusa attaches his head to a machine and cranks it so that his ideas run into the machine and it performs wonderful calculations. Then Mr Clevver grabs the handle and cranks until no ideas are left in Eusa, and walks off with the machine, leaving Eusa simple-minded and unable to control how his ideas will be applied. The Mincery wishes to rediscover a computer, yet is unwilling to see itself as Mr Clevver or accept that such technology will lead to violence.

Riddley's society is divided between those who distrust all innovation and those who would like to regain some technologies. Riddley himself is taken aback to learn that the previous society had all the marvels in slightly under 2,000 years by their counting system, whereas his has gone some 2,400 years and has no technology to show for it—no rockets, space stations, or TV. The book consists mostly of Riddley's exploring various attitudes toward such change and the power that change might enable. Sometimes he wavers toward power and wants to gain it. Sometimes it scares or disgusts him, particularly in the form of torture. Sometimes he feels that if power comes, you let it flow through you but do not actively engage it. When standing on the edge of a ditch surrounding what was once an accelerator ring, he feels power, as if the power is taking him sexually, and that sexual reaction makes him understands why some people would pursue it blindly. Other insights make him leery.

Hoban's crucified savior obviously reminds us of a Christian moral standard, and Hoban makes allusions that could be a Christian subtext. At times, for instance, various characters of his take on responsibility for deeds or disasters, their own and those of others, as an almost physical load; similarly, characters in Miller's *Canticle* accept such burdens. His Jew, Benjamin, sees himself bearing the weight of his entire people, and Benjamin's friend, Dom Paulo, admits that as a monk and priest, he is responsible for all the sins of all monks and priests back to Christ, an impossible burden, yet one that a priest cannot escape. Eusa's Orphic head, cut from his body, warns the Ram against wanting to do the bad thing and build more bombs, so once they kill Eusa, the burden of that wrong is now on them. After parting from Lissener, Riddley realizes "I had Lissener on my back plus a woal lot moren him I cudnt even say what all it wer and more and more I wer afeart it wer coming to some thing I wernt going to be hevvy a nuff for" (111). Abel Goodparley, once Pry Mincer, and now tortured and blinded, says he has so many "Drop Johns" on him that he is tired of living. Drop John is a conflation of the Hangman puppet and the Ghost puppet from the Punch and Judy show who haunts the murderous Punch in some versions. Goodparley's former partner, Orfing, says dismissively that the blinded Goodparley is "the reales part of you. It's the Littl Shyning Man of you innit" (175). In Christian terms, some kinds of suffering do make one like Christ. Because Goodparley had told Riddley that the 1 Big 1 came out of SPIRIT OF GOD (155), Riddley sometimes yells that phrase without any sense of what it might mean. Hoban's post-Christian world is littered with fragments of old myths.

Hoban's vision of human nature suggests that he considers humans deeply flawed.[16] Not only did cleverness bring about the 1 Big 1, it now brings about the 1 Little 1—gunpowder. Riddley himself puts some of the pieces of the puzzle together, and gunpowder is recreated from formulas handed down among dyers and charcoal burners. The first explosion causes two accidental deaths, and the second explosion was detonated deliberately to kill a tangled orgy of Lissener and his Eusa Folk, who are trancing down to a level where their minds become collective and can bring up advanced theory. The actions in the novel certainly suggest that any return to the old technology will result in evil and violence, and so should be avoided. Instead of pushing Christianity, however, Hoban invents a quasi-mythology of Punch and Judy conflated with the legend of Eusa.

Riddley is introduced to a Punch and Judy show through Goodparley, who secretly possesses a bag of Punch and Judy puppets in addition to his bag of Ram-sanctioned Eusa puppets. A few appear in both shows. The most important of these is Mr Clevver, who is none other than the Devil or Mr On-The-Level from Punch and Judy. What most strikes Riddley about that show is that Punch will always kill the other characters; that's his nature. Those characters include his baby, as in the Bad Time story in which parents sacrifice their child for a meal. What seems to matter to Hoban is our killing off our children's future and even our children in our pursuit of technological advancement. As Riddley ponders Punch, he wonders: "Why wil he all ways kil the babby if he can?" (220). Given the nature of the new evil let into the world with nuclear bombs, evil that produces deformed children, that is the question for us all. Part of the answer is our lust for power.

Hoban even includes a bit of Orphic mythology. The heads on poles have Orphic resonances, since his head, after being torn off by maenads, floated down the river across the sea to Lesbos, where it became an oracle. More specifically, Eusa's head was torn off his body, and it floated across the water to the Ram and preached its message of woe before falling silent and disappearing. Hoban would also seem to have in mind Celtic myth; the heads of Brán the Blessed, Mac Dathó, and Conaire Mór, all prophesied or spoke after death, and Celtic warriors traditionally cut off the heads of vanquished enemies.[17] Symbolic heads flourish in Celtic art.

Another figure with mythic qualities, albeit enigmatic ones, is the carved Green Man that Riddley discovers beneath a stone in the ruins of Canterbury Cathedral. It serves him as a meditation device; while he stares at it, pictures form in his head. He makes intuitive connections, some having to do with power, some with the local politics, and some with the nature of life. The male head with vines growing out of its mouth suggests that after death, all we do is feed the plant life, though Riddley admits that this is a mostly a message for men, since women, by having a child come out of their womb, know they are making new life and something of them is passed on.

The ruins of the cathedral also house an area sacred to the feminine, and we see another vaguely female force as the embodiment of death; she appears to men as a hag who claims them through sexual congress. She has iron teeth between her legs (and a red-hot iron willy for the ladies). She rides a rat. These are not the sometimes handsome or heroic gods of early mythologies. These mythic figures lack an elaborate mythological cycle of stories, but insofar as many of them concern death, the 1 Big 1, and the damaged nature of the resultant world, they belong to a larger picture, one that relates to how humanity got itself in this impoverished state. Complete, networked cycles of mythology are probably mostly the creation of later ages looking back. What Hoban gives us is the confused, complex picture with its different levels of seriousness and joke. Like actual religions, all these levels work to give humans a place in their universe and give some sense of meaning to their lives.

If Hoban had merely imposed the Eusa story on some future society, it would not carry as much resonance as it does when he works it into all levels of his creation. His children's chanting rhymes are crucial to this effect. "Fools Circel 9wys" appears very early in the novel, and will haunt the action throughout:

Horny Boy rung Widders Bel
Stoal his Fathers Ham as wel
Bernt his Arse and Forkt a Stoan
Done It Over broak a boan
Out of Good Shoar vackt his wayt
Scratcht Sams Itch for No. 8
Gone to senter nex to see

> Cambry coming 3 times 3
>   Sharna pax and get the poal
>   When the Ardship of Cambry comes out of the hoal. (5)

The first units are the names of towns in a circle around Canterbury: Herne Bay, Whitstable, Ashford, Folkstone, and Dover. For obscure reasons, Deal becomes Good Shoar, Sams Itch is Sandwich, and Cambry is Canterbury—its name having gone the same road as Canterbridge when it became Cambridge. Sharna pax is sharpen ax and the pole is called for because heads are put on poles for telling. The Ardship or Archbishop is for the chop. In Riddley's time, the Ardship's title was kept for the leader of the deformed Eusa Folk and belonged to Lissener, who was being taken in a circle through these towns and interrogated, none too gently, in all of them. When he reached Cambry, he expected to be executed or tortured to death, and so broke away with Riddley's help.

"London Bridge is Falling Down" as a playground game has a capture element, and "Red Rover" has a breaking through the line routine. "Oranges and Lemons," made famous by George Orwell in *1984,* has the same capture element as London Bridge, as well as the threat of an ax as chopper to chop off one's head. In Riddley's world, those particular nursery rhymes have disappeared, but others with the same activities have come into existence. Riddley refers to playing a child's game of the Ardship being caught but bursting out—he liked breaking out like that. A work chant starts "London Town is drownt this day/ Hear me say walk a way/ Sling your bundle tern and go/ Parments [Parliament's] in the mud you know"(9)—clearly recording a disaster as memorable as London Bridge falling down, a tsunami or seiche perhaps, rushing up the Thames estuary through London. Such rhymes can gain power. Riddley is distinctly upset to hear a boy making fun of his trance connection: "Riddley Walker wernt no talker/ Dint know what to say / Put his head up on a poal/ And then it tol all day" (63). Talk of one's head on a pole leads to "bad luck go away" signs and then shunning, until perhaps one becomes a scapegoat and has one's head put on a pole.

Readers can quarrel with Hoban's realism—as those linguistically inclined have strenuously done, saying language would have mutated to incomprehensibility in 2,400 years of non-technological living. They can also argue that his characters are not as heavily bound by myth as many low-tech cultures have been. Possibly that expectation of heaviness and the intolerance that mark our sense of religion come from monotheistic roots. From what relatively little we know about ancient Greece or about the Germanic tribes, heresy hunting and auto-da-fe for issues of belief were not the norm. Native Americans seem not to have been bothered by the way myths differed among neighboring tribes, so the implied tolerance is not impossible. Riddley seems to acknowledge some kind of female divine power, though it is more a mystery than divinity, and might just be the province of women in his culture and not of men. His band does not enforce belonging with sexual taboos, eating taboos, clothing taboos, or behavior taboos that we can see. Gender differences may be significant, in that we see no connection-women or ministers, and literacy appears to be confined to those functionaries. While we know that some groups have attacked one another to get land, we hear nothing that suggests these are motivated by any kind of religious fervor. That does not mean that everyone is part of a big, happy family. Riddley is aware of minute shifts in public opinion about himself, and worries when he senses a widening gap between himself and his group. The Eusa myth influences people, but does not rule them dictatorially. Overall, the story works because it explains how their way of life came into being. It gives meaning to their low-tech suffering amid ruins of past splendor. It makes sense of how they fit into history. It supplies a rudimentary morality that decries tearing the little man in two and warns against cleverness and second knowing, with their emphasis on accumulating goods and making manipulative changes.

The richness of Hoban's imagined world gives substance to his mythology. He is extremely aware of how misunderstandings can lead to solemn nonsense, but at the same time, he shows how a set of moral values can emerge from such nonsense. He knows that the complexities of history will be lost, but recognizes that a story about individuals such as Eusa and Mr Clevver may well be retold and handed down. We see the many forms that the human search for meaning takes, the many ways Hoban's characters satisfy that urge—through rhymes, rituals, tells, and connections. In Riddley's ruminations about the puppet shows, we see how a kind of art functions in this society, and, indeed, are witness to the rebirth of secular drama. Riddley's Punch show will be the first non-Mincery-sanctioned entertainment for his culture. Punch will continue to be violent and kill the other puppets, if only because a puppeteer can only wear two hand-puppets at once.[18] That apparent limitation will nonetheless allow Riddley to explore tensions in the social fabric, and let him play with subjects on which people feel hostilities; it will let him get them to laugh at extreme behaviors. Riddley's confidence at making connections by drawing on his inspiration of the moment will also give him the confidence to improvise business on his little stage. He goes off, imagining himself rhymed:

Riddley Walkers ben to show
Riddley Walkers on the go
Don't go Riddley Walkers track
Drop Johns ryding on his back. (220)

The Ghost of the Hangman puppet, Drop John, is the burden of guilt, personal and collective, and historical, that descends to him as part of this impoverished culture. He seems happy with the road he has chosen, however. It permits him to remain nomadic, whereas the people he grew up with are squeezed by farms or pushed into laboring for the Mincery to dig up metal artifacts. Taking the road as he does also removes him from the quarrels about what power his society should seek and what they should try to accomplish with it. He is free to make up his own mind. In becoming dog-friendly as he has, and his living without any more possessions than he and his partner can carry on their backs, he is living much more closely than possible before to First Knowing, being at home in the world and the dark. The mythic material in the story suggests that not many humans achieve that state, so he is doing well. By giving up most kinds of power, he gains a satisfying life.

Myths about Myths: Moore's *Watchmen*

Alan Moore undertakes an unusual project. The background to his work is what I call the invented mythic world of Superman, Batman, Captain America, and others, who flourished as popular cultural embodiments of shining American power in the 1940s and 1950s. Whereas American power as good, clean, and liberty-loving was plausible to some during that earlier era, it was much harder to take seriously in the 1970s. Vietnam changed that, and Watergate undermined any faith in politicians. Moore wants to examine such power-figures as Superman in the context of the 1980s (he published Watchmen in 1986–87), but those characters legally belonged to others. Furthermore, DC Comics and Marvel had no wish for their cherished icons to be exposed to a more critical standard than that of earlier decades. Eventually Moore and artist Dave Gibbons decided to invent a handful of superheroes and study the species in that fashion. The result is invented myth about quasi-myth, or metamyth. What Moore and Gibbons ended up focusing on was power and the ethics of power—not surprising, since power is what differentiates such superhumans from ordinary humans.

Actually, their collection of costumed vigilantes (as objectors called them) are mostly just humans in excellent physical shape and trained in fighting; in that respect, they resemble Batman rather than Superman. However, we wouldn't really have superheroes without someone who can go beyond the human, and we get that in Jon Osterman or Dr. Manhattan, a physicist destroyed by a nuclear accident who managed to reassemble himself atom by atom, and who has, therefore, control over matter as no other human. Moreover, what he assembled is not truly human; his body can change size, can exist without oxygen on Mars, can teleport, and can disappear. We also have what might be called a Nietzschean superman in Adrian Veidt; though human physically, he is credited with the highest IQ in the world and has assembled a world-class fortune from scratch. Thus, he combines a brief career as a superhero with capitalism on the grandest scale. Like several others, he sees that the Soviet Union and the United States are about to destroy the world through their nuclear escalation in this slightly altered world (America won the Vietnam War and Nixon is in his fourth term as president). His brains and his fortune allow him to create the illusion of invasion by space aliens in order to bring the two superpowers together in a common cause. His illusion kills off several million people in New York City, so is very credible. As far as he is concerned, the ends justify the means, since nuclear war might destroy all earthly life. He sees himself controlling this newly pacified world from behind the scenes, so he also stands to benefit from the massacre.

Power at the atomic level and power based on brains and a huge fortune—these are two, but we are shown other kinds of power as well. One is a kind of moral purity. The masked figure known as Rorschach had been a child from an abusive home, the victim of bullies in school, reform school, and jail. He has, though, an absolute sense of what he considers evil and complete willingness to do any damage to or kill someone who is doing wrong. Although thoroughly repulsive in behavior, we grudgingly come to admire his integrity. He knows that Adrian Veidt or Dr. Manhattan will kill him because he refuses to hide this trick on the world that has killed millions, and even more important to him, he refuses to forget that Veidt murdered another of the masked group, The Comedian, because The Comedian had stumbled onto Veidt's plan. Dr. Manhattan does indeed kill Rorschach, and Rorschach pulls off his mask to show his full hatred and contempt for those who countenance murdering the Comedian.

The Comedian had embodied yet another kind of power; one might call him the tarnished descendant of the shining superpowers of the 1940s, and indeed, he is visually based on Marvel's Captain America. He serves as an agent for the U. S. government, and so is allowed to practice his violent skills since he does that government's dirty work for it. He has been in Vietnam, and relishes the violence and battle. His eyes and teeth gleam as he wields a flamethrower. We see him kill a woman whom he impregnated and who has attacked him for abandoning her. We know that he has attempted rape of a female masked hero. His huge muscles make champions in the iron-pumping world look puny. His willingness to throw his weight about probably stands for the United States intervening in various parts of the world, though many of its interventions in the Middle East come after *Watchmen* was published. Much is made of his being completely amoral, of his enjoying his power and violence for their own sake, and not worrying about the morality of his power. He can compel, so why shouldn't he? That sums up his approach to power.

Acker worries about male misuse of power over females; that generates and ruins humanity's entire world. Hoban worries about the power that results when clever people create bombs and other weapons of large-scale destruction; he feared destroying the world rather than thinking in terms of creation. He also senses power as a visceral sensation, one that can addict people on the personal level. Clearly, nuclear power also worried Moore, with the United States all too likely to deploy it while challenging, or being challenged by, the Soviet Union. Unlike the others, one of his characters—Veidt—has a utopia in mind and has the power to encourage it to come into being, but why should we expect that to work? Humans will never agree on what constitutes utopia. Adrian may be making rational decisions, but they will not. Given his treatment of his helpers—he poisons them when he is done with them and blows up the artists who helped him create the alien monster—we can only assume that he will automatically rub out the people who disagree with his edicts, which would tarnish any vision of perfection. Dr. Manhattan will presumably go off on his own and set up his own realm—he talks of creating human life elsewhere—so perhaps he can think of different qualities to build into his creatures. In his superhuman form, though, he shows himself so little able to interact with humans or care about them that one doubts how well his judgment would operate when creating his own life forms. The image most frequently associated with Dr. Manhattan is clockwork, cogs, and gears, not promising as a basis for designing people, unless they are to be robots.

In other words, we have not come up with a way of using power safely or wisely. Rorschach's is true vigilante justice. Most readers, I suspect, feel no compunction about the child-murderer whom he kills, but generalizing his morality means that you must trust the vigilante's beliefs, and too many vigilante or honor killings murder people who do not seem guilty to the wider world: minorities by race or religion or sexual orientation, or those disempowered by female gender in a male-centric culture. We are unlikely to accept that attitude as proper or moral. Dr. Manhattan's power is so far beyond what is possible that it is a thought experiment only: create new humans somewhere else. Since Dr. Manhattan says nothing about whether he would design them differently, we have no idea whether he would come up with something workable if he did. Supposing he did indeed improve humans, he might produce a peaceable kingdom like that in Margaret Atwood's *Oryx and Crake* or in Vonnegut's *Galápagos*—creatures who strike us as more animal than human, and therefore unable to wipe themselves out with machines. He would have to find some way around our basic irrationality, as gradually teased out by the many experiments of psychologist Daniel Kahneman, for instance. Dr. Manhattan would have to find a better balance of the intelligence and hierarchical drive that Octavia Butler identifies as humanity's problem.[19] How would he handle the greedy cleverness that Hoban targets, the desire always to build a better mousetrap, to make everything better, bigger (or smaller, if electronic), more powerful, and faster. Insofar as he thinks in terms of clockwork, he might produce Houyhnhnm-like humans. Moore gives us no answers. Dr. Manhattan does not represent any usable answer to power.

Adrian Veidt is the closest to an answer given, but Moore treats this option more as tinsel and glitter and nostalgia than as real or plausible. Veidt does have logic on his side if nuclear war would have wiped out all (or almost all) life, scenarios played out in Nevil Shute's *On the Beach* and Miller's *Canticle for Leibowitz*. No humans and indeed no land animals will survive, maybe just deep ocean dwellers. Most scenarios for nuclear disaster do allow for a few survivors, however, in which case Veidt's logic may be flawed. Yes, he only kills three million, whereas a nuclear disaster leaving only a small population would kill vastly more people, but he will only be able to control his population by killing all who resist his regime. What defines "better" under those circumstances? Is one better off living in a heavily regimented utopia governed by someone who is, after all, mortal? Would one be better off living as Riddley Walker and his folk? Moore does not answer, but Veidt's fascination with death-obsessed Egyptian pharaohs and great conquerors make us distrust his ambitions as morbid or psychologically suspect. The very end of *Watchmen* suggests that Moore prefers us to know the score and make our own decisions. Rorschach's journal will probably be published, in which case the public may eventually figure out that the invasion was a manipulative illusion. Moore also upholds personal relationships: two minor masked vigilantes, Silk Spectre (Laurie) and Nite Owl (Tom), are trying to escape Veidt's surveillance and are living disguised and on the run. Laurie also reconciles with her mother, and that is one of the last scenes in the book. Moore would seem therefore to be upholding human messiness and illogic over other systems, but that leaves us admitting that humans may wipe themselves out or reduce life to the level seen in *Riddley Walker* or worse even. He does not find any way around power. Power is there. It is dangerous. No matter what, it will kill.

These three authors all end with major characters trying to live outside the regular patterns. Acker's "pirates" and other women seem to try to live with absolutely minimum income or connection to the world of getting and spending. O and Ange, indeed, end up in fantasy—winning a treasure and running with it, though that treasure may be a metaphor for sexual ecstasy. Riddley ends up trying to support himself as the first non-licensed showman, a precarious arrangement that could get him killed at any time. He will be always on the move, never safe, never sure of his next meal. He welcomes independence and freedom from the rules made by others, but will have to be both clever and lucky to survive. Ex-superheroes Laurie and Tom are trying to slide through the cracks; they hope Veidt will accept that they are keeping mum about the invasion, but know that he may decide their knowledge is dangerous. How they will make a living is not clear. They both once had power, and Tom had a lot of money, but they cannot draw on that if they are on the run. They have gained a personal relationship, but may find life hard indeed. These three authors find no answer; can a very different kind of invented mythology offer any different result? For that, I go briefly outside Anglophone literature and turn to Italo Calvino's cosmicomical stories.

Mythologizing the Universe: Calvino and Gaiman

Power is not the first thing that Italo Calvino thinks about when producing mythical figures. Instead, he mythologizes science. Each of his cosmicomical stories starts with some scientific commentary or a bit of history of science. He introduces us to the Big Bang, the first light, the first color, crystals, various theories of how the moon came into existence, dinosaurs, the first birds, the first sign, the nature of space, and probability—to name only some of his topics. What makes them seem mythic is the presence of a consciousness or a group of mentalities at such originary moments. The audacity of a consciousness existing before and during the Big Bang is breathtaking. Calvino cheerfully stretches our minds and violates all of our commonplace assumptions. He does not call his figures gods and nobody worships them, but their presence at—and sometimes their causal relationship to—events makes them at least nominally god-like. The figures do not evolve a mythology; instead, they mostly undergo endless variations on the same story. Consequently, that repeated tale of thwarted desire becomes a signature for this universe. In each story, old Qfwfq tells us about his youth, and all subsequent description in the story is given by young, effervescent Qfwfq as he tries and fails again to win a female being. Underlying all of this is an unusual interpretation of material reality, one that Calvino refines and plays through again and again, as if hoping it will solidify into something like belief or assurance. For Qfwfq, power is seeing pattern in chaos and thereby finding meaning; that is all the power he demands. In other words, power is completely mental, and governs the relationship we feel to material reality, not to each other. This is unusual indeed, so how does it work, if it does?

Because witnessing the Big Bang is so mind-blowing a concept, let us take that story. Calvino starts with a summation of something Edwin P. Hubble said about galaxies' velocity being establishable by extrapolating back to the moment when *"all the universe's matter was concentrated in a single point, before it began to expand in space."*[20] Old Qfwfq asserts the "we were all there" since everything that became the universe was all at that one point. Calvino plays with our inadequate vocabulary for describing that situation. One cannot say they were packed like sardines because "there wasn't even space to pack us into" (43). The inhabitants he names clearly all inhabit an Italian apartment building, and include a variety of different types, including Mrs. Ph(i)nk$_0$ and her friend De XuaeauX, and a family of immigrants, among others. The men all vie for Mrs. Ph(i)nk$_o$'s attention. Qfwfq remarks: "The happiness I derived from her was the joy of being concealed, punctiform, in her, and of protecting her, punctiform, in me; it was at the same time vicious contemplation (thanks to the promiscuity of the punctiform convergence of us all in her) and also chastity (given her punctiform impenetrability)" (46–47). Her expressed wish that she had some room so she could make some noodles for her male admirers caused everything to fly apart in the Big Bang. As a result of that wish to nurture, we now have space, fields of wheat, mountains producing water, calves, and the sun to ripen the plants, but Mrs. Ph(i)nk$_o$ has become the energy-heat-light of the universe and fills it with her nurturing power, while all her admirers mourn her loss. When any two of those admirers meet in later years, meaning in our present time, they all sigh when they think of this woman, and long for the contraction of the universe that will bring them all back to one point again.

What we have here is Qfwfq sighing for a female force and unable to gain even a modicum of her attention exclusively for himself. We have her transforming in a fashion that makes her permanently unavailable, at least until the universe contracts again. The power of her generous, nurturing wish brings the universe into being, though she could not have predicted that result. We find beings who are able to live through billions of years, undergoing whatever metamorphoses are necessary to meet new conditions. Given such immortals, death is abolished as a concern. The one thing we do not get in this particular story is the clash in Qfwfq's value system of separate grains of being versus those individual bits being melded into a paste, or sea, or soup. Even in one point, they are aware of their separate existences, and are not melted together. That makes this one of his sunnier and less anxious stories.

As I have argued elsewhere, Calvino has a very deep-rooted way of thinking of reality, whether material or intellectual.[21] Everything consists of numberless units. The eye or I, the consciousness or cogito, confronts these. When that consciousness can keep them separate, order them, and arrange them, then it is happy and comfortable with the world. This is the closest that Calvino comes to identifying a kind of power—the power to name and derive meaning from classifying and ordering the cosmos, a scientific impulse. When that cogito is unable to control the units and they all run together into an undifferentiable mass, then the cogito is devastated and feels defeated. It feels threatened and fears being engulfed by that mass. In Freudian terms, we get oral power expressed by calling the universe into being or by ordering and naming the units; opposing that is the oral-stage threat of being swallowed up. Control is clearly an issue; this consciousness is insecure and hesitant, and wants to be on top of things. Qfwfq represents this consciousness, and he is indeed insecure, as well as jejeune, jealous, and sometimes preposterous. As a character, he tends to remind us of some of our own weaknesses and longings; we do not respect him much, but we wince at his errors and at times vibrate with fellow feeling. Calvino's liking for multiple units is obvious in his later fiction—the tarot cards, the cities of Marco Polo, the meditations of Mr. Palomar, and the beginning chapters of novels.

Within the cosmicomical stories, these multiple units may be atoms, meteors, signs, or things to bet on. We see Qfwfq attempting to deal with ordering things in "Crystals." He loves crystals for their atomic order; his inamorata prefers the flaws—after all, flaws or contaminants are what make rubies red, for instance. Back when the world was cooling and Qfwfq thought everything might crystallize out into huge uniform solids, he was content. He lives, though, in the New York City of today, where that ersatz crystal we call glass covers everything and produces false-crystal buildings. Glass is "a paste of haphazard molecules which has invaded and cemented the world" (180–81). Qfwfq is more explicit than usual about his habit of mind: "Rationalize, that's the big task: rationalize if you don't want everything to come apart" (184). "I play the game, in other words, the game of pretending there's an order in the dust, a regularity in the system, or an interpenetration of different systems, incongruous but still measurable, so that every graininess of disorder coincides with the faceting of an order which promptly crumbles" (182). As Qfwfq looks around, he realizes that modern society is based on crystals, whether in TV, photography, or ice cubes, and yet the functioning comes through flaws in those crystals. He cannot separate them, and sees that as a kind of defeat, but not a bad one, since the crystals are still there. He ends with a reference to Thelonius Monk and jazz, a regular musical pattern (crystal) that is then varied (introducing flaws) for a greater total experience.

In "Blood, Sea," we get a more thorough defeat. Jealous couples in a car along a coastal road irritate and bait each other in such a fashion that the driver shows his temper by taking flashy risks and then ends up shooting off a cliff and drowning them in the sea. The blood inside them (which was once the outside sea to unicellular selves long ago) is now again joined to that undifferentiated mass. In "The Soft Moon," Qfwfq survives the world being enveloped by undifferentiated moon glop, but it takes millennia to escape from that paste and re-establish life on a new surface. In that story, the paste is linked to unpleasant femaleness, and we also find that pattern of being overwhelmed by a female in "The Origin of the Birds." Qfwfq resists the bird queen Or's trying to wipe his mind:

> For a fraction of a second between the loss of everything I knew before and the gain of everything I would know afterwards, I managed to embrace in a single thought the world of things as they were and of things as they could have been, and I realized that a single system included all. The world of birds, of monsters, of Or's beauty was the same as the one where I had always lived, which none of us had understood wholly. (177)

When he reveals that he has not forgotten his former life, he is attacked, and barely escapes. He loses his new love and her world and his understanding of the nature of reality. He is left with fragments of a picture that he cannot integrate in his mind.

At other times, the undifferentiated mass is not gendered or is even part of masculine rivalry, and Qfwfq deals with the infinite multiplication of signs that he and a male rival make or erase or deface ("A Sign in Space"). In "The Light-Years," Qfwfq makes a blunder and then sees signs from other galaxies that beings there saw him (he thinks). He tries to erase the blunder, tries to do things that will put him in a good light, but he cannot ensure that he will be observed, and for all his frantic attempts, he finally realizes that he can never change their opinion because they are receding beyond the horizon from which he or his signs can be seen. In this instance, his losing control and being unable to fix things brings a kind of peace, if not a happy one. Qfwfq now cannot wait for all the galaxies to fly so far apart that all his observers become unreachable and he, unobserved.

For all that Qfwfq's personality inclines him to jealousy, hyperexcitability, and boundless desire, and these are often portrayed in irritating ways, the primary reader response that Calvino engenders, in me at least, is wonder. What Qfwfq sees matters more than what he feels. The ineffable amazement of first light, or first bird seen, or the pleasures of collecting newly minted atoms, all suggest that the material world burgeons with newness and beauty, with strangeness and glory that we have ceased to see. Instead of taking sides in Qfwfq's arguments, I just want to shake him and tell him not to whine or worry about details, but just to look and revel in the wonder of it all. His petty jealousies or puppy loves may keep him from being overwhelmed by all of the infinitudes to which he is exposed, but we as readers are not directly exposed to the wonders, so wish he would not intrude irritating sentiments into the staggering vistas that he opens for us. For all that Calvino may not be thinking explicitly in terms of alternatives to power, he has produced one. Pleasure comes from emotional response to one's surrounds, to the universe, not from amassing wealth or the ability to force others to do what one orders. One derives one's pleasures from sensations and experiences that belong to everyone and to no one. These experiences are free, if only we would learn to value them. They can richly furnish our minds. We can contemplate what we have seen, and reignite wonder or find meaning by fitting what we observed to patterns stored in our minds. That identifying of pattern produces resolution and satisfaction.

Each story is a further creation myth, with new wonders for us, or if not a creation, then a situation that is totally beyond our experience or ken. Furthermore, each starts with a nugget of scientific fact or theory, so Calvino's myths—as stories about the beginning of the world—are not antiscientific or risible from a scientific viewpoint, as are the notions of forming earth and Heaven from the skull of a giant or creating all the species and putting them on a human-built ark. Calvino does not so much explain the universe as exploit scientific theories for the wonders hidden within them. We do not take Qfwfq seriously as someone who could exist—immortal or unkillable as he is—and we know that the situations he describes are highly stylized or simplified. Calvino is not offering us science as such, but science mythologized or science as story. Qfwfq is not a conventional god and has no ties to religion. At most, he is a human focalizing viewpoint that brings us to where we can see the world humanly that is normally described in scientific terms. In a sense, Calvino reverses the belief that myth is science childishly misunderstood, and gives us science imagined as myth.

At the same time, Qfwfq's all-too-human behaviors remind us that we too are part of this universe, and that our desires may in some way be responsible for further creations and developments. One of Calvino's best examples of this appears in "The Spiral." Qfwfq is a mollusk this time, and although he and his kind do not have eyes, he starts extruding a colorful shell in order to make himself stand out and be noticed by his inamorata. Later, Qfwfq sees his original mollusk love in all the other female beings of his world and feels an overwhelming desire for all these emanations of the female in the world, and cannot understand how, as mollusk, his creating a need for eyes did not therefore give mollusks eyes too. He had assumed (he claims) that eyes would come as a result of his creating the colored shell, but those eyes came for other creatures, not for himself and his mollusk love: "Shapeless, colorless beings, sacks of guts stuck together carelessly, peopled the world all around us, without giving the slightest thought to what they should make of themselves, to how to express themselves and identify themselves in a stable, complete form, such as to enrich the visual possibilities of whoever saw them" (149). He runs through a long list of sea creatures near him who develop eyes, notes the underwater fisherman looking through a face mask, a captain through a spyglass, the zoologist focusing his camera, and the school of anchovies so tiny and young that they seem nothing but an eye-dust. He ends with a *mise en abyme* of vision: an image of the two mollusks appears inside the eyes that see them and echoes about in the mirrored hall of the retinas, "in our true element which extends without shores, without boundaries" (151). Their true element is retinas, eyes, being seen, whether by a school of infant anchovies or a zoologist.

Here and other places, an action by Qfwfq ripples outward and down through the ages. Qfwfq both observes and yet participates in creation, in bringing the new into the world. So presumably does everyone else, ourselves included. Calvino is more concerned to create a sense of wonder than to consider the consequences of our actions, but that warning is at least implicitly present. The sordid squabbles that characterize Qfwfq's families and friends remind us that we hardly measure up to the beauty around us.

Calvino gives us amusing fables that domesticate the abstractions of science. He gives the galactic- and even universe-sized events a human perspective. Unlike Acker, whose personal experience blackens the world in her myths, Calvino plays with some of his own anxieties, but manages to submerge them in the material cosmos. Both Hoban and Calvino grasp the fact that we respond to individuals rather than to more abstract histories or scientific analyses. Hoban puts aside national war-mongering, theaters of operation, chiefs of staff, strategic decision-making, and the like in favor of Mr Clevver and Eusa's actions; Calvino realizes we will open ourselves more readily to scientific abstractions if they are filtered through an individual's perspective. Acker, Hoban, and Calvino found the idea of starting from scratch intellectually appealing, but have developed it toward different ends and with very different tones.

Actually, all three also invoke the Orpheus and Eurydice story. For Acker, Eurydice is the one who matters, since her experiences in Hades and death have not been told. For Hoban in *The Medusa Frequency*, fixated as he is on heads "telling," Orpheus's head is the mytheme that draws his attention. Calvino tells the Orpheus story twice, once as a story about Qfwfq and Rdix in "The Stone Sky," and another time rewritten as "The Other Eurydice," where Qfwfq's role is assumed by Pluto and Rdix is called Eurydice, but most of the story is the same, word for word. Both tell of losing the Eurydice figure from Hades to the upper realm, rather than the other way around. She originates in Hades and escapes with Orpheus, up into the world of sounds. Pluto finds those sounds an impossible jangling, maddening assault, and cannot understand why anyone would wish to endure them. He calls them an acoustic glue, one of those pastes that Calvino so dislikes. Those sounds of jukeboxes and ambulance sirens and battles seem to Pluto a very poor sort of world, the best that Olympus could do, but not at all what he had in mind for the subterranean world of order and compactness. That Calvino interchanges Qfwfq and Pluto reinforces our sense that he is working mythographically in the cosmicomical stories and feels his stories to have mythological resonances. Like Acker, he finds inspiration in a variant on Orpheus's descent, and the Orpheus myth yet again proves its adaptability. Like many other Qfwfq stories, this one records resistance to the enveloping complexity and chaos that make up modern life.

In terms of their invented mythicness, Calvino's stories are entirely situational, not concerned with elaborate or varied story. The positive emotion they stress is wonder. Whereas any action Qfwfq tries is blocked, he is always free to enjoy the universe that unfolds before him. Of the authors I know, the two who come closest to advocating something like this cultivation of pleasure in all that is around one are Aldous Huxley in *Island* and Richard Powers in several novels (*Prisoner's Dilemma, The Gold Bug Variations, Generosity,* and, most recently, *Orfeo*). When one derives sufficient pleasure from one's experiences in sight, sound, and studying, then the desire to accumulate goods or try to conquer others seems unattractive and uninteresting by comparison. If properly conditioned and encouraged, one learns to find one-upmanship inferior to being awed or surprised by nature, science, art, and learning, and by organizing the units, one sees into a meaningful universe.

Neil Gaiman's *The Ocean at the End of the Lane* would seem to have nothing in common with Calvino, and yet more than once I was struck by resemblances. His nameless child protagonist undergoes an experience very like that of Qfwfq when Qfwfq marries the first bird: For a moment Qfwfq's mind encompasses all of two worlds. He strains to hold on to those insights, but the birds wish to tear his former world from him, and he prefers to cling to his own mind and world and lose that of the birds. Gaiman's boy, when told to step into the magic ocean, sinks down, finds he can breathe the water, and suddenly finds himself understanding everything.

> Lettie Hempstock's ocean flowed inside me, and it filled the entire universe, from Egg to Rose. I knew that. I knew what Egg was—where the universe began, to the sound of uncreated voices singing in the void—and I knew where Rose was—the peculiar crinkling of space on space into dimensions that fold like origami and blossom like strange orchids, and which would mark the last good time before the eventual end of everything and the next Big Bang, which would be, I knew now, nothing of the kind.
>
> I knew that Old Mrs. Hempstock would be here for that one, as she had been for the last.[22]

He is told he cannot stay in this ocean or his consciousness will dissolve into the All. When he emerges from the water, "for one final, perfect moment, I still knew everything: I remember that I knew how to make it so the moon would be full when you needed it to be, and shining just on the back of the house, every night" (145), but he loses that knowledge. His companion Lettie says "Be boring, knowing everything. You have to give all that stuff up if you're going to muck about here.... And you really do have to give it all up if you want to play" (146). Understanding everything is possible for that brief moment of insight, but cannot be retained in the ordinary world.

Another Calvinoesque moment occurs when Lettie's mother shrugs off possible damage to our world with the comment, "It's only a world, after all, and they're just sand grains in the desert, worlds" (160). This, though, is partly her response to the tragedy, namely that Lettie is badly hurt, as near death as is possible for her immortal sort, and she is lowered into the special ocean, and the protagonist is told she will come back, but whether in months or centuries, no one knows. He doesn't see her again, though he is told that when he visits her ocean, he is being drawn there by her and she is inspecting him, to see how he has grown up.

Lettie, her mother Ginnie, and Old Mrs. Hempstock represent an attractive version of the Maiden, Mother, and Crone. In *Sandman*,

Morpheus is hounded to death by the Furies, who are cast as those three functions of womankind. They pursue those who shed the blood of kin, and drive Morpheus to choose death. They are not evil; they are just enforcing a rule that is awkward in its absoluteness, but a rule that may indeed be the oldest law in human experience. They are not presented as understanding, sympathetic, or attractive, however. In *Ocean*, the triad is far more likeable. They feed the boy delicious farm food, milk warm from the cow, honey with honeycomb, his favorite jam, and shepherd's pie. They help protect him from a being who has wormed her way to England from another plane of existence, and who torments him and nearly gets him killed. He in turn proves remarkably sensitive to aspects of their nature that we as readers do not necessarily pick up. He asks Lettie how old she is (eleven), and then later asks her how long she has been eleven, meaning not months, but for how many eons. He senses that she is not an ordinary mortal. She is ever the maiden, even as Ginnie is ever the mother, and Old Mrs. Hempstock is always the old woman. He intuits that they somehow came into being without men, and do not need men, though Hempstock men apparently exist, and some Hempstock women are scattered through the world. These three, though, have been around for all time. Old Mrs. Hempstock remembers when the moon was formed and indeed remembers the Big Bang. Their farm was in the Domesday book, and they talk about the cheese they make and how it was valued by twelfth-century princes Dickon, Arthur, and John. They had to deal with another such invasive spirit being from another plane in Cromwell's day.

Gaiman thus gives the eternal feminine some novel qualities. These women do all their own farmwork, whether mucking out or milking and reaping. They are of the land, and have no obvious wealth. While their rambling farmhouse now boasts an indoor lavatory, it is inconveniently far off, so chamber pots serve at night. They have and can drive a car, but this modern touch does not seem central to their lives. When the boy was going through a bad patch—no friends, no one came to his birthday party, a nagging sister, and parents who were less than competent at making money or at understanding their children—these women give him a haven. His exposure to the other planes of existence under Lettie's aegis may well account for his becoming a writer. Through their passing remarks, such as the one about worlds being like grains of sand, his sense of the universe is expanded. That aspect of his mind that inclines to fantasy is given a baptism of fire when he goes to the place with an orange sky with Lettie and becomes the unwitting portal for the spirit monster. The three seem to be the power behind our world, but Lettie is a friend, and her mother and grandmother are helpful without being gushing or especially taken by this ordinary mortal boy.

The power that matters in this picture of the world is female. It grows plants and tends animals. It cares little for government or nations, and has no interest in wars. When this world is invaded from another plane by a female power, they drive it off, but this is an irritating chore, not their way of defining themselves. We do see power being misused by that invading female spirit. Not only does she grievously abuse the boy, playing on all the ways she can make the adults disbelieve him and consider him a contemptible liar, she also causes trouble by buying people with surprisingly small gifts of money. We are, apparently dreadfully easily bought, if only we knew. Gaiman is not mythologizing the cosmos to give us a sermon on power, but by imagining beings with such magic, he can hardly avoid the issue. We are reminded of ways that power could be employed, ways that are much less destructive and troublesome than the more usual aims it serves, particularly in male-centered stories and cultures.

Again, as in *The Sandman*, Gaiman emphasizes the need to take responsibility for one's actions. Both the scavenger birds and the female monster, Ursula, claim that the boy is theirs, because part of Ursula is inside him. If they do not get what they were summoned to take, then they will destroy the world. Rather than let that happen, the boy tries to turn himself over to them. He knows that he became a portal because he disobeyed Lettie and dropped her hand when he should not have. He sees himself, however inadvertently, as the cause of the trouble, so tries to right it. Lettie, however, sees the blame as her own for involving this mortal in her clean-up operation. If she had not taken him along to the place with the orange sky, none of the subsequent problems would have arisen. Therefore, she insists on protecting him and is herself very badly injured. Lettie shows more sense of obligation to this particular world than do her mother and grandmother. When one has such a particular attachment, Gaiman argues, one must be prepared to sacrifice even oneself. Gaiman makes no direct claims for this willingness to die to protect others, but the beginning of the novel is given an autobiographical feel. That feel may be completely fictional, but it intensifies our sense of what matters, and leads us to speculate that the boy's later artistry gains depth and power from his actions here.

Invented myths almost naturally raise the issue of how power should be exercised. In Gaiman's *The Sandman*, Dream's refusing to draw on his immortal powers to help his son Orpheus win back Eurydice sets off the long chain of actions that will end in Dream choosing to die rather than have the Furies keep damaging his kingdom and murdering its inhabitants. Their power for one transgression is greater than his; he has shed the blood of kin, and so can only fight a losing action. Once you imagine someone with superhuman qualities, you assume powers not available to the rest of us, and then have to figure out how they could or should be used. Acker, Hoban, and Moore end up writing a kind of metamyth—myth about the nature of myth—and they find power a largely insoluble problem. Barthelme's version of metamyth demonstrates the power of myth, our entanglement in past myths, and our inability to escape them completely. Unlike Barthelme and Acker, Gaiman in *Ocean* gives us a female image of power, and a transmutation of the power inherent in sacrifice into storytelling power. Only Calvino escapes the problem of power by inventing a completely different system of rewards and pleasures. His way of escaping the power of money or running a company is to advocate wonder, to encourage us to fill our mind with beauty and visions that encourage awe. Even he, though, cannot escape the impulse to compete for a female, so competition is not completely excised from his world. He, however, comes closest to offering a solution to the problem, and his approach has similarities to that advocated by Powers in *Orfeo*.

Other solutions exist, but tend to be dishonest. The original Star Trek TV series nostalgically goes back to the knight-in-shining-armor power that was found in the Second World War Superman and Captain America. The Starship Enterprise supposedly represents humanity rather than just the United States, but in most respects, it is American liberal democracy writ large and lauded to the skies and beyond. The Star Trek quasi-mythology has admittedly been so successful that it comes close to having spawned a new religion; at the very least, some trekkies consist of a cult. They want to believe that they would expend might only for right causes, and they assume the right action would be obvious.

Mythology serves as a tool to examine the problem of power, mostly in terms of one person to another or one person toward society. Because what gods and immortals have that humans do not is such power, they provide natural excuses to look at it. However, personal power has not always been the concern of gods and demi-gods. In the Renaissance, they were seen more to represent governance and the problems of governmental power.[23] Even Orpheus was valued not for his trip to the underworld, but for generating social harmony. In the Romantic period, their power was that of the imagination and poetry or of nature. In our age, devoted as it is to the individual, individual power emerges as the problem to be explored. Acker, Hoban, and Moore show their focalizing characters at odds with social power, and show them trying to escape its grasp. Barthelme's characters are trying to escape the power of myth. Calvino alone recasts the terms of the problem, decides that we need new ways of feeling happiness, and describes what could be a major revolution should it ever happen in Western thought and culture. Powers too makes a similar argument, and mythology lets him put his idea across. Both he and Calvino define happiness in aesthetic and intellectual terms, and greatly reduce the importance that power would have in society.

5

Situational Myth

Posthuman Metamorphoses

McIntyre, McCaffrey, Simmons, Doctorow, Piercy, Stross, Rucker, Tidhar

Let me summarize a few distinctions among myth, mythology, mythic worlds, and their invented equivalents. Myths are inherited stories about cultural heroes, gods, and demi-gods, and they are often originally associated with a religion no longer extant in the culture that is deploying them artistically. Myths are cultural artifacts, and knowledge of them provides cultural capital—proof of high-culture learning as well as satisfying and puzzling stories. For the Western world, the primary myths are Greco-Roman and, for unbelievers or relaxed believers, Judeo-Christian, but education has supplied us with at least casual acquaintance with North Germanic, Celtic, Egyptian, Hindu, Slavic, Native American, and other mythologies. As Asia and Africa grow in global influence, some of their cultures' myths will presumably enter common knowledge. Some myths may still be religious truth in their own culture or among fervent believers, but from the viewpoint of artists employing them as "myth" rather than doctrine, they circulate as story for whatever effect the writer hopes to achieve with them.

A mythology is a network of related stories that has coalesced from individual mythic stories. This body of stories is open to development by a variety of writers of different eras. Homer (whoever he or they may have been) gave us the Trojan War and the Odyssey. Virgil combined the war with Mediterranean wanderings, attached them to Aeneas, and developed the story with the founding of Rome in mind. Medieval writers took obscure characters such as Troilus and gave them major roles, and justified new viewpoints by inventing Dares and Dictys as sources for new siege of Troy stories. In literary usage, mythology is highly collaborative in the sense that writers feel free to add to and alter the received stories. We see this in the independent developments in Iceland and Germany of the *Völsungasaga* and the *Niebelungenlied*. Wagner's additions are just one more such contribution to the branching tree of story.

Mythic worlds are the most difficult to define. Most obviously, they add nonmaterial dimensions to the material world. In keeping with this sense of Greco-Roman myth and influenced by Christian myth, mythic worlds often have postmortem dimensions, and may have explicit beginnings and violent endings. These could be called situational myth since creation and apocalypse are situations found in some mythologies, and they frequently recur as literary situations. These worlds encourage larger-than-merely-human actors and actions. Witnessing creation from a quasi-human perspective as an event that is limited in time rather than spread over billions of years certainly goes beyond normal human possibility. We get such mythic creation in Kathy Acker, Neil Gaiman, and Italo Calvino. Apocalypses flourish in genre fiction, be they nuclear, ecological, plague-driven, or extraterrestrial, and the chief question in readers' minds will be to wonder whether all land-based terrestrial life will be destroyed, as in Nevil Shute's *On the Beach*, or whether some plucky small band of humans will survive and try to build a new civilization.

But what of invented mythology? And how do such quasi-mythological worlds differ from fantasy? The fullest and most perfect example of an invented mythology that I know is the gradual development of the Arthurian story. This elaborate cycle of stories did not grow from a discarded religion, but simply absorbed the Christianity prevalent in medieval culture. Most of the actors are humans, not gods, though occasional figures from the realm of faerie give us nonhumans capable of suprahuman actions: Morgan le Fay has powers not found among mortals, and the Green Knight can survive having his head chopped off and have it speak when he picks it up. We know too little about Celtic religion to be very sure of mythic remnants, but the grail has been linked to a legendary magic cauldron as well as to Joseph of Arimathea from the Bible, and other stories may have Celtic roots, even if those are probably too distant to be recognized and understood as such by the artists.

One of the salient characteristics of the Arthurian material is its highly collaborative nature. Some early British authors developed the tale as one of conquest and empire on the continent, but others later focused on the internal rise and fall of a society whose chivalric institutions tried to encourage good and prevent evil. In Malory's case, this was a desperate thought experiment about knighthood carried out during the War of the Roses when knights were anything but desirable forces in society. The social tensions explored in the Middle Ages, which include the conflicting demands of Lord, Lady, and God, become something different in the hands of twentieth-century writers. We see spelled out our materialist society's craving for magic (Mary Stewart), feminist desire for recognized female power (Marion Zimmer Bradley), or our desire for a historically realistic yet admirable figure (Jack Whyte, Rosemary Sutcliff) who can achieve what Arthur supposedly did but be purely human. We want to know how a powerful but good leader could arise. Power and goodness seem incompatible to us now, but we yearn for that combination.

Modern creators of similar stories are up against limitations that did not face medieval writers: intellectual property laws and copyright. Tolkien created a world with a complex mythic scope, and in a different era, it might have taken root and drawn other writers to work with his characters and history, but anyone trying that now would be sued by the Tolkien estate. We get films, but their departures from the original text are not great compared to what a medieval writer might have felt free to undertake, and they usually come into existence only after the author or estate has agreed to the changes and has been paid. Films of current literature simplify, but rarely go in an entirely different direction or radically change the outcome or introduce new major characters. Plenty of authors do not want their world meddled with by others. In the realm of graphic novels, Alan Moore was not allowed to mess with extant superheroes from Marvel or the DC Universe in *The Watchmen*, so had to invent equivalents to Superman and Captain America. Neil Gaiman did not allow others to meddle with his Sandman for thirty years, though he ultimately changed his policy. The world of fanzines offers the closest to that kind of collaborative contribution in the literary world. Fans of Mercedes Lackey's Valdemar series, for instance, have written stories set in that world of heralds and their equine companions, and Lackey has encouraged (and doubtless to some extent controlled) these efflorescences by editing them and publishing them in collections.

With something like the Valdemar stories, original and volunteer, we look at the fuzzy border between quasi-mythic material and fantasy. Despite the abilities for "mind magic" and even true magic in that world, I would call that not suprahuman but just fantasy. We get a bit closer to mythic with stories based on worlds containing elves and dwarves. They represent a collaborative long-ongoing imaginative effort, and any writer can decide to incorporate them and know that readers will expect a certain kind of cosmos with such inhabitants. When Raymond Feist, Katharine Kerr, or Robert Jordan introduce elves or dwarves, we know with considerable accuracy what to expect, and enjoy watching for the minor departures from the norm that make any one version of such peoples special. They are nonhuman, but not particularly suprahuman (aside possibly from long lives and sometimes for magic), and while they may ultimately derive from the mythological cosmos of some pre-Christian European world, the connection is very, very distant. I would call them fantastic, albeit with faint mythic roots.

With current speculative fiction, we are getting a collectively imagined world that probably does qualify as invented mythic: the realm of the posthuman. The basic situations recur from author to author, and they offer serious departures from reality as we experience it, but departures that may someday be brought into being by technology. We are trying to imagine life in a radically different world that we or at least humans may nonetheless inhabit. These dimensions beyond the material embody just enough possibility that they give far more substance than elves and dwarves do for us, and go beyond mere fantasy. For speculative thinkers who believe in the technological singularity, they represent a world with the nonmaterial layers of a mythological world, so I shall look on the postsingular as quasi-mythic worlds. Whether the authors writing the fiction believe is another matter; they employ that postsingular mythic world for their own artistic purposes, and collectively, they are adding to our understanding of what such a world might be.

Early science fiction relied on certain violations of what we take to be possible or probable, particularly faster-than-light travel, communicative and benign aliens, and the ability of humans to live unprotected on Terra-like planets without the bacterial problems anticipated by H. G. Wells in *The War of the Worlds*. For all the marvels produced by the technology in such fiction, the humans remained for the most part completely human, with all the limitations that we have had to endure throughout history, including death. Suddenly, that is changing. Current speculation in fiction and cultural philosophy do away with such limitations, and one of the most grandiose prophets of this promised world is Ray Kurzweil. For Kurzweil, the human form is plastic in more senses than one: we change it through forced evolution or mutation or surgery and we supplement it with metal, plastic, silicon, biological nanobots, and electronic additions. AI is another way of going beyond the human, particularly when embedded in android form. So is uploading the contents of the brain and achieving electronic existence as a thinking being, while leaving the meat behind. At present, writers agree on the fictive possibilities inherent in this new way of envisioning humankind. No grand mythology has yet emerged in the sense of a story cycle focused on a particular person such as King Arthur. What we get instead is situational myth, a new world with qualities that in some sense go beyond the material and make it quite different from the world we know. In it we find speculative possibilities based on potentially living forever; changing our physical form in ways that would allow us to live in many different environments; and voluntarily giving up bodily existence for the life of disembodied intelligence. This constitutes an invented mythic world and produces suprahuman characters in terms of lifespan and even intelligence. We can see what it adds to our sense of the human. It grows out of a world of shared beliefs; many authors contribute to it. Their stories may not be cumulatively linked, but the image of this world and kind of life is growing rapidly and is becoming more coherent and consilient.

Human Plasticity: Vonda McIntyre, Anne McCaffrey, Dan Simmons, and Cory Doctorow

Reading Ray Kurzweil's *The Singularity is Near* is an experience. In his lexicon, everything is possible and much sooner than you think. He led major breakthroughs as the designer of scanners, Optical Character Recognition equipment, and text-to-speech synthesizers. He identifies three fields that will completely transform human experience: genetics, nanotechnology, and robotics.[1] Back in the 1980s, nanotech was only beginning to be conceived of, and genetic and robotics were in their infancy, so authors then imagined what we would now consider only the early steps along the paths those fields would later make possible. Vonda McIntyre and Anne McCaffrey are two who treated mutation and cyborg combinations as desirable and productive, and such anxieties as they register are minor—perhaps because what they describe seemed so close to impossible in their era. What they describe also takes place on too small a scale to make humans as a group feel threatened. Theirs is purely a fantastic handling of the ideas, and that is a distinction to keep in mind. Theirs is fantasy, whereas more dedicated posthumanists are promulgating a mythological world with dimensions of reality that we currently lack.

At the heart of Kurzweil's argument is the law of accelerating returns in technology. Technological progress rises exponentially, not linearly. The curve starts upward slowly, but once it reaches the "knee," it turns sharply upward. By his reckoning, our next hundred years of progress will not resemble the last hundred years, but will shoot up at the equivalent of 20,000 years of progress, or achieve about a thousand times as much as we did in the twentieth century. By his reckoning, the point at which everything will be rocketing skywards is about 2045. His enthusiastic vision pays no attention to the fact that those baffled by a new cell phone or car GPS or programmable thermostat will soon be the detritus of the new society.

If the exponential curve is his first argument, his second is that all matter corresponds to information. Any atom, even in a lump of granite, is at a particular atomic state and so can represent a datum. All matter can be made to serve as a pattern of information, so all matter is ultimately computational power. To a non-specialist, this seems like an awfully big "if," but several authors have accepted the argument as they build their postsingular worlds. Computers will soon surpass human intelligence, and they have three great advantages: they have direct access to the web, their "minds" can be transferred from machine to machine, and their signals are three million times faster than human electro-chemical signals in the brain.

Nanotechnology will let us replace aging parts of our bodies; respirobots will be able to carry oxygen around and do away with heart and lungs, for instance. Nanobots will extend human experience into virtual reality. They will reverse pollution and will manufacture new goods out of our civilization's trash landfills. You get the general picture. Yes, drawbacks exist; malicious tamperers and terrorists will launch the equivalents to internet viruses, but we do not close down the web and its possibilities because we are always fighting off such attacks. Electromagnetic pulse weapons could devastate such electronic systems. Nonetheless, Kurzweil feels that the benefits far outweigh the problems.

Since some of Kurzweil's predictions have not yet come to pass in the time he specified—such as those on the diving cost of photo-voltaic solar panels—I am interested but skeptical. His ideas, however, are dear to the hearts of many technologically inclined writers, and they tackle the benefits and disasters that might accrue to us as we transfer our "self" into electronic existence, or deal with a post-scarcity Economics 2.0 world where nanobots can break everything down into component atoms and then manufacture anything atom by atom, or we can replicate for ourselves a body when the current one is damaged or aging, or transfer ourselves entirely to a Virtual Reality Earth.

Early approaches to some of these themes that will become serious challenges to our concept of human life turn up first in the realm of fantasy. Anne McCaffrey's *The Ship Who Sang* appeared as a book in 1969, but one of its component stories goes back to 1961. Her ship people were babies born defective; their bodies are enclosed in a fluid-filled column and their brains are attached electronically first to educational equipment and eventually to the controls of a space ship that zips around the star systems, spending only hours or days in transit. Hence, we have cyborged bodies made desirable, since the alternative might well have been death or extreme disability. These brainships are also beneficial to society, so society has no reason to ban this or the other brain-machine combinations that run some of the communication services on a planet. McCaffrey will explore various ways that her ship people (mostly female) can interact with their mobile human partners, called brawns (mostly male), but much of what these stories do is show women who are seen as less than able-bodied being, in fact, completely competent and emotionally well balanced.

That this is fantasy is shown by McCaffrey's assumptions and techniques. In *The Ship Who Sang*, she shows people leaving their human bodies behind and existing in some other form that can survive in a hostile atmosphere on another planet. The mechanics of this transfer remain the mumbo jumbo of fantasy; no scientific attempt is made to explain such changes. Three people make this transfer; their bodies, however, are left alive if senseless, back on the ship, and those are evidently going to be maintained back in their original world. The cost of caring for human vegetables is not weighed in this fantasy future, which is one thing that makes it fantasy.

When we move into the 1980s, we find slightly more thought given to the processes of change that are otherwise still fantastic. Vonda McIntyre's *Superluminal* deals with two kinds of changes. Some of her humans expose themselves to viruses that help them grow webbing between their fingers and toes and change their metabolism so they are unbothered by ocean temperature and can breathe the way dolphins do. They can mix with other humans if they wish, but they have formed breakaway communities that mostly shun ordinary humans in favor of dolphins and whales. Her other altered humans submit to an operation that replaces their hearts with mechanical pumps; this lets them survive dimensional jumps in space transit and thus pilot superluminal (faster than light) space ships. The first development is thus an induced mutation; the second is a form of cyborg melding of human and machine. Humans both make themselves more at home on Earth by populating the waters and more suited to travel to other planets, all of which amount to variants on the American frontier experience of more land to expand into and more resources to cultivate, though mostly without sentient inhabitants to be displaced and massacred. These books are standard fantasy/speculative fiction, and I would not call them mythic or even quasi-mythic, but they represent a nontechnical response to ideas that will become more central and more challenging to our sense of human form as the requisite science advances.

We also find a different kind of change to human form, not in shape but in longevity. Basically, humans do away with death and old age as we know them. Genetic advances let us alter telomeres, grow replacement organs, and generally renew our bodies. In other fiction, we are able not only to renew our bodies, but can store cloned replacement bodies against need. Should we be killed in an accident, we can be brought back to life by implanting stored memories in the cloned body. Yes, we would lose awareness of the time since the last mind back-up, but we need not fear death in the usual sense.

Dan Simmons shows us people living the deathless life in *Hyperion* (1989), and a life in which transit to other planets can be instantaneous via farcasting and apparently without cost. He does not call it teleportation, but that seems to be the means. The pilgrimage to the monstrous Shrike, the invocation of Abraham and Isaac when Sol Weinstein is called on to sacrifice his daughter, and the strange effect of the Time Tombs, which all take up much of the story, prove to be a smoke screen for the more pressing issue of advanced intelligence. What happens to us when we create intelligence greater than our own? Why would a greater intelligence wish to put up with us, especially if we do not die off after eighty or a hundred years? If this intelligence is hidden in location and exists electronically, do any of our technological inventions provide immunity to AI tampering? The Hyperion series involves a three-way clash of the sentients of the galaxy: humans of a technological and empire-building sort; the "swarms," which seem to be human-derived, but much altered and very eco-oriented (they prefer to adapt to worlds rather than terraform them); and the AI hive mind, which has achieved bodilessness in the various kinds of transport portals and farcasting systems that permit instantaneous transit and communication all over the galaxy. The clashes are complicated by both the AIs and the humans being convinced that they are bringing into existence an Ultimate Intelligence (or God). Simmons writes an extremely complicated plot, but underneath it is anxiety about creating our superiors. Because we initiated their existence, we think we control them, but if we truly do, that is slavery.[2] The name Hyperion and Simmons's heavy investment in John Keats comes from Keats having focused on the Titans being overthrown by the younger Olympians. If that is the natural outcome, how ought we to proceed in our quest for more and more competent computers? We too would be overthrown.

Another author to tackle implications of singularity's promises is Cory Doctorow. I am not sure that he meant to give us what I see as the lesson in *Down and Out in the Magic Kingdom* (2003), but to me he seems to show us serious unsolved problems in this future world of immortality, mind-downloading, and post-scarcity conditions. Death basically disappears. If this ever happens, the effect on fiction as we know it will be drastic, and very possibly the effect on life will be just as bad. If we are that close to immortal, most stories and actions lose their interest and intensity. Who cares if a character gets killed; he can come back. One character obsesses over figuring out who assassinated him, but he is partly kept from solving it by one of the conspirators backing up her mind just before planning the assassination, planning the action, and then getting her body disposed of and her back-up mind installed in a clone, with the result that, in her new form, she knows nothing about the plot. She can swear under oath that she had nothing to do with his murder. Life and death no longer work as we understand them, and we find caring for the characters a bit difficult. They seem real only to the extent that they behave shabbily and seem boringly ordinary; whatever advantages infinite life offers cannot be made very real in the novel without making it uninteresting, and if this transformation of life offers no advantages, no improvement in overall happiness to those living it, we might well wonder whether this particular technological miracle will bring benefits. Yes, one can choose to die when tired of life, but one can also get oneself stored for a hundred or a thousand years, and see if reentering life seems worthwhile after that retirement. How the world would respond to reanimations from the distant past is not explored—though it should be—nor is the cost of preserving them in a suitable condition. This is a post-scarcity novel—one of the quasi-mythic post-singularity conditions—in which raw materials and energy are abundant enough to supply almost everything humans want through nanobot manufacture. Instead of currency, people gain social capital by means of accumulated Whuffies, something analogous to Facebook "likes."

Post-scarcity conditions bring their own challenges to novel writing. If nanomanufacture can take any matter apart and assemble whatever we need through nano-construction and 3-D printing, for instance, then what have we to desire or work for? We can even grind up asteroids rather than tear up Earth and derive power from solar mirrors. What Doctorow gives his characters to play with is . . . Disney World. They devote themselves to one of the displays, to upgrading it and making it even more attractive through highest of hi-tech virtual-reality developments. They work as adhocracies. That his group devotes itself to a mindless amusement is perhaps a fundamental statement about this mode of life. If achievement, creation, and triumphing against odds have all pretty well disappeared, then entertainment is what remains. If characters haven't found an adhocracy they wish to join, they may get yet another doctorate—simply for the sake of doing so rather than for using it. Or they may compose music, or anything they like, but whatever they do is simply whatever entertains them. Doctorow's character realizes that he doesn't know what he wants to do in life or with his life, and this would seem to be a serious problem for the designers of the brave new world postsingularity. None of the authors I have run across who are exploring this situational mythic future seems really to have taken on this issue. Scarcity, achievement, and desire are important to traditional concepts of worthwhile living, at least in the West. The alternatives tend to be meditative, achieving a state of mind that is untroubled and free from desire, or achieving a link to the divine. Even those goals might come to seem inadequate if humans were to live essentially forever.

Artificial Intelligence: Marge Piercy

Altering the body, whether in shape or with mechanical supplement, or making it immortal or close to that, all take us into a different world, one whose implications we are only just beginning to think through. Artificial intelligence takes us in a slightly different direction, and has a truly mythic analog: the golem. Marge Piercy investigates the implications of such created intelligence in her 1991 book *He, She and It*. Her cyberpunk near-future Jewish collective creates an android that can pass for human. Every few chapters, one of the android's programmers, a visionary older woman who sees to it that the android will behave in ways that women appreciate, recounts a version of the golem tale for his edification. We as readers see Avram (the android's inventor and "father") and Malkah (its partial programmer and golem story-teller) as jointly equivalent to Rabbi Loewe; the Prague midwife/female scholar Chava corresponds to the younger programmer Shira. The golem Josef and the android Yod become human enough to fall in love with those younger women. We definitely have a mythic-legendary story growing out of a religion that serves to probe our future. What does it achieve?

First, a word about the world Piercy has created. This is a cyberpunk world of international conglomerates imagined along Japanese lines; you join one after your university training and expect to stay loyally with it for the rest of your life. These conglomerates have taken over all aspects of life, and nation-states hardly exist anymore. Like many writers of the era, Piercy relies on Western images of Japanese business relationships, so the companies are extremely hierarchical, prestige-conscious, and conformist. Marge Piercy establishes futuristic "strangeness" by positing the working outfit being a backless business suit that showcases elaborately developed muscles. We gradually learn that essentially all living has to take place under domes, because the atmosphere is badly damaged and the sun's rays are deadly. Furthermore, many creatures have perished and much of the land is now desert. Humans have lost fertility, and most children are conceived and born only through laboratory manipulation, and are apparently even nurtured in artificial wombs. Shira, the young woman whom we follow, joins Yakamura-Stichen (Y-S) after her education, in part as a rebellion against her home in the Jewish collective. She marries a Jew and has her son in the old-fashioned physical way, and dotes upon him. Her marriage, though, falls apart, and to her horror, Y-S's court awards total custody to her ex-husband. She leaves Y-S, goes home, and is hired to help civilize the illegally constructed android so that he understands people better and can pass as human.

Outside the domes of the international conglomerates live the poor in the "glop," a continuous city from Boston to Atlanta and over other parts of America as well. This is straight cyberpunk, borrowed from Gibson's *Neuromancer*, whose BAMA sprawl is Boston to Atlanta, but similar to ChiPitts for Chicago to Pittsburgh, and SanSan for San Diego to San Francisco. Also borrowed is the image for people jacking into the net; what they do in both books is visualizable, and paths are visible, not just electric equivalent to zeros and ones. Gibson too went in for Japanese-style conglomerates and attributed to them ruthless control of people, with assassination always an option. In Piercy's story, Y-S gets wind of the illegal android, and is ready to do anything to take him over, multiply him, add him to their arsenal, and they would think nothing of eliminating the Jewish collective Tikva to do so.

People can lengthen their lives, replace injured or diseased organs, and spend much of their time communing with computers in ways that suggest they have almost become half-computer themselves. Yod is a mixture of mechanism and biological materials, so he looks human, though his skin feels dry and he does not sweat. Shira long resists considering Yod anything but a mechanism; she calls him "it," and talks about him with others while he is present. For a long period, she resists the idea that he has feelings that can be hurt by such an attitude, though gradually she observes what seem like human responses. Basically, Avram or Malkah has found a way of creating a machinic equivalent to pain and pleasure, and with those, a mechanism can quickly become more and more human. When Shira finally gives in to Yod's polite importunities and takes him to bed, she finds him the ideal lover (whom she later learns was programmed and trained to be good in that fashion by Malkah). At this point, however, we really have to admit that Yod seems to deserve recognition as a person, perhaps as a nonhuman person (as Shira calls him), but nonetheless a person. He was designed as a weapon to protect Tikva, but he has become human enough to fall in love and to value his life, and not wish to be a deployable human bomb. All sorts of interesting issues arise. Should he be paid for his services? Can he make up a minyan? That last sent six rabbis away blissfully happy at the chance to argue over such a wonderful question.

As Malkah recounts the story of the golem, we see how Rabbi Loewe grows dubious that the golem should be allowed to continue. Josef clearly is falling in love, and any such alliance with humans should not be allowed. The golem is the strongest "man" in Prague, and the rabbi is very old; when he dies, will anyone be able to control the golem? No. Hence, since the recent anti-Jewish riots have subsided, Rabbi Loewe puts the golem into a once-and-future state. He is not actually destroyed, and a sufficiently learned kabbalist could bring him back to life if the need were great enough, but he may no longer live. Josef resists and clearly does not wish to be thus annihilated, but the magic words rob him of any ability to resist. No matter what he may feel or think, he is a tool and made to serve aims imposed on him.

Piercy clearly thinks that some of the issues that bothered the Orthodox rabbi of the sixteenth and early seventeenth century are no longer that important. Marriage and sexual relations would be okay. So, we suspect, would making up a minyan. She is far more sensitive, though, to the issue of creating a being for purposes other than those that such a being forms for itself. This is slavery. Humans have always wanted someone or something to do the dirty work for them, and even in this very egalitarian collective, when the dirty work involves dying to protect them, the idea of an android doing it instead of a person seems at first like a good idea.

Yod fulfills his purpose and takes out all the upper echelon officers of Y-S by blowing himself up. Beforehand, he destroys Avram and all Avram's notes and information on creating androids, so Avram cannot impose his will on a similar being. Tikva is safe for a while at least. This leaves the grieving Shira and others who had come to value Yod as a person. Shira finds some duplicates of the programming, and thinks longingly of creating her lover again, but eventually sees that she too would be creating a being to do what she wants and be her slave, rather than one free to form his own goals. She destroys the duplicates so that no entity like Yod can be brought to life and then exploited.

Piercy thus imagines one kind of human-machine amalgam and works out what seem to her the drawbacks to such a project, drawbacks felt in the original story but not seen in terms of slavery. The issue would be harder to decide if the personality were in a stationary computer, not one that could join a family as a family member, but one that still had the capacity to feel pleasure and be hurt. Heinlein imagined such a combination in *The Moon is a Harsh Mistress*, but the consciousness of that mainframe computer was "killed" in a bombardment, and it was not sacrificing itself specifically to spare people. We instinctively make a distinction between something seemingly alive and able to move around and something we may consider non-living (such as a mainframe) and unable to move around. However, if a mechanical creation can feel pleasure and pain, that distinction will be difficult to maintain with any fairness, and if it can conceive of and resist its own "death," even if that is just being unplugged, then we have to see whether such an act is equivalent to murder. In many ways, Piercy's book shows its age; this is a future of ecological impoverishment and regimented scarcity. Piercy's judgments are obviously humanist, not posthumanist or postsingular, and she is arguing for the ethics of being human. What will happen to such ethics if we go into a posthumanist existence involves issues that we are just beginning to consider.

Posthumanity to the nth Degree: Stross, Rucker, and Tidhar

I don't pretend to understand all of the variations on the human condition being played out by Charles Stross in *Accelerando*. Minds are completely uploadable and downloadable. Bodies are evidently quickly replicable, even those long dead. Minds electronically multiplied become separate entities, so many versions of what were once one person can be operating at the same time, thus reifying the multiple-selves theory discussed in Chapter 1. You can "fork" and have a "ghost" of yourself go on an expedition to the edge of the universe, even while electronic ghosts of yourself serve as gatherers of information in the net, so that a question no sooner forms in your mind than one of them collects possible answers. They presumably can do the sorting and winnowing for your personal needs that Google cannot. You can also live many parallel lives, trying out combinations of career and partner to see which combination is best. Less satisfactory alternatives can be erased. Because electronic entities can create their own virtual realities, a group of people can go to the region of Jupiter in something the size of a beer can, yet they experience it as spacious quarters and if they wish, they can have a Versailles-like throne room. In one version of her life, a woman has a child, and that child, when grown, sues another version of his mother for some dereliction when that particular version was not even aware of his existence. People often choose to take some down time and are dead for a few decades, yet some electronic version can be consulted even during that time, and it can watch the news reports and can decide to bring its originary self back to life. Such a being is decanted into a body (if that's what it wants). It staggers out of the rehabilitation center and ask the nearest wall for some clothes, describes a simple outfit, and has it manufactured and extruded in a moment.

Pretty clearly, one effect that Stross wants is for us to feel technologically backward. We need to put more effort into understanding the latest developments and not allow ourselves as individuals to fall behind. Keeping up with the latest is going to mark all lives from here on out, so we need to start practicing that outlook as the most basic necessity for post-singularity life. You link without wiring to the equivalent to the internet and merely by thinking, you pose your question or demand your service. You need to keep upgrading whatever hardware is installed in your skull so you can take advantage of all this computational power.

The fact that death is not final has some weird effects on society. In one area of a settlement, children torture and kill each other with gay abandon, since their parents can put them back together or otherwise resuscitate or produce another copy of them with no trouble. How Stross describes this is telling: these kids dive "into an exciting universe of myth and magic where your childhood fantasies take fleshy form, stalking those of your friends and enemies through the forests of the night."[3] All throughout his story, I felt narratively lost, since I hardly knew which version of a person we might be following, or how I should respond to Manfred Macx, earlier the principal character, apparently long dead, who turned up in the form of a flock of pigeons and then proceeds to extract himself and recondense as a single entity from that multitude. All of a sudden, though, Stross started using terms like myth, and I think he was having trouble ending this multiply forking story without resorting to that earlier kind of story structure and earlier guarantor of meaning beyond the material realm in which we function.

Pamela, once Manfred's wife, a woman who, from some viewpoints, has seemed like the wicked witch, hands some "encrypted tokens" to an avatar of Manfred, and these are called "a trail of bread crumbs leading into a dark and trackless part of mindspace" (395). Aineko, a being in cat-form that may be some kind of minor god or alien with a mentality superior to any embedded in humans, demands that Manfred's avatar run a dangerous program and be erased at the end. Both the temporarily meat-embodied human who has that original Manfred mind and his bodiless avatar are not happy at the prospect of erasure, even though it has fewer consequences than God's demand that Isaac be sacrificed. What happens plays off against that central biblical myth. Instead of sacrificing the son, the embodied, three-armed child who is also a reincarnation of Manfred kills the cat. Even this act, however, is hardly what it would be for us. Manfred senior, if I may call him that, realizes that the cat is removing himself from their lives and thinks that a violent end will be psychologically satisfying to those whose lives it had manipulated; after all, the cat admits to having made Pamela and Manfred hate each other all those decades ago because Manfred would be far more productive a creative genius if not comfortable and sexually satisfied as he had been with Pamela. This allows Stross to bring the story to a close by having them walk off together and give their relationship a second chance. The cat's body may have been bloodily killed, but its mind has presumably taken another body, and will go its merry way, undeterred by this temporary death.

Post-singularity speculation raises some serious issues. If we reach the computational and nanorobotic stage that we can do away with scarcity, such that everyone can have basic food and clothing and shelter for free in some space colony, then what else remains to do with one's apparently infinite life? Stross has a sharper answer than any I saw in Doctorow's *Down and Out in the Magic Kingdom*. We must keep trying to improve our computational ability and intelligence, because sooner or later we will run across alien intelligences, and we risk being destroyed if we are not up to that challenge. Our natural curiosity (and our need for asteroid matter and energy) will drive us to explore first our own solar system and then our galaxy. In his further future world, the inner planets have all been turned into usable matter, computational power, and energy. Taming wormholes through space and making them usable will presumably give us a major goal worthy of our best efforts. If we do run across superior and hostile intelligences, including our own augmented descendants who do not see why we should be taking up room or energy in the universe, we will need strategies for escaping their predations. Believing in any of these is a stretch, but these problems seem more worthy of human endeavor than improving a display at Disney World.

Let us consider yet another attempt to imagine this brave new mythic world, Rudy Rucker's *Postsingular*. In it, we see four attempts at technological advancement. The first involves nants (nanorobots) who try to consume the world and us, but who translate us into virtual reality. A madman launches these nants on an unsuspecting world, and they nearly succeed in absorbing us until someone makes them swallow an autistic boy who had been able to memorize all the digits of a program needed to reverse the nants and make them work backward and return our world to its former state. The next attempt consists of orphids. These multiply intelligence throughout the world. People are always linked to the net and can see anything, including how people look under their clothes or how they behave in the bedroom. Privacy, obviously, disappears completely, and one's very thoughts are detectable. For the most part, this is treated as good, and we develop greatly expanded brains with memories stored up in the net. Then the mad-scientist figure who launched the nants tries again with an "improved" model. His rejection of Earth is complex, but one reason is a dislike of its messiness. He wants a "clean" world; in his VEarth (virtual Earth), dogs and dogshit will not exist, for instance. The fourth wave consists of a kind of telepathy that does not rely on technology but on unrolling the eighth dimension to infinity. This version makes the previous versions obsolete, and gets rid of the second wave of nants. Teleportation also becomes possible. While not exactly Heaven and Hell, this vision of the future does produce at least two layers of reality beyond what we think of as the material, although both nants and orphids have material existence. With the final telepathy, however, we move to a fully mythic-like nonmaterial dimension.

So, what do people in this world live for? Thuy creates a metanovel, a work of art that is experienced as virtual reality by her audience; it includes music, art, and what she experiences and thinks. She considers herself an alchemist, "transmuting our lives into myth and fable."[4] Jayjay studies physics. Both are living homeless, and using the orphidnet to locate free food and temporary shelter. They initially suffer from a kind of addiction to the web—visualized as Big Pig, the central AI, on whose tits they and others fasten and absorb whatever knowledge they want. Big Pig, though, develops its own consciousness, and it encourages nants because they consume all matter and turn it into computational power, from which Big Pig will gain more memory. Whether we look at Big Pig or humans, or nants or orphids, what we see is the illimitable desire for more memory and computational power. We can never have enough, and no obstacle will be permitted to remain; if the obstacle is legally protected, then someone will remove it illegally.

In addition to unlimited computational power to be provided by nanobots, even at the expense of human life, we are exposed to the ideal that our being translated to virtual reality might not be such a good idea. Jayjay experiences a dream-vision supplied by Big Pig as to what would happen in terms of the computer power needed to supply high resolution to virtual reality. Those with money get higher resolution, and those with less get jagged, pixelated edges and simplified shapes. As the population rises (and does not die), everyone suffers a diminution of resolution. If your wife runs away with another man, having emptied the joint bank account, you may find yourself unable to pay for your resolution, and much of your body may disappear. What was once billed as a clean, utopian existence proves to be far from ideal. Wealth and poverty have not disappeared in this version of the future.

Rucker supplies a utopian ending—telepathic connectivity not reliant upon electronics or mechanism, the "end of the Digital Age" (320). "Omnividence, telepathy, and endless memory were the natural birthrights of every being on the globe" (318). Further, all nature becomes conscious. Rucker ignores the problems implicit in the plants we eat becoming conscious, for instance, or animals presumably better able to communicate with us as we slaughter them for food. Possibly both plant and animal protein will be vat-grown. He leaves unanswered whether such telepathy gives infinitely extensible life span or at least virtual existence after the body's death. In a sense, he takes the dream of singularity to its implied ideal, a kind of transcendence, an escape from human limitations, even though he slams early, mechanical attempts at the same result. By creating an ideal and presumably impossible version of postsingular goals, he attacks the electronic version implicit in Kurzweil's prophecies; he plays with those throughout the novel, but ultimately rejects them. They are too susceptible to attack or corruption, even if the extended memory and understanding they lend us is extremely attractive. As long as our network is programmable, it is vulnerable to attack. Indeed, one could say that as long as our mental existence is material in its existence, it can be hacked. Viewing all matter as computational power is dangerous in its consequences. Once we gain true telepathy, those objections seem to be met, but at that point, we have moved into pure fantasy and are no longer dealing with this urgent, if invented, mythic future.

Not everyone projecting such a post-singularity future takes a positive view of the developments. Interestingly Lavie Tidhar projects all sorts of electronic, robotic, and biological additions to human life, but not the post-scarcity economy. The Israeli spaceport he shows in *Central Station* is a multiethnic, multi-religion, and multi-hybrid city area in which most humans are cyborged in a variety of ways, whether with machines, biological materials from elsewhere in the solar system, or genetic tinkering. Evolution in all these combinations has been stimulated such that a new kind of human is beginning to appear among some street children. The solar system is inhabited and exploited, and a virtual reality world offers employment for those who prefer to make their living that way. Not all the genetic combinations are harmless. A vampiric type of being exists, but she sucks data and memories from people. Although rumor of her presence drew a mob, a few humans are willing to try to help her so that she can fit in without damaging others. Tidhar's is a useful corrective to the more cheerful visions that assume the disappearance of economic want. Some of his people are quite poor. One character is so much older than anyone else that he may be a version of the wandering Jew, but his occupation is junk collector. Insofar as Tidhar denies the rapturous and glossy version of the future, his *Central Station* stands outside the growing post-singularity myth-world, a critique with the doubting but hopeful suggestion that if we develop many kinds of human hybrids and evolutionary variants, perhaps we will worry less about religious hostilities. In this regard, his world reflects some of the advantages postulated by Donna Haraway in her Cyborg Manifesto, namely, "Single vision produces worse illusions than double vision or many-headed monsters."[5]

Stross and Rucker both work within Kurzweil's projected quasi-mythic world, explore it, and show some possible limitations and drawbacks. Tidhar's world is anti-mythic. He suggests that even with vastly greater artificial intelligence and far more sophisticated genetic abilities, we will nonetheless rub along pretty much in the same old way—not ideal, not free of want, and often dissatisfied with life. In earlier mythology, Adam and Eve were drawn to the tree that promised knowledge; we too want knowledge, in part because knowledge becomes power and enjoyment. How to reduce the effects of power and increase those of enjoyment underlies Rucker's material. In Rucker's mind, our desire for enjoyment is too easily corrupted into an addiction, whether to the experiences with Big Pig or the drug sudocoke. Such a drug is always a threat to more intellectual types of enjoyment, a problem for thinkers who feel that pleasure should be our goal. Stross, by contrast, makes the intellectual goal crucial to eventual survival. Of all the authors considered so far, only Italo Calvino and Richard Powers have managed to imagine knowledge and experience as enjoyed for their own sake. Calvino goes furthest, and his cosmicomical mythologies present admiration, wonder, and delight as the attitude and life to be cultivated for interacting with our universe.

6

The Contemporary Functions of Myth as Artistic Tool

Pynchon, Arthurian stories, Faber, Pullman, Morrow, Ducornet, Marcus, Atwood, Vonnegut, Naylor, Morrison, Silko, Östergren, Winterson, Grossman, Rucker

> *I don't want to be excessively bitchy about this, but nice little Johnny Updike knows the way to make minor league critics happy—you take a certified Greek myth, preferably a touch obscure, build your book within its frame, like a monkey in a cage, season the fodder with Greek, and you're the number one horse on the pole for the National Book Award.*[1]

However snidely he puts it, Norman Mailer has a point. Myth is a handy tool, as many writers have found (himself included), a Swiss Army knife that offers many ways to tackle problems. But what problems? In this chapter, I wish to spread out at least some of the tool-forms taken by myth and show their various functions by focusing on how deploying myth lets the authors react to the hegemonic culture—in these cases, Western civilization, or, more narrowly, Anglophone culture. The default positions in that culture are largely white, male, and (if religious) Judeo-Christian, but also materialist and scientific. Not surprisingly, one or more of those characteristic value clusters is likely to be the problem to which the tool is being applied.

Myth as Cultural Capital

The development of myth or myth-like situations in contemporary fiction seems to have three basic forms: borrowed, invented, and situational. The first is the explicit presence of well-known mythic characters or mythic stories derived from previous cultures. They may be given their original names (Orpheus, Osiris, and Odin) or may have modern names and be mortal rather than divine, but still have an explicit connection to their mythic inspirations, as do Lobey and Mishka Bartok to Orpheus. These gratify educated readers, and make them feel knowledgeable about this ancient lore that is rapidly disappearing from general education, thanks to the plethora of images and stories that now floods us from the Web, television, film, games, and social media. Games that pit Thor against Gilgamesh do not give meaningful knowledge of that lore.

Consider an example where myth as overt borrowing appears in an exemplary postmodern text: the Orphic strand in *Gravity's Rainbow*. Tyrone Slothrop, a major character, resonates with Orphic elements.[2] One manifestation attaches to him, for instance, by way of a pinball machine. The pinball is being menaced (via reference to Offenbach's *Orphée aux enfers*) with Folies-Bergère maenads. Orpheus's descent into the underworld is suggested when the pinball gets stuck against a pin, and "having looked into the heart of the solenoid, seen the magnetic serpent and energy in its nakedness, long enough to be changed, to bring back from the writhing lines of force down in that pit an intimacy with power, with glazed badlands of soul, that set them apart forever" (GR 594–95). Slothrop, however, bears the mythic burden of Orphic identity before and after this clonic spasm. He beds, but fails to save, a nymphet Eurydice (480, 540) from a decadent underworld on the boat named *Anubis*. He wanders the hills naked, playing his harmonica (also called a harp and mouth harp) to the beasts, birds, and insects. After he learns about the bomb dropped on Hiroshima, a subhead appears "Orpheus puts down Harp" and we hear nothing more about his music. He eventually disappears, "Scattered all over the Zone" (726). Meantime, *Gravity's Rainbow* as film is showing at the Orpheus Theater in Los Angeles, and that theater appears to be the target for a missile. To judge from its billboards, that theater has recently shown Ingmar Bergman's apocalyptic *Seventh Seal* and Jean Cocteau's *Orphée*.

Pynchon does a lot with Orphic and musical material in *Gravity's Rainbow*, but his chief Orphic character is Slothrop, whose mysterious end corresponds to the sparagmos of the mythic musician. We do not necessarily predict Slothrop's end, but we think "Right, got it!" when we learn that he has become "scattered" in the Zone, this end being linked to his mother holding a martini, a modern version of the intoxicated maternal maenad. Myth here provides some orientation. This particular example is routine and easily parsed by anyone who knows the Orphic story.[3] It gives some shape to an otherwise puzzling tale that refuses to "make sense." Taken literally, what does Slothrop's scattering mean? Something postmodern that denies realism and reflects a lack of unitary self, but nothing we can explain in everyday terms.[4] Were this a realist novel, he might die in some Zone brawl, or be kidnapped by Tchitcherine and stashed in a Russian work camp, or he might somehow deal with his AWOL record and go home to the States, marry the girl next door, and be nagged and manipulated by his mother. Any of those would make ordinary sense in a way that scattering does not. With the Orpheus story hovering above him, however, we accept the impossibilities and feel that his otherwise strange disappearance is, if not explained, then at least appropriate. The Orphic element gives readers a sense of satisfaction at understanding something implicit, at knowing the relevant myth and catching the reference. It lets us have our cake and eat it too: we are both puzzled by something that does not fit our everyday, materialist expectations and yet also gratified. The tension and discontent that puzzlement would leave is released. Release of tension is one factor that contributes to our sense of meaning. Myth thus makes us more comfortable in complex recent fiction.

Cultural Compensation

Invented mythology allows us to engage with our culture in a different fashion. The Arthurian world that coalesced in the Middle Ages gives us Western culture's most complete and convincing example of this form of mythic thinking; it has continued to grow and be rethought and reconfigured right up to the present. It exemplifies a collaborative process of invention and reworking to supply lacks in changing cultures. While Star Trek and the Marvel and DC universes may achieve similar status, that process will take many decades or a cataclysm that destroys most of our heritage and leaves us just fragments from those sources. That pattern of myth invention is exemplified in *Riddley Walker*, where misunderstood and elaborated bits taken from the life of St Eustace serve to explain the United States and nuclear war.

Quasi-myth or invented myth is a borderline category that rather quickly slides into romance or fantasy. In the case of the Arthurian story, though, it accumulated into a rise and fall story cycle, and we still draw on and reshape that story, even though knights in armor have long faded from our life of automobiles and computers. Such knights are essentially as remote from us as the warriors of Troy, so why do we still find them of interest? In Malory's day, armored men were very much alive and were killing each other with great enthusiasm during the War of the Roses. We do our killing with missiles and planes and without steeds or swords, so what is the attraction?

Here I think we see at work that ability of mythic materials to supply something seriously lacking in the current culture: cultural compensation. In its earlier medieval English stages, Arthurian conquests on the continent may have compensated the Anglo-Norman populace for the shaming loss of territory in France. By Malory's time, one prominent lack was the ideal behavior attributed to knighthood; instead, dirty and treacherous little battles were being fought, and many people got sucked in against their will through their feudal ties. Plenty of noncombatants got trampled in the confusion. The relative cleanness of Arthurian ideals and quests, the way that many such were handled by individuals rather than armies, and the high standard of moral behavior by Round Table knights were sadly absent in the York-Lancastrian politics that Malory had experienced. Today, what modern Arthurian tales supply is again various things lacking in current cultural values.

An obvious example of such complementary invented myth is Marion Zimmer Bradley's *The Mists of Avalon* (1982). She tells the story from the perspective of various women—Morgaine, Igraine, Viviane, Gwenhwyfar, Morgause, Nimue, and others. She creates an original cultural mythology in that many of the women are raised on the Isle of Avalon as votaries of a Celtic mother goddess, and they are fighting to defend their worship and lore, their magic and empowerment, from encroaching, masculine-centered Christianity. The women are powerful, and in that capacity, they call attention to the relative powerlessness of women when Bradley was writing. Bradley also gains shock value from rewriting well-known characters. Instead of embodying motiveless malignancy, Morgaine and others have a defensible and plausible rationale for their actions. They are involved in feminist politics, in earth-valuing and protecting, rather than being archetypally evil, which is an effective and artistically interesting development. Were the same story projected with non-Arthurian names, we would never feel the shock of recognition that we feel when Morgaine and Morgause are presented as reasonably positive figures rather than as vicious troublemakers. The same story with different names would not create anything like the same impact. A major part of myth's effect comes from our prior knowledge. Such prior knowledge is the cultural capital that gives one kind of mythic literature its weight and gives it a layer of meaning not available to pure fantasy.

Less obviously making a point is Mary Stewart's tetralogy on Arthur, starting with *The Crystal Cave* (1970). Her focal figure is Merlin, so of necessity she deals with magic, but she reduces the inexplicable and truly magical to a very small part of the story. Most of what Merlin does could be explained as engineering or psychic flashes of insight. What Merlin and Arthur between them do is give the world a sense that actions are fated and fit into some grand plan. Stewart seems to cherish this sense of a world that has promises of greatness—and of doom—but at least its developments are planned, not random, and its doom does not mean the end of the world. A higher power exists. Fictionally, she values this sense of living in a world in which actions have meaning and belong to larger patterns. One might call this just the fantasy that romance gives us, but many a fantasy exists without giving us this strong a sense of meaning. One has only to read Stewart's own non-Arthurian romances such as *Nine Coaches Waiting* and *Airs above the Ground*, to see just how lacking in mythic weight and meaningful action they are. Known stories can impart a sense of density that original creations are unlikely to achieve, unless those stories persist for centuries. They must sink in and become part of the audience's cultural knowledge before they can have this effect of conjuring a sense of meaning. I enjoy some of the fantasy series by Mercedes Lackey, Anne McCaffrey, Raymond Feist, and Katharine Kerr, but they are not set in our world and have no cultural resonance. They remain just fantasy, whereas Arthurian material gives that little extra buzz that comes from being known from childhood, from taking place in known lands, and from being a story that is known to other educated people.

A Scots-Canadian writer who has explored Arthurian territory is Jack Whyte. His is the most researched in terms of Romano-British background and history, and he tries to imagine an Arthur who might have arisen out of that history. Rather than magic, what his version embodies is the wish for a leader who is both powerful and good. Whyte's multivolume saga gets rather lost in the details, as reviewers have complained, but even in the figures prior to Arthur, in *The Skystone* (1996), Whyte seems concerned with how integrity and power can be found together. Our cynical age has seen too many politicians exposed for corruption or misbehavior to give us faith in anyone using power except for selfish ends. Nor do we have much hope that leaders will make strong, effective decisions. In this Never-Never-Land of the past, however, these combinations seem possible, and we revel in that kind of world. One can argue that pandering to this desire for honorable leaders is politically irresponsible or just a version of opiate for the masses, but the audience desire for such a combination is being recognized and offered as compensation for cultural lacks.

We see something similar in T. H. White's *The Once and Future King*. The anxieties arising at the outset of the Second World War make their way into Arthurian form; T. H. White's Arthur, or Wart as he is called, is a boy who has only average intelligence and physical ability—not a heroic type at all—but he means well and tries hard to do the right thing. He more or less bumbles his way to success until treachery overcomes him. This picture of the well-meaning, ordinary Briton (or British soldier), published at the beginning of the Second World War, is not unlike Tolkien's picture of hobbits, and represents a new kind of hero.[5] Tolkien's Frodo does succeed in destroying the Ring. Arthur must fail, though T. H. White implies the descent of the story to Tom of Newbold Revel, also known as Thomas Malory, and thereafter to writers of the present, so the death of the man Arthur does not kill the effectiveness of his story, and its ideals live on.

Cultural compensation sometimes, indeed often, serves morally dubious aims. For British readers, historicized Arthurs fight against colonizing Angle and Saxon invaders. Uneasiness over Britain's colonizing role and its empire won through conquest and control thus undergo easy erasure as readers enjoy the position of fighting heroically against colonizers. H. G. Wells tapped into that same reverse psychology in his *War of the Worlds* where his empire-ruling Britons played the victim and fought colonizing Martians. Similarly, early American science fiction played with various scenarios of America being invaded at the times when America was sending armed forces to Haiti or the Philippines and starting its own overseas empire.[6]

Criticism of Christianity's Mythic Core

If a writer is a nonbeliever, then certain biblical stories are mythical, and can be manipulated to criticize the dominant culture and its values. The myths that have drawn most recent attention are Christ and Eden, and I would like to consider what several authors do to employ the myths as tools against their country's general culture. Christ being so central to Christianity, treatment of that story as myth amounts to full-out attack. Michel Faber, Philip Pullman, and James Morrow all go after the majority religion in the Western world, Christianity.

Faber's *The Fire Gospel* (2008) explores all too briefly what might happen if an amazingly preserved manuscript in Aramaic dating from earlier than the Gospels is found. In it, Jesus's story is told without any miracles, and features death without resurrection. In essence, Faber strips the story of its mythical and miraculous content. Jesus is just a good man publicly urging others to be good and to uphold obvious values. Faber spends a lot of time on the sleazy discoverer of this manuscript and on the murderous pressures brought to bear on him to renounce the truth of his finding and declare it a forgery, but from what we see of various Christian reactions, most people would feel that their religion had lost its value without the magic implied by resurrection. Faber's book, incidentally, is one of several in the Canongate Myth series that will be considered in this chapter.

Pullman must like doubles. He doubled worlds in his *His Dark Materials* series. His *The Good Man Jesus and the Scoundrel Christ* (another Canongate book) doubles the messiah. Jesus preaches down-to-earth and ordinary goodness, as does Faber's Jesus; Jesus's twin, Christ, wants a great, new, institutional church to grow from this, and he emphasizes and embellishes all traces of the miraculous. Christ is guided by a stranger, possibly a fallen angel or Satan himself, and in order to bring his desired future about, Christ permits himself to be mistaken for Jesus the preacher, and is crucified. Both Faber and Pullman are challenging the foundational miracles claimed by Christianity. They cannot believe in them, and ask whether anything worthwhile is left when we shear away that mythicized component. That Pullman would be hostilely skeptical toward Christianity is to be expected from the *His Dark Materials* trilogy, in which we see a very moth-eaten God rebelled against and evidently die. Like Faber, he acknowledges the side of Jesus that simply preaches practical goodness, but also recognizes the side making far greater claims, claims that would be the words of a madman if uttered anywhere or any time were they not presented in the Bible. As C. S. Lewis puts it in *Mere Christianity*, we have either to accept his statements about being the son of God, or he is a lunatic and should be utterly rejected.[7] These authors are trying to get around that issue, and Pullman finds a logical (if fantastic) answer to Lewis's alternatives: postulate twins!

James Morrow's *Only Begotten Daughter* asks a more unusual question, namely what would happen if God produced a second offspring today and if that proved to be a daughter? Within his mythic world, he permits Jesus, Satan, and the daughter, Julie, to have miraculous powers, but locates the story in a slightly altered United States. Most of the novel is concerned with what Julie should do with the powers she has initially, and when she loses those, then how she can best spend her life.

Most of Morrow's characters refer to God with female pronouns. Hence, everything must be reversed. We have a celibate Jewish hermit who helps support his life by participating in an experiment that involves his producing sperm once a month for a sperm-donor bank, and their experiments with some of his sperm miraculously start an embryo, no one knows how. The apparatus that serves as artificial womb is implausibly simple, but a girl is born nine months later. She would have been destroyed when Revelationists firebombed the building had Murray not stolen his developing germ plasm in its womb just before that raid. Also sharing the abandoned lighthouse with Murray Katz and his immaculately conceived daughter is a lesbian and her sperm-donor child Phoebe.

Julie shocks her father early by walking on water and by developing gills so she can breathe under water. She causes fireflies to blink out messages and brings a dead crab back to life. At each such childish act, Murray angrily chides her and even slaps her over the crab. He is desperately afraid of what will happen to her life if her miracles become known. He imagines her, held captive and forced to heal person after person, situation after situation. She would be blamed for anything that went wrong and would lose all personal life. Her final juvenile miracle is to give sight to a boy who had been blind from birth, the son of the Revelationist leader who is trying to trigger the second coming of Christ by causing city-destroying disasters on Earth.

Julie is much influenced by science, and tries through a newspaper column to persuade people to accept uncertainty. When the Revelationists attempt to destroy Atlantic City in order to usher in the millennium, Julie's powers let her prevent the worst of their damages. She becomes a target, and eventually accepts the Devil's invitation to live (comfortably) in Hell. There she helps her half-brother Jesus heal the pain and thirst of the damned, but after several years, she decides this is not what she was supposed to do and returns to New Jersey, only to find it entirely changed. Furthermore, she finds that the Devil has stripped her of her powers. Her newspaper columns have become the gospel for a new underground religion, and New Jersey is now a Revelationist republic that burns and tortures heretics. She is crucified by the Revelationists and her body is slung into the bay. A philosophical sponge whom she had known as a child cleans her wounds, and absorbs and changes the poison she had been given while crucified. She escapes and eventually tries to reach her communal family again.

Morrow shows many forces at work. Julie tries to persuade people to live by logic and science, but returns to see that her advice has been translated into a faith whose adherents look to her for salvation. No single human, however divinely gifted, can heal all the damaged people who would demand healing. Even if her laying on of hands can heal a person, her human energy would not suffice for millions. Jesus was a local phenomenon, but Julie lives in the world of total communication. What then are those powers good for? Occasional displays to make a point or prevent a massacre near where she lives, perhaps, but on the scale of the world, that does not do much, and our culture would not trust or accept anyone with extraordinary (and therefore threatening) powers. When she loses her divine abilities, she runs a mobile soup kitchen and tries to help those in need. While that is never enough, it may do almost as much good as more exalted powers.

Her experience with the sponge leads her to consider the possibility (suggested by the sponge itself) that the sponge is God: "Faceless, shapeless, holey, undifferentiated, Jewish, inscrutable ... and a hermaphrodite to boot. Years ago, I told you sponges cannot be fatally dismembered, for each part quickly becomes the whole. To wit, I am both immortal and infinite." To this statement from the sponge, Julie says weakly "there's not much comfort in that .... Sponges can't help us." To which the sponge replies, "Neither can God."[8] In *Towing Jehovah* and *Blameless in Abaddon*, Morrow's characters find no satisfactory answer to how a supposedly good God can permit evils on earth. In *Only Begotten Daughter*, we find this interesting comparison of God to a sponge. Something can be immortal and infinite and yet not in any sense powerful or helpful. This concept of God may be as philosophically misbegotten as Anselm's ontological proof of His existence. We easily spot possible gaps in the sponge's logic. The sponge's claim, however, is intriguing and amusing.

Although one might expect a feminist take on the new child of God being female, that does not seem to be Morrow's chief concern. The various characters who imagine God to be female cannot in fact make any better argument for Her existence than can previous theologians for a male deity. Switching to a feminist theodicy gains us nothing in explanatory power. What matters is more what would happen to a Messiah if one turned up in the modern age of communication and celebrity. How could such a person not be totally overwhelmed? Throughout Julie's life, she tries to establish contact with God the Mother, but never succeeds. Morrow seems to think that God is Santa Claus for grown-ups, so her lack of success is not surprising. Like Pynchon, Morrow seems to feel that the most practical thing humans can do is help make life easier for those who have a hard time: in this case, drive a soup-dispensing truck. You cannot make life better for everyone, so do what you can locally.

Broader Engagements with Judeo-Christian Culture

Instead of attacking the dominant Judeo-Christian faith, some authors try to reinvest the myths with power. Pat Robertson's 1995 novel, *The End of the Age,* describes the Rapture as it might be experienced by those alive in the year 2000. We get a secularized, Alien-orchestrated version of that physical rising up into the empyrean in Spider and Jeanne Robinson's trilogy, *Stardance, Starseed,* and *Starmind* (1979, 1991, and 1995). For a writer who has focused on the power attributed to God when He creates our world, though, I turn to Rikki Ducornet. She draws on Jewish-Kabbalistic, Christian, Islamic, and pre-biblical Egyptian gods to try to energize our minds with the idea of the miraculous power of God's word—and metaphorically, the power of all words. As she puts it in her Afterword to *The Jade Cabinet* (1993),

> I was infected with the venom of language in early childhood when, sitting in a room flooded with sunlight, I opened an alphabet book. B was a Brobdingnagian tiger-striped bumblebee, hovering over a crimson blossom, its stinger distinct. This image was of such potency that my entire face—eyes, nose and lips—was seized by a phantom stinging, and my ears by a hallucinatory buzzing. In this way, and in an instant, I was simultaneously initiated into the alphabet and awakened to Eden.[9]

Her various characters are often overwhelmed by such experiences. In *The Jade Cabinet,* the narrator's father, Angus Sphery, spends his life looking for the language God spoke, the primal words of power that through sheer utterance could bring whatever they named into being. He seeks that language in everything from the patterns on butterfly wings to the babblings of Bedlamites. So convinced is he that the primal language could be accessed that he has his first child, Etheria, raised without any spoken sounds so that when she started to express herself, she would do so in the language of paradise. All that did, of course, was to render her unable to speak, though she did eventually learn to understand and to write.

An architect is equally convinced that he knows the primary starting point for Creation, namely certain perfect geometric shapes, and he goes mad when trying to find evidence for these under the Egyptian pyramids. Egyptian hieroglyphics seem equally imbued with magic, for they are pictures of what they represent, unlike our words and letters. What these and other Ducornet characters seem to strive for is a return to Eden and Creation, to perfection before the fall, but perfection that includes many people living in geometric cities, and the power to create by word alone, without industrial complexities. In another novel, *Gazelle*, Ducornet pays more attention to the Egyptian side of this concept of power. The perfume-distiller sees creation in terms of odors. The father, the daughter, and the perfume-maker read the story of a student of magic who discovers the Ism-el-Aazam, the hidden name of God. By using that sacred name, the student could make anything he asks for come into being, including his deciding in old age to go back in time and make a different decision so that different results lead to a different life for himself and others. Also in Egypt, though, the old gods with their animal heads remain in the guise of similarly headed Djinn, and they are the powers invoked by a desert magician in that novel for trying to woo back an errant wife.

Ducornet suggests that thinking of Creation through words or other pure principle is powerful and enlightening, but at the same time, she shows most of her characters chasing their mystic ideas into forms of insanity.[10] Angus Sphery wastes his money and ruins his academic reputation by giving extravagant support to a freak show hunger artist who appears to speak no known human language, and who, he thinks, is therefore speaking the primal tongue. The architect, thanks in part to being caught in some cave-ins when exploring under pyramids, spends the rest of his life in Bedlam. Radulph Tubbs, the industrialist who marries Etheria, spends many years consumed with depression and mad thoughts that arise from the speechless but incandescently beautiful Etheria's having left him. The narrator thinks that Etheria became a stage magician, and if so, her acts make her look as if she is floating in the air. For all that she was deprived of the chance to learn speech, she may have acquired some compensatory channel to magic power, which is part of this "primal" complex. Our narrator, her less than beautiful sister, consoles herself with her Christian faith (and with her father's friend, the Rev. Dodgson, who delights in nonsense logic), but her religion just attributes magic to others, and she takes that magic on faith.

Ducornet's other characters want immediate personal demonstration of that mythic power, and they mostly come to bad ends, though emotionally, they often seem exalted and soaring. Madness and rapture seem near-allied in Ducornet's imaginary. The rapture fuels her interaction with words, her writing, but the insanity warns us against trusting such rapture. Whereas other writers have invoked myth for intellectual reasons, hers, like Kathy Acker's, are emotional.

Another writer responding to Jewish sense of the power in language is Ben Marcus. *The Flame Alphabet* (2012) rests on the premise that words spoken by children—just Jewish children at first, but then maybe all—have the power to sicken and destroy adults. We never learn how far this language plague has spread in the world, but we see the local adults sickening, finding themselves increasingly unable to speak, hear, or even think, read, or communicate through any word-oriented means. Babel is invoked as a background myth, though the curse of many languages seems pale beside this language plague. A mysterious character sometimes named Murphy responds contemptuously to the protagonist, Sam's, mention of Babel.

> Mythology is the lowest temptation. You want to talk about first causes, I'd go back before the Jewish child and city mythology, the most sickening specimens of speech. We subscribe to these supposedly important stories, religious stories, and we ignore their inanity, how moronic and impractical they are. Can we prove the stories don't make us sick? Because they happened long before we were born, we somehow decide they are extraordinarily important and we shut our brains down, we turn into imbeciles, we let the past start thinking for us. *That's sickness.* [11]

The principal article to analyze the novel does so in terms of its handling of anti-Semitism. Inbar Kaminsky links this novel to Philip Roth's *Nemesis* since both authors create a plague narrative to reflect the workings of anti-Semitism.[12] Our first inkling of trouble comes from the voice of Esther, Sam's daughter. Sam and his wife belong to a mysterious sect of Jews who go to hidden cabins in the woods, listen through strange electronic means to a rabbi's recorded sermons, and are bound by the terms of belonging never to discuss or mention what they hear. Some of Sam's musings on the power of God's words reminds us of Rikki Ducornet's Kabbalistic concerns with primal language. What struck me, though, is an entirely different layer of meaning in the book: the dissolution of a less than satisfactory marriage, and the admittedly scarifying hostile comments made by the fourteen-year-old Esther to her parents. Sam's complete inability to understand what his wife needs or wants, his heavy assurance that he is doing the right thing in regard to his wife, and their joint inability to interact satisfactorily with their daughter is another manifestation of how words can poison, can make personal relations impossible.

Marcus reminds us that our cultural acceptance of certain myths defines us as a culture, and makes us vulnerable to particular insanities. Rabbinical veneration of the word and the endless words poured out in discussion thereof mark Judaism. Whereas Ducornet saw the possibility of rapture at such insight—rapture dangerously allied to madness—Marcus only presents the madness in this novel. The madness does not just remain an internal problem to Jews; the adjacent Christian culture has its own mad myths, and those trigger unthinking reactions to rival myths. The words and the mythic stories they form are indeed at the root of cultural clashes.

Eden has provoked many writers to think about the culture in which we live. If they are not haunted by the kabalistic power of the creative word and primal language, then it is the unfallen existence compared to flawed human nature. Kurt Vonnegut tried such a devolutionary story in *Galápagos* (1985). A small group of humans were marooned on the Galápagos Islands just as a plague wiped out humans in the rest of the world. As we leave them a couple of generations on, they are rapidly turning into something like seals. Their needs are met through fish and seaweed, and their "big brains" (to whose peculiarities Vonnegut attributes all sorts of irrational and destructive decisions throughout the plot) are no longer needed, and are shrinking. Big Brains are not only able to generate complexities, such as technology, but are also very liable to irrationality and self-destructive actions, so Vonnegut decides we would be better without them. Other writers have similarly focused on our mentality for reasons that explain our inability to construct utopias or even just behave decently and sensibly. Octavia Butler, in *Dawn* (39), put it down to our having two characteristics: we are intelligent, and we are very hierarchical. That latter makes us bend our minds to ingenious ways of putting down rivals.

More recently, Margaret Atwood, has written a very elaborate and extensive trilogy that explores the possibility of beginning again in an Edenic fashion. The first volume, *Oryx and Crake* (2003), shows how humanoids created through genetic manipulation can be launched as an alternative to our destructive species. When a female is fertile, males around her turn blue and offer her flowers. She accepts four of them and the rest promptly lose their color and desire; the four winners mate with her and serve as co-fathers. They too, though, lose their color and she her smell, so that life is mostly peaceful, non-sexual, and undisturbed by rivalries and competition. Many other changes affect how they interact, but basically very steady and nonviolent behavior is programmed into them. Unfortunately, the plagues designed to remove ordinary people do not prove entirely effective, so ordinary people and some who have been brutalized by a prison system involving freeing the fittest who survive a murder fest put some very dangerous opponents up against the innocent Crakers (as they are called). *The Year of the Flood* (2009) and *Maddaddam* (2013) chronicle the gradual development of the Crakers, their being taught to read and record wisdom, their development of a sense of the world. Much of the trilogy shows how some eco-oriented, mostly pacifist, unaltered humans try to mesh with the Crakers, protect them, and work out a viable future. In one regard, the gamers, coders, and biologists who created the Crakers failed: they tried to eradicate religion, but we see a sense of worship toward crude monuments representing dead helpers. This may just lead to respect for the ancestors and a sense of history, or it might evolve into religion. If it does, the long-term future for the Crakers may not be smooth, even if the violent humans can be dealt with.

A different version of Eden, one distanced by a metaphoric sleight of hand, is Thomas Pynchon's invoking Lemuria and then California as paradise in *Inherent Vice* (2009). When Lemuria sank, its fleeing inhabitants landed in California and, at least until the Spaniards and Anglos came, had a relatively Edenic existence. Pynchon calls attention to various forks in the path of history taken by cultures, and he grizzles over America's having taken the wrong paths. America did this on the issue of slavery and humanity's relationship with nature in the colonial period, a point he stresses in both *Gravity's Rainbow* and *Mason & Dixon*. He also points out that Puritan fixation on being the Elect caused them to neglect the Preterite, the outcasts, those of lower class unable to get up the social ladder. America also welcomed Reaganite politics in the 1980s (an issue in *Vineland* and one "prophesied" in *Inherent Vice*). The myth, however, comes in when he considers California, the golden land that so many find worthy of being Eden but now ruined by shoddy developers.

The protagonist, Doc Sportello, reluctantly takes LSD in hopes of locating his missing ex-girlfriend by means of the drug vision. While tripping, he finds himself in the "ruin of an ancient city that was, and also wasn't, everyday Greater L. A.," and it is sinking into the ocean.[13] He climbs up and up, and then is helped by a Lemurian spirit guide, Kamukea, who helps him fly over the ocean, gives him a view of the girlfriend in a boat and a vision of the evil energy operating in that drug-running boat, *Golden Fang*, and then leaves him "to find his way out of a vortex of corroded history, to evade somehow a future that seemed dark whichever way he turned" (110). Doc dreams of "the years of promise, gone and unrecoverable, of the land almost allowed to claim its better destiny, only to have the claim jumped by evildoers known all too well, and taken instead and held hostage to the future we must live in now forever" (341). At the end, he hopes that the boat *Golden Fang*, now renamed *Preserved*, "is bound for some better shore, some undrowned Lemuria, risen and redeemed, where the American fate, mercifully, failed to transpire" (341). Lemuria is thus a once-and-future paradise and a tantalizing image of what California might have been but failed to achieve.

This once-and-future quality of the Edenic Lemuria myth suits Pynchon's elegiac vision in this novel. Though the story is set in 1969–70, it is written with the hindsight available from the period leading up to publication in 2009, so the Vietnam War, the hippie era, the period of Reagan's governorship, his presidency, and later international interventions in Kuwait, Iraq, Afghanistan. and elsewhere add a looming dark quality to the novel's sense of the future. Pynchon longs for something less capitalistic, more attuned to community values. He ends the book with Doc driving in a fog, imagining that someday "there'd be phones as standard equipment in every car, maybe even dashboard computers. People could exchange names and addresses and life stories and form alumni associations to gather once a year at some bar off a different freeway exit each time, to remember the night they set up a temporary commune to help each other home through the fog" (368). Doc's final wish is "for the fog to burn away, and for something else this time, somehow, to be there instead" (369). That something else is presumably a less damaged California, a less squalid and vicious America, something more humane that imitates the Edenic ideals of attributed to Lemuria.

This dream of Lemuria raises interesting literary questions, since no one takes that myth seriously in geological terms. The very idea of Lemuria only developed in the nineteenth century as imitation of the Atlantis myth, and it has no wide-spread religious backing. There never was a Pacific continent that sank, and it will not be rising off the coast of California, as it seems to at times in the novel. California was not originally settled by Lemurians. Even if there had been such a culture, we would be in no position to say that it was Edenic or ideal. What, then, does Pynchon gain by using this thoroughly fictional myth that he associates with Edenic life?

Early in the novel, Doc is annoyed by some of the alternate lifestyle types he associates with because they take Lemuria seriously. He dismisses it, but he cannot escape it, since his LSD trip involves him directly with a Lemurian, and this Lemurian seems also to be the spirit guide of his LSD supplier. That this guide would appear in both their visions adds to the guru's insistence that everything is connected, and Doc's correctly seeing his ex-girlfriend's location in the vision is another bit of evidence for connection and multiple layers of reality. Pynchon is a playful writer, so speculating on the reasoning behind his choices may be unwise. Given his linking the Lemurian guide also to Hawaii and to his sense of Lemuria as a place with ideal climate, I suspect it is just a catchy way of saying that a different path would have been possible. California need not have been treated the way it was. Its original Native inhabitants need not have been driven off and slaughtered to make way for suburban spread. Their way of living would have come much closer to the ideal than anything established by Western Christian civilization. We have wrecked all the places that seemed paradisal to early explorers. The Lemurians might in a sense signify those who wish to get back to such a state of being, those who sense their loss and would welcome the chance to return—the hippies and others devoted to alternatives who flourished so briefly and were washed away by the rising Reaganomic tide.

Challenge to Judeo-Christian Culture from a Minority Position

We find cultural compensation and myth operating differently when deployed by minorities within the larger Anglo culture in America. Consider the African American myth of flying Africans. Both Gloria Naylor in *Mama Day* (1988) and Toni Morrison in *Song of Solomon* (1977) draw on that folk myth.[14] It derives from the landing of slaves at Dunbar Creek on St. Simons Island. In 1803, a group of Igbo captives chose death over slavery, and marched off into the water, heading back to Africa. Accounts vary as to how many drowned and how many were recaptured, but enough survived to spread the story and tell of how those who marched into the water called on the "Water Spirit" to take them home.[15] As the story became embellished over time, some versions say that they flew home, and that is the version that attracts Naylor and Morrison. A story of bravery, despair, and rebellion becomes a mythic tale of magic, of ancestral African superiority to earthbound whites, and of a few people managing to manoeuver in a dimension that is not accessible to humans, the air. Although Gloria Naylor's novel begins with the sale slip for the ancestral woman, Sapphira, no one remembers her name, and her descendants frequently assert that she was no slave. She got their island from Bascomb Wade, probable father of at least some of her seven sons, and got it deeded to them and their offspring. She also apparently soared away from a particular east-side cliff. The realist part of the reader's mind assumes that she jumped off the cliff, but the magic version in folk memory claims that she flew off to Africa. Naylor admits the suicide possibility obliquely, since the wife of the seventh son committed suicide by diving down into a well, and the two women are frequently linked. Sapphira's flying away, though, gives a magic start to this island culture, to the magic of a place that belongs neither to Georgia nor to South Carolina because it is directly and equally off-shore from their border. That hint of magic also paves the way for Mama Day's female-patterned magic based on healing, herbs, and vodoun.

In Morrison's *Song of Solomon*, Milkman Dead hears of flying Africans, but really starts paying attention when he learns that his great grandfather, Solomon, was supposed to have flown away and back to Africa. Solomon even tried to carry his youngest son, Milkman's grandfather, but dropped him. Finding such an illustrious ancestor does much to reorient Milkman Dead's life. He changes from a lazy, self-centered man into someone who tries to do and be better. When Milkman makes a leap between tall rocks that might well kill him, he proves his manhood by not holding back; he may fall, or he might be stabbed or shot by his former friend, but the danger is his to face, and he will do his best. The myth thus inspires him, and our final glimpse of him is of his being in the air. Again, the myth offers cultural compensation in that some African Americans can fly as no white can do. It also fights against white cultural assumptions that devalue everything about those with dark skin. Morrison invites readers to learn, as Milkman does, to take charge of their lives, and to African Americans she offers the story of ancestral magic as encouragement.

We find a different kind of mythic deployment in Leslie Marmon Silko's *Ceremony* (1977). This takes us to a world unfamiliar to readers who are not Native Americans from the Southwest. When readers do not know the myths, how can the myths function in a work of art, or do they become inert? At first reading of this novel, one is likely to say that this is not a postmodern work. Nonetheless, it aggressively challenges the nature of reality as defined by Western civilization. Ontological questions are central, and the characters are very far from being comfortably unified. They are torn by conflicting cultural discourses, the claims of Western and Native cultures. We see this clash when Tayo remembers a biology class.

> The teacher brought in a tubful of dead frogs, bloated with formaldehyde, and the Navajos all left the room; the teacher said those old beliefs were stupid. The Jemez girl raised her hand and said the people always told the kids not to kill frogs, because the frogs would get angry and send so much rain there would be floods. The science teacher laughed loudly, for a long time; he even had to wipe tears from his eyes. "Look at these frogs," he said, pointing at the disc[o]lored rubbery bodies and clouded eyes. "Do you think they could do anything? Where are all the floods? We dissect them in this class every year."[16]

This kind of culture clash makes the personalities of most of the characters multiple; they think like Anglos in some circumstances and like Native Americans in others, and cannot join the two world pictures. While that is not postmodern in its more European senses, it does embody the nonunited self and it explores ontological issues.

I first read the novel influenced by my work with the hero monomyth and, therefore, saw it as a perfect, but routine, monomythic quest story. And so it is, but that reading pares away the hinted-at significance of details—heading west or north, looking toward Mt. Taylor, and the like. Reading the novel as a monomythic quest turns it into a romance and divests it of novelistic and mythic complexities—the wealth of detail that builds layers of meaning. Roland Barthes pointed out that the "effect of the real" in realistic novels comes from a superfluity of ordinary detail. I have also argued that certain kinds of detail can create an "effect of the historical."[17] The mythic overlay that Silko gives to her locations and directions suggest what might be called the "effect of the spiritual." She builds a world on which divine figures and locations exist. I won't say they are superimposed on the physical landscape because they are, within their own system, more importantly present than the mountain or ravine is there physically. Their presence makes that mountain what it is, calls it into existence within that world picture.[18] They are non-material yet anchored to the material landscape. Someone with the right spiritual training and outlook might be able to cross over in spirit and carry out some quest or ask for help, but others would not be able to access this nonmaterial level.[19]

Because these myths are not familiar to Euro-American readers, we need to see what they add to the novel. According to knowledgeable critics, Silko tweaks, alters, and combines mythic materials from the various southwestern tribal traditions.[20] She has also drawn on material collected and published by anthropologists, so this material is at least nominally in the public domain and accessible, while some sacred elements are altered to protect them from profane eyes. A reader whose background includes these Laguna and greater southwest traditions presumably grasps far more immediately than most Anglo readers the significance of Spider Woman, the spiritual implications of heading west versus north, or the mythic inhabitants associated with Mt. Taylor. Eurocentric readers may grasp from hints the possibility that such details as a direction or a landmark have meaning, but can only find that meaning by reading the many articles that explain this material. Given Native American preference for not revealing spiritual matter to outsiders and the practice of some Native American writers of altering colors and details to protect sacred lore, the Anglo reader cannot be sure of what constitutes an authentic myth and what is merely myth-like.

A book like *Ceremony*, obviously filled with mythic references, works in at least five ways for different audiences. Laguna audiences who object to public dissemination of sacred material might stop reading and reject the book unless they sense that the material has been altered or if they know the material present is already public in anthropological studies. If they are not bothered by this exposure of their stories, they can share the sense of valued cultural capital and the values of interconnectedness. They see the most clearly how Tayo develops spiritually. Native Americans more generally, and if they have any training in their own spiritual traditions, probably get most of the embedded world picture if not all of those specific mythic and local references. Zealous believers in some other religious tradition might reject the novel for its alien mythology, as some medieval Christians did stories with classical mythological material, and as some Christian Native Americans or some Evangelicals might do. Nonreligious Anglos can recognize their own being outside the cultural circle, but can at least absorb direct statements about the fragility and interconnectedness of everything, and the impossibility of saying that a person or thing is all good or all bad. They will sense the extra mythic dimension, but will be unable to access it without considerable research.

This last audience, however, will probably resist some native concepts, such as witchery. Particularly if someone is accused of witchery and shunned or killed for it, those readers will resist fiercely, witchcraft not being recognized by the scientific values of the West, and being now defined as the imposed name for terrible prejudice. They will resist Tayo's sense that his cursing rain in the Philippines caused the drought he finds in the American southwest, but they can accept the reason that cursing is considered a spiritual error. A more serious problem arises when Abel kills an albino Indian in N. Scott Momaday's *House Made of Dawn* (1968) because he is sure without evidence that the albino is a witch. However much Anglo readers try to understand, they are unlikely to accept murdering such a person as acceptable. The seriousness of such a resistance correlates to the seriousness with which we are willing to take the overall picture; few readers would take Mailer's Egyptian world seriously, so we do not worry about magic attacks on characters or killing someone for wielding hostile magic. Silko's vision of closeness to the land resonates with various ecologically active strands in recent Western culture, so many readers will be at least interested in entertaining it seriously. Those readers are left dangling, positive about some of the vision, but resistant to other parts.

Silko employs myth even more syncretically in *Almanac of the Dead* (1991), for she draws on African and Central American myths as well as myths of the Southwest Indians. Indeed, she and her characters recognize as valid any attempt to get back to prescientific and pretechnological culture, so Neopagans and Celtic healers are mentioned as potential members of the masses whom she wishes to see resist the ruling technological culture. The goal is to get back to a spiritual understanding of the Earth, learn to live with nature rather than destroy it, and learn to feel the presence of spirits.[21] Those familiar with the myths will make more of the symbolism involving sacred twins than outsiders will, but again Silko can make the spiritual and political messages clear without many of her readers knowing all the mythological resonances. Even to those ignorant of the details, the mythic elements give a sense of fatedness to the action; they make the actions predicted, not random, and therefore give overall meaning to political action. Silko's own sense of the spirits pushing us toward actions good or bad is apparently quite personal; she felt so compelled to write this book under pressure that she says she felt as the spirits pushing her, and even as she finished it, she saw the Zapatista movement in Chiapas begin to take the shape of the fictional movement she describes in the book.[22]

Myth Attacking Myth

Myth can be manipulated to challenge the very idea of gods. We saw in A. S. Byatt's *Ragnarok: The End of the Gods* that gods may be stupid, bullying, impractical, and selfish. Why did some ancestral northern Europeans worship these brutes—not that we really know much about the nature of that worship? Byatt's interest in them—and her argument—seems to be that their stupidities make them exactly like humans, and like those gods, we are stumbling toward the destruction of the world, and have no idea of how to stop that movement. Ecologically, we head almost blithely toward disaster. The Norse gods at least cared about dying bravely; that, rather than the death of their world, was what they could control.[23] We cannot even claim that our culture encourages us to face death calmly and valorously. In that novel, Byatt enjoys the stories, but shows no respect for these products of the human imagination as gods. Myth lets her attack our idea of gods, perhaps our felt need for them, and, by implication, the human tendency to assign the blame to them for whatever is going badly rather than take responsibility and work to solve the problems.

Byatt's was a Canongate Myth novel, and not the only one to build on Norse mythology. Klas Östergren's *The Hurricane Party* is another, and while originally written in Swedish, its being published in that British series is my excuse for discussing it here. Östergren describes a diminished future world, one in which people have to live in shelter and cannot spend much time under the sky, a civilization that scrounges bygone technology if it still works, such as typewriters. The country seems Scandinavian in that even though the main character, Hanck, is fired from his civil-service job, he does not starve or lose his living quarters. Religious books that educated people read include the Bible and the Quran, but Hanck gradually learns that Odin, Thor, Loki, and the others reside someplace near and hold occasional banquets on a nearby island. Hanck only learns of this when his only son, a chef at one of these banquets, is killed by Loki for sneezing, and Hanck has to do a lot of detective work even to find out who the feasters are. While apparently the Norse Gods, they are also shadowy rulers of the local city, and they operate more like mobsters running rackets.

Again, we have an array of deities who fail to garner much respect from us as readers. For the most part, they try to embarrass their fellow banqueters and are accused of various adulteries and thefts, above all by Loki. As in Byatt, Loki is the most interesting character, but far less attractive. In this novel, he appears to be a psychopath. He deliberately causes trouble, attacks all the Aesir and Vanir, and tries push them into civil war simply because he is driven to make trouble. He likes to stir things up and see what happens. He cares nothing for their feelings and nothing for others, including the young man he killed. He does not care what the results will be. He clearly spends a lot of his time in exile or shunned, and that does seem to bother him. He cannot be disposed of because he is an immortal, and he is apparently less of a threat when under Odin's eye than when roaming beyond the horizon doing things that no one can see or prepare for, so he is periodically accepted back.

The name Hurricane Party refers to the practice of neighbors gathering, bringing foods and supplies to some safe shelter before a bad storm, since many individual houses will be rendered uninhabitable through flooding or wind damage. Loki's drive always to needle and insult turns this banquet into a hurricane party.[24] The storm that is coming may well be Ragnarök. Given the timeline of divine lives, the storm is unlikely to be immediate, but the constrained and oddly limited nature of the human civilization we see suggests that ecological degradation is far advanced. Loki's psychological drive very likely reflects our human drives to keep stirring things up, altering them, "improving" them, but paying no attention to the long-term costs. Byatt's Loki, though superficially more attractive, is in many ways the scientist who is fascinated by his study of phenomena, but who does not consider long-term implications of the knowledge he makes public. Östergren's Loki is driven by urges he feels no need to control; the fact that they work against his society does not register with him. If he is the archetypal human, or represents our essence, then we truly have no conscience, and the eventual result will be disaster.

That flawed gods reflect modern culture also features in Neil Gaiman's *American Gods*. While that book has become a TV series that sees these gods as immigrants, Gaiman's original suggested a clash between two parties: the old gods derived from the Old World, and those who grew spontaneously in America, namely Media, Technical Boy, the Black Hats, and various less solidified gods related to the stock market and other modern forces. The old gods are limited, sometimes dishonest and selfish, but their flaws seem somehow human compared to the hideously slick and completely insincere Media. Insofar as we worship with our pocketbooks, Media, Technical Boy, and various representatives of modern fast transportation and money-making, are definitely our gods. Seeing them as such, though, proves rather sickening. They have lost any positive human qualities. The old gods are at least a mixture of virtues and vices.

Other Targets for Myth in Literature

Three novels in the Canongate series address personal problems in society: Jeanette Winterson's *Weight* (2005), David Grossman's *Lion's Honey: The Myth of Samson* (2005), and Margaret Atwood's *Penelopiad* (2005). Winterson and Grossman both approach the problem of people who struggle because they feel themselves to be outsiders or otherwise separated from or punished by society.[25] Both their heroes, Atlas and Sampson, are abnormally strong, a characteristic that is usually approved by society. Both authors seem intrigued by this paradox of being physically strong but socially weakened by that very attribute. Atwood looks instead at the way that all women have been made to feel separated from the society that matters and has power.

Behind Winterson's sense of the weight of being different are the pressures of being adopted and being lesbian. She has explored these at length in other fiction. With Atlas, though, he carries the weight of the whole world. Just to be sure we recognize that value, she gives us a recapitulation of the creation of the world along scientific lines, showing the wonder and glory without relating it to Genesis. Rather, she narrows it down eventually to Poseidon (Atlas's father) and Earth (his mother), and she lyrically eroticizes the caressing tides and interactions between ocean and land. The chief action of the book is the time when Heracles temporarily holds up the world while Atlas, freed, gathers for him Hera's golden apples of the Hesperides, a dangerous feat. Atlas wants to remain free, but Heracles cunningly tricks him into holding the world just a moment while he adjusts padding for his shoulder, and then Heracles skips off, leaving Atlas once more holding that weight. Both strength-heroes are puzzled and irritated by a question that Heracles raises: Why are their fates what they are? We follow Heracles to his eventual death, brought about indirectly by Hera but also by his own actions and nature. When Atlas learns of that, it is the last news from Olympus he gets. Christ changes the world. Technology sends satellites up. He rescues the Russian dog, Laika. Having a canine friend makes him see things differently, and the daring idea grows that he should just set the world down and free himself—which he does.

Winterson switches back and forth throughout the novel, talking in her persona as writer of the work, as someone who has as many layers of emotion and experience as the earth has geological layers. She feels their weight. She herself feels the angers of both Atlas and Heracles, the sense of wonder as to why she has these burdens. She says she undertook to retell this story so she could give it a different ending, Atlas setting down his burden. Here we see myth being applied to a very specific set of personal problems, but at the same time offered for anyone's personal problems. We see using myth as a way for the novelist to free herself from the burden by reshaping the story. Myth thus becomes a medical tool. When she was a child, she evidently had a lamp that was a globe. Those memories perhaps suggested this myth of carrying the world, but Winterson's weaving in scientific history of the world gives her version a sparkling, wondrous edge, extra flavors and lovely moments to savor. Mixing planetology, personal history, writerly concerns, and Greek myth produces something that pulses with energy, light, and emotion.

Grossman's novel on Samson focuses on Samson's being specially devoted to God but not meshing comfortably with his peers, and getting into trouble through using his strength in frustration or anger. He has been told that he has a particular mission predestined for him by his specially heralded birth, but he never can get clear what it is, and never manages to undertake it. Unlike Winterson's Atlas, Samson can never put his burden down, never enjoy the vision of beauty in the world that Atlas at times achieves. Insofar as Samson is implicitly endowed with a mission he cannot understand, he seems to be being set up in part as representative of Jews as the Chosen People, but also possibly as the individual writer struggling with the question of what life should mean. Atlas and Heracles were similarly bedeviled by the question "why?" Like Heracles, Samson's life ends through acts of his own, but Heracles was not trying to kill himself. Samson at least carved out a bit of meaning for himself by killing a large crowd of Philistines and avenging on them his slavery. What is frightening about this vision is its insight into terrorism. Those who never feel they fit in, never feel at home, never find what seems like their purpose in life, are likely to find suicidal terrorist action an effective way to create a sense of purpose. Grossman's use of this myth as a prototype of current problems makes all too much sense to me as reader.

Margaret Atwood's *Penelopiad* rethinks Penelope and Odysseus very plausibly.[26] For a start, Atwood does not idolize Odysseus; she sets him up as a clever con-man, a manipulator who instinctively and probably uncontrollably manipulates those around him. He is not totally lacking in honor, but he does his best to avoid situations that would demand that he behave rightly at cost to himself. Penelope is smart, and while not overly in love with him, recognizes his being about as good as she could get, so she makes herself into a model wife. What set Atwood off on this mythic story is Odysseus's brutal decision to hang the twelve handmaids of Penelope, supposedly for their sleeping with the suitors. As is made completely clear, they have no choice, and indeed they willingly supplied Penelope with very helpful information in her attempts to outwit these suitors. She does not think they deserve that end, and the question about which this story circles is an attempt to see why they should be so treated. Penelope narrates most of the tale from the from the land of the dead. The handmaids, also haunting the land of the dead, serve as chorus to comment on the actions.

Atwood gives us a negative view of this aristocratic and patriarchal society. Many women are slaves and have no control over how their bodies are used. Whatever guest might father a child, that child still becomes a slave or servitor, and has no standing. Even Penelope, as daughter of a king and legal spouse, has practically no standing, and her wits are needed to protect what little power she has. Once Telemachus has grown, he is stupidly eager to challenge the suitors and to start bossing his mother instead of being guided by her. Penelope does not come up with any answers. The maids who were hung were those whom she had particularly cultivated and encouraged, and who had helped her to unravel her daily weaving in secret. Eurycleia picked out the ones who had been impertinent to her for hanging, but Penelope had never let Eurycleia into her confidence, in part because the old nurse saw her as a rival for Odysseus's affections and confidences. We see a twenty-first century-courtroom scene where the judge dismisses various charges against Odysseus, with the scene breaking up as the ghosts of the maids call on the Furies to avenge them, and the lawyer for Odysseus calls upon Pallas Athene to defend him. Penelope ends with comments on life in the Underworld;

she occasionally intrudes on earthly séances, and feels amazement at the trivial things about which people want information from the dead—stock prices and personal health issues. Her cousin Helen often gets summoned or gets looked up by the recently dead, but Penelope does not get that kind of attention. Many of the dead drink of Lethe and are reborn. Odysseus does so compulsively, and has been many things: "He's been a French general, he's been a Mongolian invader, he's been a tycoon in America, he's been a headhunter in Borneo."[27] They all end badly with suicide or murder or death in battle; the vengeance of the maids continues to hound his spirit. Penelope sees no point to going through life again. One might be even worse off the next time around. In the maids' next to last choral song, they point out that Odysseus might have buried them properly and asked their forgiveness, but he did not, so they will never forgive him and will haunt him forever. An unpleasant end, but then he and his culture apparently saw no problem with arbitrarily hanging them, so Atwood asks the questions that never troubled Odysseus and his patriarchal society and keeps those questions alive.

Replacing Religion with Technology

When we look at current invented mythology, the most interesting created situations appear to be technological. Where those realms may once have been Heaven and Hell, or land of the dead and Olympus, now they tend to be electronic. Electronics still rely on material metal and silicon, but the virtual worlds "inside" or reached in the internet by the computer are only slightly more accessible than Heaven or Hell in the Middle Ages to someone housed in a body, and, as in *Postsingular*, these electronic realms often merge with or take characteristics from telepathy or telekinesis. Metamorphosis has come into its own again, and writers explore possible changes to our mortal body or try to make some part of us immortal. Whether we gain the ability through space travel and aliens, or whether it emerges from experiments in quantum entanglement, nanotechnology, genetic manipulation, robotics, computational power, or cloning, we are looking for ways of greatly extending life, possibly without any necessary end. Eternal existence as a soul or spirit or shade or ancestor is part of many religious value systems; as posthuman thinking develops, however, this mythical state has shifted to bodily immortality and eternal youth (via clones) or to potentially immortal electronic life. This seems to be an extension of mythical modes of thought.

Mythic worlds that offer immortality either in the form of electronic existence in web-based virtual reality or in the form of cloned bodies clearly push us into the realm of fantasy, but unlike some kinds of magic, these are not ruled out by the laws of science as we understand them. Indeed, this topic appeals to popular and elite tastes alike. One can identify with characters undergoing the transformation, but one can be equally wrapped up in the technicalities of how this might be achieved. That demands a good deal of arcane knowledge involving current research, computers, nanotechnology, and the like. This is not material known from childhood, as mythology might be for the child of well-educated parents, but it does demand intellectual engagement, and it pushes readers to try to compare such theory with actual possibility. The more technical the descriptions, the less this operates like genre fantasy, which I would crudely simplify as elves, dragons, space opera, and magic. Elves and n-space drive need no explanations; translation into electronic form can be handled that way—hey presto!—but it can also be approached by means of equations and advanced post-singularity theory. By some definitions, these future worlds are fantasy, but their concern with extended life and virtual (nonmaterial) life or actual immortality seems to me to put them into the realm where myth is an appropriate term for the type of situational subject matter.

Ordinarily, we do not think of technology as creating a mythic world, one with an extra level of reality different from the material world, but Pynchon manages to do this even with slightly outmoded technology. In *Bleeding Edge* (2013), he takes something that actually existed in 2001—the deep web—and shows how it functions as an auxiliary world, a layer of reality where people with sufficient technical knowledge can pursue secret or nefarious goals. They can experience entering it personally through virtual reality gaming structures. In that novel, Pynchon is more concerned to write a detective story than to expand this mythic level. To some extent, the deep web just gives him another way of playing out his "paranoid" politics, a place where secret networks can aggregate and spread. Very convincingly, though, he shows us a layer of our own reality that is much like the underworld of Orpheus, say, a place not easily visited and one that may bring death to those who enter unprepared. Because he locates the novel at the time of 9/11, he is not forecasting a postsingular world, but he anticipates some of the web's attractions that will be so important to those describing possible futures. By giving his paranoia a high-tech gloss, he is building a bridge between his earlier forms of paranoid fiction and postsingular projections.[28] Pynchon in *Bleeding Edge* gives us what is only marginally a mythic world, but he attests to the way that even mainstream literature is responding to our cultural drive to let our electronic inventions intervene in our lives and function in the way that divine beings and locations would once have functioned in earlier cultures.

Many kinds of metamorphosis figure in current speculative fiction. Writers tackling the implications of our going beyond Kurzweil's singularity are trying to imagine a new form of humanity, one that enjoys (or suffers from) a totally new relationship to the world. Rudy Rucker's *Postsingular* (2007) explores several forms of metamorphosis and imagines several possible stages in the development of human hyper-intelligence. Owing to the way that any matter, even a stone, can be transformed into computing memory, both the original and second wave of nanorobots or nants would multiply and consume the globe, and at best give human consciousness a life in virtual reality, though if the nants tired of us, we might cease to exist. An alternative version of nano-networked intelligence, called orphids, creates a Gaian organism that gives us instant and complete connectivity, an organic internet to the nth degree. People can access it simply by thinking, and indeed are mostly completely connected unless they deliberately cut themselves off. These orphids are in us and on us and on and in every other thing around us. Once the orphid net is well established, however, it develops its own artificial intelligence far superior to any human intelligence, so that configuration also proves ultimately to be a threat to humans. Rucker seems to take a bleak view of what will happen once superhuman intelligence develops, so much so that he can supply a happy ending only by having humans conveniently develop omnividence, telepathy, and teleportation. These no longer rely on any material, computorial basis. The drive for more and more memory and for more and more calculations per second can disappear in this exalted form of telepathic sharing.

This rollicking jaunt into a possible future will strike some readers with a distressing sense of déjà vu. The internet is wonderful, but hackers are constantly launching viruses and malware, either for fun or to steal information. This future-analog of the web will be similarly vulnerable to viral nants or their equivalent. The ads that appear in the sky, targeted to appropriate portions of earth, are all too reminiscent of the targeted ads that bedevil search engines—ads blinking and crawling in the very wide margins of the screen or interrupting the text, showing items that you have looked at on the web. Those ads continue to scream at you even after you may have purchased the item. Rucker's system is susceptible to misdirection; the madman who twice tries to reduce material existence to virtual reality through nants can so control communications that information supposedly sent to the police in fact comes to him. Furthermore, if the newly elected president does not do what the madman demands, the madman implies that (a) the president's large margin was owed to virus-controlled computers, (b) the count can be redone, and (c) the public can be made to forget the previous supposed outcome of the election. Given that the viral nants are microscopic and enter people's brains, his ability to manipulate public memory is no idle threat. The more we satisfy an insatiable desire for more memory and computer power, the more we open ourselves to the possibility of such a take-over of our minds.

Even if we can set to one side the threat of a madman (and why should we?), this hyper-connected system quickly develops its own artificial intelligences, and they develop interests and desires of their own that do not favor the continued existence of people. The orphidnet's central intelligence, nicknamed Big Pig, is quite happy at the thought of turning humans into virtual humans; by devouring the world, its matter will produce vast amounts more of memory and computing power, and Big Pig wants that more than it wants humans, however amusing or intriguing they may be. We cannot imagine what Big Pig is thinking or computing; we can only acknowledge that its hunger for more computational power is analogous to our own.

Several times in a few years' time-span, Rucker's fictional world narrowly misses tumbling into apocalypse. Some of the threats come from Christians who believe in the Rapture and want the world to end. Most of the trouble, though, as well as the advances and enjoyable additions to life, comes from people who enjoy learning about new technologies and thrive on their challenges. Although loss of privacy with the orphidnet would bother many people for a while, we seem to be giving up privacy to Facebook, Twitter, Alexa, and increasingly to government and employer, and street-side and corridor surveillance as well. This will just be one further step, with the compensation of infinite voyeurism and the creation of such computing power that you need just think a question to have configurations in this net go and look for answers for you. Nor is the gain only in science. One of the characters is writing a metanovel; the power available lets her create scenes and transfer them with sound, vision, smell, feel, and every dimension of experience into this web, and the consumers of the novel will enter into her experiences as virtual reality. Computer gamers can enter their worlds as never before, with all the implications that has for entertainment and education.

For similar myth-like metamorphoses, we can refer to the futures envisioned in the novels of Charles Stross and Cory Doctorow. This Kurzweilian future is gaining coherence, though often without Kurzweil's unshadowed optimism. Computational capacity and memory become the new currency of society, replacing money or making wealth much less central to experience.[29] Once the sheer number of connections exceeds those of brain synapses, new forms of intelligence become possible. People may be able to become virtual, but they might also find themselves superseded and eliminated. Rucker helps us see that the resolution possible for such virtual reality affects how "real" it would seem, and he draws on our experience with digital photos and pixels to help us imagine what low-resolution virtual reality would seem like compared to multidimensional, sensory life we experience now. His analogy with pixels effectively suggests that the complexity of human character, when reduced in resolution, would be two-dimensional and simplified to stereotypes.

Some writers—Greg Egan in *Permutation City* (1994) and Charles Stross in *Accelerando* (2005)—imagine this mythic metamorphosis of humans to virtual form in relatively positive ways. Indeed, one of Egan's characters kills his meat body to escape physical existence once he has uploaded his mind. Rucker's *Postsingular* is more rollicking in tone, but much more dubious about whether we will reach this new ideal state or whether it would be ideal; we may instead wreck ourselves on the way through inadequately developed nanotechnology and imperfect conceptualizing of the implications. Rucker's metanovelist, Thuy Nguyen, describes such novelists as alchemists who are "transmuting our lives into myth and fable."[30] So, in his way, is Rucker: he creates both a mythic world, one with alternative levels of reality, and a mythic situation, metamorphosis or rather several possible metamorphoses. The world is being transformed into computational power, and humans become variously part of a vast conscious network or, later, telepaths whose control of a hitherto unknown dimension will presumably let them figure out ways to escape mortality. Projectors of postsingular worlds are also postulating AIs that far outstrip human intelligence and therefore function like gods in other mythologies. Through the work of many contemporary authors, metamorphosis is the new dominant myth of our high-tech culture, and artificial intelligence is supplying new gods. Our posited ability to change our existence from the body to electronic or even telepathic form has rightly been called the Rapture for Nerds.[31]

Conclusion

I have referred often to literary situations that give us a sense of meaning. I had better clarify the factors that seem to give such a sense of meaning to literature with mythic components. We derive versions of meaning from many situations. Genre produces one kind of sensed meaning. We feel gratified when we anticipate a resolution and it comes; that resolution satisfies our feeling that the right thing happens, and when a "right" thing happens, we feel the acquiescence and gratification that seem to make something meaningful to us. The sense of rightness can be as simple as the good ending happily and the nasty being punished, but in a more sophisticated and philosophical vein, we can consider a thoroughly suspended and unresolved work, or a tragic work, to be "right" for the point it is making about life. Rightness inheres to an emotionally or intellectually appropriate resolution. Rightness also operates at many levels, and it will differ with the reader's personal background and intellectual concerns.[1] A reader who despises genre fiction will get little sense of gratification at the destined ending being reached, but most readers will at least acknowledge the appropriateness of the ending to the type of characters involved.

When responding to genre, but also when we read about human behavior, we try to match new phenomena to patterns we have already experienced, and when we can place that phenomenon in our mental structures, we again feel gratified, and perhaps proud of ourselves for making the match. The pattern we recognize and suddenly understand may be a psychological quirk, our way of identifying living phenomena by genus and species, story patterns, and any sequence that, once known, lets us predict what will come. Simply identifying an Orpheus story, particularly when Orpheus is not named, or a dying god story or a variation on virgin birth will feel good to our pattern-seeking drive. A similar satisfaction arises from our recognizing that we are dealing with an unreliable narrator, or our diagnosing an autistic character and guessing how that behavior will affect the story.

Yet another way that something feels meaningful is when an object comes from some historical period in the past that we care about; seeing or touching that object, or passing on what feels like an authentic version of that story, makes those with an interest in history feel a bit of connection to that past. Lisa Zunshine mentions our projecting a sense of essence on a genuine Roman coin, and our feeling something when we handle it that we would not feel on handling what we knew to be a modern copy.² While this sense of connection is probably stronger for a physical artifact than for most stories, those who value the genealogy of stories also value the sense of being the inheritor of such richness. We like to sense the connection, be it to Beowulf (in *The Hobbit*, Gardner's *Grendel*, and Headley's *The Mere Wife*), Sigurd and the Volsungs in Wagner's Ring, or Orpheus in a myriad of modern works. Depending on how well we know and value the original, the modern film where Beowulf beds Grendel's beautiful mother may feel counterfeit to the purist, though not to someone whose concept of heroes grows out of our sexualized era and not to someone who disbelieves in the goodness of heroes.

Meaning can also be derived from a portrayal of values or events that we find lacking in our current social patterns. The Arthurian story exemplifies this *compensatory function* throughout its history for white inhabitants of England. It compensated for loss of continental holdings; it supplied ideals of aristocratic behavior when those were brutally lacking; likewise, it freed empire-builders from uneasiness by letting them identify with heroic fighters against colonizers. Given the obvious gaps in a purely materialistic interpretation of life, mythic and quasi-mythic material also supplies a sense of our world or our human life being part of a larger plan. Arthur and his knights belonged to a larger system; the classical Gods belong to such a system with its inherent values.

Rightness, pattern, linkage to the past, values lacking but desired, and having a large-scale purpose and grand pattern: most of these can be found in various concentrations in myth-inflected literature. They can be found in other literature and other art as well, but they take easily recognizable forms in contemporary novels that employ myth.

I have been reading in neurocognitive theory in hopes of finding explanations for the artistic function of myth in literature. All of these patterns just mentioned have their place in the neurocognitive-literary field, but that just gives new names and scientific trimmings for something we know or feel anyway.³ The most helpful material I found—and this is a contested area—concerns the distinctions that theorists are trying to make between normal left- and right-brain responses, normal equating to right-handed people. (Some prefer a tripartite system brain functions that belong to the reptilian (old), mammalian (middle), and human (new) parts of the brain.)⁴ What some call the right brain seems the area more likely to be affected by various aspects of myth. The left brain for right-handed persons concerns itself with specifics, immediate objects and how we can employ them, and the distinction between real and unreal. The right hemisphere apparently takes a much more holistic view of everything around us and how we relate to it. In protecting us from predators, it has to be very quick at recognizing patterns, and its sensitivity to anything that doesn't fit makes it susceptible to interpreting faint flickers in our surrounds as "spirits."⁵

In other words, our sense of religion and of invisible forces arises from right-brain functions, though logic is imposed on them by the left. The right hemisphere provides us with our theory of mind and supplies a lot, if not all, of our understanding of facial expressions and actions of others. The right side seems to be the source of empathy. The left side, however, seems to concern itself with story endings as pattern, and as young children learn the shape of narratives, their developing left side is what insists on the happy endings or changing given endings to fit their sense of what the end should be.[6] While both hemispheres necessarily contribute to any interpretation of experience we make, the left hemisphere is more analytic, less emotionally engaged, and primarily concerned with things it considers real, not the unreal. Someone who is heavily left-dominant is unlikely to be personally interested by myth, fantasy, or other "unreal" phenomena. Someone more open to impulses from the right brain is more likely to respond positively to literature involving these elements.

A sense of rightness, a recognition of matching a pattern, a feeling of something missing, and a feeling of connection—these seem to me to explain why myth in its various forms still operates on many readers through literature. Let us look at various mythic materials and see how they relate to these four situations and how they make something feel meaningful, at least to someone susceptible to these arguments.

Historically in Western culture, mythology has supplied something lacking in a culture. The Christian cultural system in the Middle Ages and Renaissance, for instance, banned nudity and sexuality, except as sanctioned within modest and private matrimony. Mythic stories of a distant pagan past let an author gratify audience interests in love and lust, and they let visual artists satisfy interests in naked bodies. Adam and Eve's experience does not get that many elaborate renditions in literature until Milton, but they get drawn and painted with great frequency. Their near-nudity is acceptable even on church walls and windows. Troilus may end up well punished for his illicit love, but Chaucer's audience could enjoy his raptures in the interim. In the Renaissance, Orphic harmony supplied a symbol for good government, but also suggested that lack of harmonious agreement was the norm and the longing for harmony was either a kind of desperate nostalgia or a strategy of oppression with those in power dictating what defined harmony.[7] In the Romantic era, mythology let poets resurrect the natural world as a desirable realm that was being destroyed by the rising capitalist system. By bringing us back to what we can sense, by pointing to ways we can enrich our minds and memories that do not depend on money, the artistic cultivation of myth offers an alternative to the norms of the increasingly consumerist culture. Particularly in the Romantic projections of myth, we get an attempt to reconnect humans to nature. The move tries to integrate us to the broader world, and give us a sense of purpose and function within that broader system. One could argue that this mythic strain in the postmodern world represents a romantic element that has continued since the original romantics, emerging often at a popular level when too despised by the most prestigious definers of taste.

In the contemporary world, as in previous eras, mythic and quasi-mythic material offers compensatory visions of many things felt to be lacking in current culture. Not everyone responds to these. Even among those people who do not believe in any kind of divinity, however, who are skeptical scientists, or who simply accept materialist explanations for reality, some find satisfactions in mythic material. Mythic material offers importance for the individual, a role that our population of billions denies. Myth supplies layers of reality beyond the material. The promises of postsingularity offer a new cultural myth of transformation, new ways of transcending death, and new superhuman powers that may seem equivalent to those previously attributed to gods.

Myth gives importance to characters within a novel. In *Gravity's Rainbow*, Slothrop becomes both more explicable and more important when linked to Orpheus; in his very postmodern context, that extra explicability helps readers significantly. Silko's Tayo is definitely more important for being relinked to his people's myths. His being salvaged for his tribe will help it weather the loss of all the young men who were ruined by their war experience. Tayo wants to live on the reservation, wants to fit in, and wants to carry on the traditions that link him to the landscape, the weather, and the animals. Insofar as he behaves in the right way, he contributes to the positive balance in the fragile world, somewhat like Mailer's man making the brave decision rather than the cowardly one and therefore helping God's side of the undecided struggle with Satan. What the myths do for Tayo, they can do for others, but only if they accept the whole cultural package, and that is difficult for people who were educated in modern educational institutions. Tayo regains control of himself by following through on a mythically described course of action. Similarly, characters in *Almanac of the Dead* gain sanction for political action by drawing on prophecies that belong to an older indigenous mythic world. The myth permits them to feel important, and lets us feel that individuals can perform actions that matter.

When the individuals exalt their own status not only over that of the community but also over the natural world, then the finality or non-finality of death becomes crucial. If one gains meaning from serving a cause or trying to improve the world, life itself is the satisfaction, but when we feel ourselves to be the only thing that matters, then being snuffed out is an ultimate destroyer of meaningfulness in life. Hence a mythic world with different levels of reality can let us feel—for the length of the story—what it is like to believe that individuals last beyond life and matter in some larger pattern. Such stories can suggest without making truth claims that death is not the end of everything. Again, they supply something missing if the world is interpreted as purely material. They let us experience a world in which human life seems to have at least the general purpose of doing our best to leave things better than we found them. It feels meaningful to the characters, so insofar as we identify at all with their values, we feel what that sense of meaning is like. The myths concerned with reassuring the individual cannot prove any of this, and do not demand that we take them on faith. Instead, they accustom us to cultural values in which importance and survival of death in some fashion are assumed and feel comfortable. In this regard, the myths operate in a fashion similar to that discussed by John McClure in *Partial Faiths* for extant religions.[8] Using myth from cultures no longer present is perhaps a step further from a mindset based on weak or rationalized religious belief, but both attenuated religions and more distanced myths give us the feeling of meaning without actually trying to guarantee it.

When we turn to current invented myths, we find power to be a major issue, with the mythic stories sometimes offering a critique and sometimes an escape from our cynical and disappointed sense of how power actually operates at the corporate or national level. We feel helpless against higher-level power, and at the same time powerless as individuals. Invented myth lets us experience a relationship between individual and government that we think we would prefer. This is compensatory, but we are reminded that somehow someone might make a change for the better. We would like to believe in virtuous national action, but few nations have any right to identify with that, and those that claim such virtue do not usually seem righteous to their neighbors or to the international community. The discomfort being assuaged may be colonial, and the more historical the account is of Arthur fighting Anglo-Saxon colonizers, the more this seems compensatory, particularly for British readers. For American readers, the appeal is probably more a matter of Arthur's being a ruler who combines power with goodness. American superheroes similarly are projected as embodying American goodness.

Situational myth is the most remote from embellishments drawn from Greco-Roman, Judeo-Christian, Ancient Egyptian, Old Norse, and Native American myths, and it serves many purposes. It does not consist of a collection of linked stories, but rather it deals with one or more of a collection of situations often found in mythologies—creation/Eden/utopia/Golden Age, visit to a land of the dead, apocalypse, messiah, metamorphosis, and futures that promise extra dimensions of reality. Some of these situational myths do seem compensatory in the sense of filling cultural gaps. The frantic desire to upload one's mind into a computer and so live beyond death (or alternatively, the possibility of cloning suitable bodies) both offer extension beyond ordinary life without waiving scientific disbelief in the soul or its afterlife. Other dreams of the future involve being permanently, even telepathically, connected to an internet inhabited by AIs who help you to more effective thinking as well as gathering data for you and giving you access to anything you want. Some authors, though, offer thoughtful warnings that such altered life might not be worth the trade off, might (to invoke another myth) be putting ourselves into the hands of the Devil, and we might not like the result.

Overall, various kinds of myth can be said to amplify certain literary effects. If the myth is a known tale with known names, it focuses our attention. It gives us a context for interpreting what we read. When the myth is well known, it rouses expectations, and we feel gratified when those expectations are met, or we feel intrigued when they are countered. Mythic worlds, with their nonmaterial levels of existence, challenge the scientific vision that dominates our culture, sometimes just emotionally, but sometimes also using science (or postsingularity projections of science) to produce alternate realities. Even when we are unfamiliar with the myth, we may be able to grant that it gives a bit of extra weight to the story. People may no longer believe in Odin or Zeus, but they did in bygone eras. For someone who values tradition and values knowing about the past, this adds something to a story that rootless fantasy cannot give—call it the weight of cultural capital.

Above all, though, myth in its various forms seems able to give us *the feeling of meaning*. It takes us beyond our isolated selves and connects us to larger patterns of significance. It does not supply meaning itself, whatever that is. That would be belief. Meaning comes from inside our minds and depends upon our individual assumptions. Meaning represents a belief that something we read confirms. We can, though, through sympathy with characters, feel as if we agreed with them for the moment, and if they find something meaningful, we feel a similar sense of confirmation. This sensation of meaning would not stand up to investigation; mirror neurons may be involved, but that does not make the feeling lasting. The feeling would evaporate if we brought our individual beliefs to bear. For the period in which we read, though, and are living within the fictional world, we can (if we wish) relax our own belief systems and experience a mild version of others.

Science answers questions of how things happen. Religion and many forms of mythic story try to answer why. A sense of meaning clings to actions that have relatively predictable outcomes, at least as long as those outcomes have some positive resonance attaching to them. Even Arthur's death or mysterious disappearance somehow promises that his ideals will continue to be valued and upheld, if only because they were shining and so attractive. That is what gives this feeling of meaning. A connection to the past or to a genuinely possible but strange future also carries a bit of meaning. Something that lets us gain (or at least exploit) our cultural capital will activate that temporary feeling of meaning. We may ultimately shy away from terrible visions of the future or even from a character who does something very stupid and is predictably destroyed. We would grant that end to be meaningful, but it is not a meaning that many readers wish to respond to or absorb, though we may find it meaningful if it engages us in thinking through the implications. Meaning, at least when we are reading for pleasure, usually has some kind of positive valence, and is less frequently purely negative, though for some individuals, the negative is more challenging and attractive than the positive.

Myth can be a powerful way of activating this tenuous and gratifying feeling of meaning. That it can still do this for some people with a scientific set of assumptions about reality is surprising, but it plays on so many of our mental cultural components that it can work for at least some readers. It supplies values missing in our culture. It can also work for some people who think of themselves in postmodern terms, as we saw with Burroughs and, to a different end, with Silko, whose myths tried to help minds constructed of conflicting discourses. When it reminds us of our cultural capital, we feel a bit of satisfaction at our own learning. Invented situational myth feels familiar because we have read of other creations or apocalypses, and resistance to the idea of death as final makes us at least interested in metamorphosis, in survival in some other form. Myth as artistic tool is not under the obligation to demand belief that religion is. Instead, it gives those who are willing to respond a feeling of meaning, a sensation that delicately gives us release, gratification, and inner satisfaction.

NOTES

Prolegomenon: Myth as a Tool in the Artist's Toolbox

1 Kathy Acker, *Pussy, King of the Pirates* (New York: Grove Press, 1996), 68.

2 For the equivalent mythemes in the Oedipus story and their use in recent fiction, see Debra A. Moddelmog, *Readers and Mythic Signs: The Oedipus Myth in Twentieth-Century Fiction* (Carbondale and Edwardsville: Southern Illinois University Press, 1993). She offers a semiotics of reading texts that figure mythic subtexts. When readers possess such background knowledge of mythemes, they feel themselves to be sophisticated, elevated above merely popular taste. See Pierre Bourdieu's *Distinction: A Social Critique of the Judgement of Taste*. Original French, 1979. Translated by Richard Nice (Cambridge, MA: Harvard University Press, 1984).

3 For a detailed analysis of how we have construed myth, see Andrew Von Hendy, *The Modern Construction of Myth* (Bloomington: Indiana University Press, 2002). A good enquiry into Greek mythological belief in its original setting is Paul Veyne's *Did the Greeks Believe in Their Myths? An Essay on Constitutive Imagination*. Original French, 1983. Translated by Paula Wissing (Chicago: University of Chicago Press, 1988).

4 Malcolm Bull traces some changes in the uses of myth through the ages. See "Make Me a God." http://www.theguardian.com/artanddesign/2005/apr/30/art and *The Mirror of the Gods* (Oxford: Oxford University Press, 2005).

5 Northrop Frye makes roughly this same distinction: "We have myths of Zeus and Aphrodite; we have legends of beings, like Theseus or Oedipus. . . . Legend, then, is an early and easy-going form of tradition, before there is a general demand for history, conceived as the study of what actually happened. But the boundary line between myth and legend is impossible to draw." See "Literature and Myth," in *Relations of Literary Study: Essays on Interdisciplinary Contributions,* ed. James Thorpe (New York: MLA, 1967), 27–55, quotation p. 30.

6 Paul Ricoeur, *The Symbolism of Evil*, trans. Emerson Buchanan (Boston: Beacon Press, 1967), 163.

7 Harry Slochower, *Mythopoesis: Mythic Patterns in the Literary Classics* (Detroit: Wayne State University Press, 1970).

8   This account appears in Lindner's collection of case histories, *The Fifty-Minute Hour*, and is available on the web in two parts in its original magazine form at http://harpers.org/archive/1954/12/the-jet-propelled-couch/ and http://harpers.org/archive/1955/01/the-jet-propelled-couch-2/ (consulted July 14, 2015).

9   Milton had many reasons to discard Arthur, several of which are analyzed by Helen Cooper in "Milton's King Arthur," *The Review of English Studies* n.s. 65, no. 269 (2014): 252–65. Aside from the royalist politics of such an epic, he was repulsed by his increasing conviction that little or none of it was historical, and he rejected the sexual misbehaviors that strayed so far from his concept of chastity. The growing interest in Saxon language and law (in aid of establishing common law as supreme even over kings) also caused a slump in general enthusiasm for the Britons or Welsh. See Roberta Florence Brinkley, *Arthurian Legend in the Seventeenth Century* (Baltimore: The Johns Hopkins Press, 1932), especially chapters 2 and 3. As a result, we get plays about Saxon figures on the London Stage, and King Alfred supplanted Arthur for a while as the ancestral figure of interest. Ranulf Higden in the fourteenth century had read European chronicles before composing his own, and he is one of the relatively few voices to doubt Arthur's authenticity. See Edward Donald Kennedy, "Visions of History: Robert de Boron and English Arthurian Chroniclers," in *The Fortunes of King Arthur*, ed. Norris J. Lacy (Cambridge: D. S. Brewer, 2005), 29–46, esp. 33.

10 For the development of the Arthurian cycle, see Roger Sherman Loomis, *Celtic Myth and Arthurian Romance* (1927; New York: Haskell House, 1967); and Eugène Vinaver, *The Rise of Romance* (Oxford: Clarendon Press, 1971).

11 A helpful study of these myths is *Scientific Mythologies: How Science and Science Fiction Forge New Religious Beliefs* by James A. Herrick (Downers Grove, IL: IVP Academic, 2008). To those that I mention he also adds the myths of the spiritual race, of space religion, and of alien gnosis.

12 Ray Kurzweil, *The Singularity Is Near* (New York: Penguin, 2005). Steven Shaviro traces "the Rapture for nerds" to a character in Ken MacLeod's *The Cassini Division* (New York: Tor, 1999), 90. See Shaviro's "The Singularity Is Here," *Red Planets: Marxism and Science Fiction*, ed. Mark Bould and China Miéville (Middletown CT: Wesleyan University Press, 2009), 103–17, esp. 105.

13 For myth in videogames, see http://www.ign.com/articles/2006/05/18/the-influence-of-literature-and-myth-in-videogames, http://greece.greekreporter.com/2014/03/04/video-games-based-on-greek-archeology-and-mythology/, http://en.wikipedia.org/wiki/Category:Mythology-based_video_games, http://anothergamersblog.wordpress.com/2012/05/07/video-games-and-norse-mythology/, and others; google your myth tradition of choice with video game or role-playing game (those listed were consulted May 30, 2014).

14 My impression is that much game use of myth hardly even deserves the label of appropriation, since little but the names of gods or heroes get used. For a more conservative, literary discussion of that term, see Julie Sanders, *Adaptation and Appropriation* (London: Routledge, 2006).

15 Works like these seem better handled by adaptation theory; see Linda Hutcheon, *A Theory of Adaptation* (New York: Routledge, 2006).

16 Authors whose work sheds light on the connections between myth and the quest story so common in science fiction and fantasy would include Joseph Campbell, Lord Raglan, and Northrop Frye.

17 Good work on how to read novels with mythic elements is offered by John J. White, "Mythological Fiction and the Reading Process," in *Literary Criticism and Myth*, ed. Joseph P. Strelka, *Yearbook of Comparative Criticism* 9 (1980): 72–92. See also his more extended study *Mythology in the Modern Novel* (Princeton: Princeton University Press, 1971).

18 Northrop Frye, *Anatomy of Criticism: Four Essays* (Princeton: Princeton University Press, 1957).

19 For modernist use of myth, of course, one turns to T. S. Eliot's "Ulysses, Order, and Myth." 1923. http://people.virginia.edu/~jdk3t/eliotulysses.htm (consulted September 6, 2015).

Chapter 1

1 For a good analysis of the basic agon and some of the related issues, see John Michael Lennon, "Mailer's Cosmology," *Modern Language Studies* 12, no. 3 (1982): 18–29. Mailer concurs with Carl Jung that "having a view of the universe that makes sense to oneself" is important to mental health. See *On God: An Uncommon Conversation*, Norman Mailer with Michael Lennon (New York: Random House, 2007), 26.

2 For some of Mailer's scatological theories, see *The Presidential Papers* (New York: G. P. Putnam's, 1963), especially "The Twelfth Presidential Paper—On Waste" (269–302). For their application in *Ancient Evenings*, see Kathryn Hume, "Books of the Dead: Postmortem Politics in Novels by Mailer, Burroughs, Acker, and Pynchon," *Modern Philology* 97, no. 3 (2000): 417–44. For the connection between cowardice and cancer, see "An Interview with Norman Mailer" by Eve Auchincloss and Nancy Lynch in *Conversations with Norman Mailer*, ed. J. Michael Lennon (Jackson and London: University Press of Mississippi, 1988), 39–51, esp. 42–43.

3 Mailer discusses this Theogony with Lennon in *On God*.

4 Norman Mailer, *Ancient Evenings* (1983; New York: Warner, 1984), 436.

5 For the emphasis on Mailer's invention of Egyptian culture, see Robert J. Begiebing, *Toward a New Synthesis: John Fowles, John Gardner, Norman Mailer* (Ann Arbor: UMI Research Press, 1989); for writing, see Philip Kuberski, "The Metaphysics of Postmodern Death: Mailer's *Ancient Evenings* and Merrill's *The Changing Light at Sandover*," *ELH* 56, no. 1 (1989): 229–54.

6 Ashton Howley, "Imperial Mailer: *Ancient Evenings*," in *Norman Mailer's Later Fictions: Ancient Evenings through Castle in the Forest*, ed. John Whalen-Bridge (New York: Palgrave Macmillan, 2010), 105–22.

7 See Ian Hamilton, "Mummies," *London Review of Books* (June 16–July 6, 1983), 6; Benjamin De Mott, "Norman Mailer's Egyptian Novel," *New York Times Book Review* (April 10, 1983), http://www.nytimes.com/1983/04/10/books/norman-mailer-s-egyptian-novel.html (consulted August 1, 2015); Harold Bloom, "Norman in Egypt," *New York Review of Books* (April 28, 1983), http://www.nybooks.com/articles/archives/1983/apr/28/norman-in-egypt/ (consulted August 1, 2015); Richard Poirier "In Pyramid and Palace," *Times Literary Supplement* (June 10, 1983), 591–92.

8 *The Western Lands* (1987; New York: Penguin, 1988), unpaginated prefatory matter.

9 Wayne Pounds argues that mapping is "a principal function of Burroughs's work. On several occasions he has referred to himself as 'a map maker, a cosmonaut of inner space.'" See "The Postmodern Anus: Parody and Utopia in Two Recent Novels by William Burroughs," *Poetics Today* 8 (1987): 611–29, quote p. 627.

10 Alex Houen argues that Burroughs is concerned very literally with humans living in outer space; such "living" seems to be without bodies or without mechanisms to make survival possible, but Houen is certainly right that space attracted Burroughs. See "William S. Burroughs's Cities of the Red Night Trilogy: Writing Outer Space," *Journal of American Studies* 40, no. 3 (2006): 523–49. For emphasis on freedom see David Ayers, "The Long Last Goodbye: Control and Resistance in the Work of William Burroughs," *Journal of American Studies* 27, no. 2 (1993): 223–36. For film, Michael J. Prince, "The Master Film Is a Western: The Mythology of the American West in the *Cities of the Red Night* Trilogy," *European Journal of American Studies* 2011, [online] Document 3, available at http://ejas.revues.org/9412. For a sense of humanity's terminality, whether through virus, junk, or capitulation to control, see Kendra Langeteig, "*Horror Autotoxicus* in the Red Night Trilogy: Ironic Fruits of Burroughs's Terminal Vision," *Configurations* 5, no. 1 (1997): 135–69 and Oliver Harris, "Can You See a Virus? The Queer Cold War of William Burroughs," *Journal of American Studies* 33, no. 2 (1999): 243–66.

11 See Kathryn Hume, "William Burroughs's Phantasmic Geography," *Contemporary Literature* 40, no. 1 (1999): 111–35.

12 Especially since *Reckless Eyeballing*, Reed has been attacked for sexism; one of the better analyses of the problem as a necessary by-product of the paranoid vision prominent in *Mumbo Jumbo* is made by Andrew Strombeck, "The Conspiracy of Masculinity in Ishmael Reed," *African American Review* 40, no. 2 (2006): 299–311. Daniel Punday offers a rhetorical analysis that gives us a different way of reading the sexism: "Ishmael Reed's Rhetorical Turn: Uses of 'Signifying' in *Reckless Eyeballing*," *College English* 54, no. 4 (1992): 446–61.

13 Critics who emphasize Reed's evenhanded attacks on anyone, black or white, who holds Atonist values include Roxanne Harde, "'We Will Make Our Own Future Text': Allegory, Iconoclasm, and Reverence in Ishmael Reed's *Mumbo Jumbo*," *Critique* 43, no. 4 (2002): 361–77; and Sharon A. Jessee, "Laughter and Identity in Ishmael Reed's *Mumbo Jumbo*," *MELUS* 21, no. 4 (1996): 127–39.

14 Reed codeswitches linguistically, but also allegorically; he draws on science fiction tropes as well as Egyptian, and Jes Grew is a "virus" that infects the people and elicits drastic measures from the power brokers. See Michael A. Chaney, "Slave Cyborgs and the Black Infovirus: Ishmael Reed's Cybernetic Aesthetics," *Modern Fiction Studies* 49, no. 2 (2003): 261–83.

15 Ishmael Reed, *Mumbo Jumbo* (1972; New York: Atheneum, 1988), 182.

16 Donald L. Hoffman notes the connection between the loa as a pantheon and the multiple feel this gives to individual souls in "A Darker Shade of Grail: Questing at the Crossroads in Ishmael Reed's *Mumbo Jumbo*," *Callaloo* 17, no. 4 (1994): 1245–56. He also argues for another mythology at work, namely the grail quest. Reed's ideological support for periphery against center and centralized control also undercuts the idea of an indivisible core being. See W. Lawrence Hogue, "Postmodernism, Traditional Cultural Forms, and the African American Narrative: *Major's* Reflex, *Morrison's* Jazz, *and Reed's* Mumbo Jumbo," *Novel* 35, no. 2–3 (2002): 169–92.

Chapter 2

1 *Blood and Guts in High School* (copyrighted 1978 but first published 1984; New York: Grove Weidenfeld, 1989). The twenty-four page section entitled "The World" is unpaginated, but this quotation comes from the first page of text following the title, and other page numbers follow this in sequence.

2 For more detailed analysis of the images and their sources, see Kathryn Hume, "Books of the Dead: Postmortem Politics in Novels by Mailer, Burroughs, Acker, and Pynchon," *Modern Philology* 97, no. 3 (2000): 417–44.

3 William Gibson, *Neuromancer* (1984; New York: Ace, 2000), 6.

4 William Gibson, *Count Zero* (1986; New York: Ace, 1987), 76–7.

5 Leslie Marmon Silko makes an argument like this in *Almanac of the Dead*, when she claims that Christianity never took well in the new world, it being an import. She sees Native American religions as the natural and native spirituality that belongs here. *Almanac of the Dead* (New York: Penguin, 1991), 718.

6 A. S. Byatt, *Ragnarok: The End of the Gods* (Edinburgh: Canongate, 2011), 161. Although the title page says *Ragnarok*, the final chapter on that event spells it Ragnarök with the umlaut.

7 William Kennedy, *Legs* (1975; New York: Penguin, 1983), 315.

8 Reading aloud to the corpse takes place in *Against the Day*, and the title number in *The Crying of Lot 49* very possibly comes from the forty-nine days spent in the Bardo plane by the dead spirit. See Robert E. Kohn, "Seven Buddhist Themes in Pynchon's 'The Crying of Lot 49'," *Religion & Literature* 35, no. 1 (2003): 73–96.

9 Thomas Pynchon, *Vineland* (Boston: Little Brown, 1990), 172–73.

10 "Books of the Dead: Postmortem Politics in Novels by Mailer, Burroughs, Acker, and Pynchon," 437.

11 James Morrow, *Towing Jehovah* (New York: Harcourt Brace/Harvest, 1994), 89.

12 For more on this book, see Kathryn Hume, *Aggressive Fictions: Reading the Contemporary American Novel* (Ithaca: Cornell University Press, 2012), 96–99.

13 James Morrow, *Blameless in Abaddon* (San Diego: Harvest Book, 1996), 35.

Chapter 3

1 Such symbolic equivalence between Orpheus and The Artist is central to Maurice Blanchot's "Orpheus' Gaze" (1955), in *The Sirens' Song: Selected Essays by Maurice Blanchot*, edited by Gabriel Josipovici, translated by Sacha Rabinovitch (Bloomington: Indiana University Press, 1982), 177–81; Orpheus similarly stands for Artists in a grand way in Ihab Hassan's *The Dismemberment of Orpheus* (1971; 2nd ed., Madison: University of Wisconsin Press, 1982).

2 See, for instance, Elizabeth Sewell, *The Orphic Voice: Poetry and Natural History* (New Haven: Yale University Press, 1960); Walter A. Strauss, *Descent and Return: The Orphic Theme in Modern Literature* (Cambridge, MA: Harvard University Press, 1971).

3 Sewell focuses on those who are attuned to the musician taming the wilderness. Strauss studies the romantic and modernist descents into madness, darkness, anguish. Merrill Cole studies the homosexual and homoerotic element in modernism in *The Other Orpheus: A Poetics of Modern Homosexuality* (New York: Routledge, 2003). Ihab Hassan stresses the dismemberment or sparagmos that is necessary for the head to become oracular.

4 Kim Paffenroth, *Orpheus and the Pearl* (Salt Lake City: Magus Press, 2008); and Daniel H. Gower, *The Orpheus Process* (New York: Dell, 1992).

5 *Orpheus*, by Bryan Armor, John Chambers, Genevieve Cogman, Richard Dansky, B. D. Flory, Harry Heckel IV, Ellen Kiley, James Kiley, Matthew McFarland, Dean Shomshak, and C. A. Suleiman (Stone Mountain, CA: White Wolf Press, 2003).

6 Selena Kitt, *The Song of Orpheus* (Alpena, MI: Excessica LCC, 2010).

7 A. E. Stallings, *Archaic Smile* (Evansville, IN: University of Evansville Press, 1999), "Eurydice's Footnote," 11.

8 Carol Gilligan, *In a Different Voice: Psychological Theory and Women's Development* (Cambridge, MA: Harvard University Press, 1982), 16–23.

9 Their attraction, because it stems from shared childhood friendship, seems more personal and less a political statement than the similar relationship between Frenesi Gates and Brock Vond in Pynchon's *Vineland*. Frenesi's

fetishized adoration for uniform and power applies more generally to national values.
10. Russell Hoban, *The Medusa Frequency* (London: Jonathan Cape, 1987), 26.
11. The "idea of someone" may not be known by that someone, but he or she may hope it can be interpreted and made comprehensible by the artist using it or portraying it; this phrase and concept is also important (and not explained) in *Riddley Walker*.
12. Samuel R. Delany, *The Einstein Intersection* (New York: Ace, 1967), 148.
13. Salim Washington, "The Avenging Angel of Creation/Destruction: Black Music and the Afro-technological in the Science Fiction of Henry Dumas and Samuel R. Delany," *Journal of the Society for American Music* 2, no. 2 (2008): 235–53.
14. *The Sandman* appeared in seventy-five monthly comic book issues between 1989 and 1996. The frame-tale plot covers the period from 1916 through the late twentieth century, but stories flash back to Orpheus (approximately 1250 BCE) and maybe yet earlier for Nada (the evidence on her dating is contradictory). For the complicated publication history see the Wikipedia entry for *The Sandman*. Web. May 31, 2012 (http://en.wikipedia.org/wiki/The_Sandman_%28Vertigo%29). The Absolute edition is published in New York by Vertigo in 4 volumes (2006, 2007, 2008, 2009). For a more extensive version of this argument, see Kathryn Hume, "Neil Gaiman's *Sandman* as Mythic Romance," *Genre: Forms of Discourse and Culture* 46, no. 3 (2013): 345–65.
15. The Orpheus story was published separately as *The Sandman Special #1* (1991) and in the ten-volume version, this comes in "Fables and Reflections," the sixth volume. In the four-volume *The Absolute Sandman*, it appears in Vol. 3.
16. Although I think Orpheus is meant to be the chronological beginning of this frame, I would argue that if Nada's story really is earlier, then we get an interesting framing parallel between her being African and dying because someone in power values his own interests above hers and the sequences about African slave trading near the very end. Hob Gadling's nightmare recollections of his own actions as a slave trader show the same indifference to others that Morpheus (as Lord Kai'ckul) showed to Nada. See Kathryn Hume, "Neil Gaiman's *Sandman* as Mythic Romance."
17. See Kathryn Hume, "Novelty, Pattern, and Power in Richard Powers's *Orfeo*," *Orbit: A Journal of American Literature* 5, no. 1 (2017): 1-19, DOI: https://doi.org/10.16995/orbit.202 for an in depth analysis of the various mythemes.
18. Richard Powers, *Orfeo: A Novel* (New York: W. W. Norton, 2014), 349.
19. For almost identical genetic tinkering, see Katherine Xue; she describes how the first verse of a Danish Christmas poem was inserted into E. coli, and in the article, the achievement is treated as fascinating and not threatening. One would like to assume that an ethics board okayed these genetic high jinks, but jolly holiday experiments might sometimes be light-heartedly carried out without formal oversight. Els's experiments are not overseen at all, which causes some readers uneasiness on moral or scientific grounds. MIT scientists have recently turned E. coli bacteria into "tape recorders" to store usable,

erasable information (http://www.sciencedaily.com/releases/2014/11/1411 13142006.htm). What Els does is in fact going on around the world, despite any potential for a dangerous mutation, whether we are comfortable with the idea or not.

Chapter 4

1. For good analyses of the variations in American superheroes, see Robert Jewett and John Shelton Lawrence, *The American Monomyth* (New York: Anchor Press, 1977); and John Shelton Lawrence and Robert Jewett, *The Myth of the American Superhero* (Grand Rapids: Eerdmans, 2002).
2. See Kathryn Hume, "Voice in Kathy Acker's Fiction," *Contemporary Literature* 42, no. 3 (2001): 485–513. Acker's use of O as a name and the reference to owl masks refers us back to Pauline Réage's exploration into total female submission in the novel named O.
3. *Empire of the Senseless* (New York: Grove Weidenfeld, 1988), 12.
4. *Blood and Guts in High School* (New York: Grove Weidenfeld, 1978), 112.
5. *Pussy, King of the Pirates* (New York: Grove Press, 1996), 10.
6. Amy Nolan shows Acker blaming ancient Greece in "'A New Myth to Live By': The Graphic Vision of Kathy Acker," *Critique* 53, no. 3 (2012): 201–13, esp. 207.
7. *Eurydice in the Underworld* (London: Arcadia Books, 1997), 1–26.
8. Donald Barthelme, *The Dead Father* (1975; New York: Penguin, 1986), 38.
9. Julian Jaynes, *The Origin of Consciousness in the Breakdown of the Bicameral Mind* (Boston: Houghton Mifflin, 1976). Although Hoban was writing before Neurocognitive studies had done much with literature, he envisions with "first knowing" something similar to a right-hemisphere, holistic relationship to the universe, as outlined in Iain McGilchrist's *The Master and His Emissary: The Divided Brain and the Making of the Western World* (New Haven and London: Yale University Press, 2009).
10. For an interesting book on modern cultivation of the ability to talk with God and hear Him talk back, see T. M. Luhrmann, *When God Talks Back: Understanding the American Evangelical Relationship with God* (New York: Knopf, 2012).
11. Russell Hoban, *Riddley Walker* (1980; New York: Washington Square, 1982), 89.
12. "An Interview with Russell Hoban," with Edward Myers, *Literary Review* 28, no. 1 (1984): 5–16, quote 11.
13. For analyses of the language in *Riddley Walker*, see David Dowling, "Russell Hoban's *Riddley Walker*: Doing the Connections," Critique 29, no. 3 (1988): 179–87; Mary Maclean, "The Signifier as Token: The Textual Riddles of

Russell Hoban," *AUMLA* 70 (1988): 211–19; Natalie Maynor and Richard F. Patteson, "Language as Protagonist in Russell Hoban's *Riddley Walker*," *Critique* 26, no. 1 (1984), 18–25; Jacob Mey, "The Last of the Canterbury Tales: Artificial Intelligence in the Fifth Millenium," *Prague Linguistic Circle Papers* 1 (1995): 261–94; R. D. Mullen, "Dialect, Grapholect, and Story: Russell Hoban's 'Riddley Walker' as Science Fiction," *Science Fiction Studies* 27, no. 3 (2000): 391–417.

14 Walter M. Miller, Jr., *A Canticle for Leibowitz* (1959; New York: Bantam, 1982), 18–23.

15 This biblical echo of divinity also adheres to the Cambry female force: "Shes what she is" (160).

16 A Christian interpretation is drawn from the book by David Huisman in "'Hoap of a Tree' in *Riddley Walker*," *Christianity and Literature* 43, nos. 3–4 (1994): 347–73. David Cowart argues that though those remnants of Christian myth are there, they are "inadequate to restoring the Waste Land" and simply remind us what humans have lost. See *History and the Contemporary Novel* (Carbondale, IL: Southern Illinois University Press, 1989), 105. In the interview with Myers, Hoban states, "I have nothing to do with any organized religion of any kind. I think I'm a very religious person, but I don't go in for anything organized, whether its Judaism or Buddhism" (12), and he likes the description "freelance mystic" to describe his approach to religion.

17 According to Patricia Monaghan's *The Encyclopedia of Celtic Mythology and Folklore* (New York: Facts on File, Inc., 2004), giants, when beheaded, were able to reattach their heads, as does the Green Knight. For further Celtic lore, see her entry on "head." My thanks to Prof. Don-John Dugas for the Celtic parallels to Orphic head myths, and for information on Punch and Judy.

18 Neil Gaiman and Dave McKean make this point in their graphic novel *The Tragical Comedy or Comical Tragedy of Mr Punch* (1994; New York: Vertigo, 1995), no pagination, but the point is made when the boy watching the show sees Judy killed the first time.

19 Octavia E. Butler, *Dawn* (New York: Warner, 1987), 39–40.

20 *The Complete Cosmicomics*, Trans Martin McLaughlin, Tim Parks, and William Weaver (London: Penguin, 2002), 43. The original set of cosmicomical stories was published in Italian in 1965, with individual stories appearing in magazines before that. *T-Zero* and individual stories were published later in Italian, but are all brought together in this Penguin collection.

21 Kathryn Hume, *Calvino's Fictions: Cogito and Cosmos* (Oxford: Clarendon Press, 1992).

22 Neil Gaiman, *The Ocean at the End of the Lane* (New York: William Morrow, 2013), 143.

23 See Robin Headlam Wells, *Elizabethan Mythologies: Studies in Poetry, Drama, and Music* (Cambridge: Cambridge University Press, 1994).

Chapter 5

1. Ray Kurzweil, *The Singularity Is Near: When Humans Transcend Biology* (New York: Penguin, 2005).
2. Justin Leiber has laid out the philosophical arguments for the possible personhood of machines and some animals in *An Invitation to Cognitive Science* (Oxford: Basil Blackwell, 1991) and *Can Animals and Machines Be Persons?* (Indianapolis: Hackett Publishing Company, 1985).
3. Charles Stross, *Accelerando* (2005; New York: Ace, 2006), 392.
4. Rudy Rucker, *Postsingular* (New York: Tor, 2007), 145.
5. Donna J. Haraway, *A Cyborg Manifesto: Science, Technology, and Socialist-Feminism in the Late Twentieth Century*, 15. http://ebookcentral.proquest.com/lib/warw/detail.action?docID=4392065.

Chapter 6

1. Norman Mailer, "Norman Mailer on *An American Dream*," (1965); reprinted in *Conversations with Norman Mailer*, edited by J. Michael Lennon [Jackson and London: University Press of Mississippi, 1988], 100–103, quotation 102.
2. For analysis of the Orphic materials, see Kathryn Hume, and Thomas J. Knight, "Orpheus and the Orphic Voice in *Gravity's Rainbow*," *Philological Quarterly* 64, no. 3 (1985): 299–315.
3. For a more complex and arcane use of Orphic cult material, see Christopher K Coffman's analysis of *Against the Day* in "Bogomilism, Orphism, Shamanism: The Spiritual and Spatial Grounds of Pynchon's Ecological Ethic," in *Pynchon's Against the Day: A Corrupted Pilgrim's Guide*, edited by Jeffrey Severs and Christopher Leise (Newark: University of Delaware Press, 2006), 91–114. For an obsessive emphasis on Orphic descent and return in Pynchon, see Evans Lansing Smith, *Thomas Pynchon and the Postmodern Mythology of the Underworld* (New York: Peter Lang, 2012).
4. For a good analysis of the way that characters map onto each other and hence do not represent self-contained individuals, see Brian McHale, "Modernist Reading, Post-Modern Text: The Case of *Gravity's Rainbow*," *Poetics Today* 1, nos. 1–2 (1979): 85–110.
5. Thomas A. Shippey argues that after the First World War, traditional sorts of heroism were unbelievable, and with Bilbo and then Frodo, he launches another sort of hero. See *Heroes and Legends: The Most Influential Characters of Literature* (Chantilly, VA: The Great Courses, 2014), chapter 1.
6. H. Bruce Franklin, *War Stars: The Superweapon and the American Imagination* (New York: Oxford University Press, 1988), chapter 2, "Fantasies of War 1880–1917," 19–53.
7. *Mere Christianity* (London: Collins, 1953), 54–56.

8   James Morrow, *Only Begotten Daughter* (1990; San Diego, New York, and London: Harvest Book, 1996), 309.

9   Rikki Ducornet, *The Jade Cabinet* (1993; Normal, IL: Dalkey Archive Press, 1994), 155.

10 This identification of quest for Eden with insanity has parallels in the arguments of Donna Haraway. In her *Cyborg Manifesto*, the masculine mindset seeks Eden and unification of self; the cyborg accepts disunity, variety, and regeneration rather than rebirth. The cyborg mentality, which she sees as our future, does not believe in Eden or any kind of ideal past.

11 Ben Marcus, *The Flame Alphabet* (New York: Alfred A. Knopf, 2012), 66.

12 Inbar Kaminsky, "Epidemic Judaism: Plagues and Their Evocation in Philip Roth's *Nemesis* and Ben Marcus's *The Flame Alphabet*," *Philip Roth Studies* 10, no. 1 (2014): 109–24.

13 Thomas Pynchon, *Inherent Vice* (New York: Penguin, 2009), 108.

14 Gloria Naylor, *Mama Day* (1988; New York: Vintage Contemporaries, 1989); Toni Morrison, *Song of Solomon* (1977; New York: Signet, 1978).

15 https://en.wikipedia.org/wiki/Igbo_Landing

16 Leslie Marmon Silko, *Ceremony* (1977; New York: Penguin, 1986), 194–95.

17 Roland Barthes, "The Reality Effect," (orig. French, 1968) in *The Rustle of Language*, trans. Richard Howard (New York: Hill and Wang, 1986), 141–48, and Kathryn Hume, "The Semiotics of Fantasy in William Kennedy's Fiction," *Philological Quarterly* 79, no. 4 (2000): 523–48.

18 When talking about the nature of our two brain hemispheres and their response to the world, Iain McGilchrist makes the following relevant statement: "we neither discover an objective reality nor invent a subject reality, but that there is a process of responsive evocation, the world 'calling forth' something in me that in turn 'calls forth' something in the world. That is true of perceptual qualities, not just of values. If there is no 'real' mountain, for example, separate from one created by the hopes, aspirations, reverence or greed of those who approach it, it is equally true that its greenness, or greyness, or stoniness lies not in the mountain or in my mind, but comes from between us, called forth from each and equally dependent on both." See *The Master and His Emissary: The Divided Brain and the Making of the Western World* (2009; New Haven and London: Yale University Press, 2012), 133–34.

19 Some helpful critics who explain the mythic material include Peter G. Beidler and Robert M. Nelson, "Grandma's Wicker Sewing Basket: Untangling the Narrative Threads in Silko's *Ceremony*," *American Indian Culture and Research Journal* 28, no. 1 (2004): 5–13; Elizabeth N. Evasdaughter, "Leslie Marmon Silko's *Ceremony*: Healing Ethnic Hatred by Mixed-Breed Laughter," *MELUS* 15, no. 1 (1988): 83–95; Robert M. Nelson, "Settling for Vision in Silko's *Ceremony*: Sun Man, Arrowboy, and Tayo," *American Indian Culture and Research Journal* 28, no. 1 (2004): 67–73; Robert M. Nelson, "The Kaupata Motif in Silko's *Ceremony*: A Study of Literary Homology," *Studies in American Indian Literatures* Series 2, 11, no. 3 (1999): 2–21; and Edith

Swan, "Healing via the Sunwise Cycle in Silko's *Ceremony*," *American Indian Quarterly*, 12, no. 4 (1988): 313–28.

20. See David A. Rice, "Witchery, Indigenous Resistance, and Urban Space in Leslie Marmon Silko's *Ceremony*," *Studies in American Indian Literatures*, Series 2, 17, no. 4 (2005): 114–43 for some of her changes and alterations.

21. The tendency to sense spirits is discussed as the origin of all religion by Pascal Boyer. Evolutionarily, "it is far more advantageous to overdetect agency than to underdetect it. The expense of false positives (seeing agents where there are none) is minimal, if we can abandon these misguided intuitions quickly. By contrast, the cost of not detecting agents when they are actually around (either predator or prey) could be very high." *Religion Explained: The Evolutionary Origins of Religious Thought* (New York: Basic Books, 2001), 145.

22. Silko discusses both her sources for ideas and her sense of urgency in writing this huge novel in "Notes on *Almanac of the Dead*" in *Yellow Woman and a Beauty of the Spirit* (New York: Simon and Schuster, 1996), 135–45. Kimberly Roppolo mentions Silko's sense of being driven by spirits to write what she did in "Vision, Voice, and Intertribal Metanarrative: The American Indian Visual-Rhetorical Tradition and Leslie Marmon Silko's *Almanac of the Dead*," *American Indian Quarterly* 31, no. 4 (2007): 534–58, esp. 543.

23. Tom Shippey writes about the Viking culture as a death cult in *Laughing Shall I Die: Lives and Deaths of the Great Vikings* (London: Reaktion Books, 2018).

24. Klas Östergren, *The Hurricane Party*, orig. Swedish, 2007 (Edinburgh: Canongate, 2009), 195.

25. Jeanette Winterson, *Weight* (Edinburgh: Canongate, 2005); and David Grossman, *Lion's Honey: The Myth of Samson* (Edinburgh: Canongate, 2005).

26. Feminist rethinkings of Homer became popular in 2018 and 2019. Natalie Haynes's *A Thousand Ships* reimagines the war through the agency of the muse Calliope. Madeline Miller's *Circe* reconceives Odysseus. Pat Barker's *The Silence of the Girls* channels the Troy story through Briseis, the hapless bone of contention between Agamemnon and Achilles.

27. Margaret Atwood, *The Penelopiad* (Edinburgh: Canongate, 2005), 189.

28. For the paranoid strain in contemporary fiction, see Timothy Melley, *Empire of Conspiracy: The Culture of Paranoia in Postwar America* (Ithaca: Cornell University Press, 1999); and Patrick O'Donnell, *Latent Destinies: Cultural Paranoia and Contemporary U.S. Narrative* (Durham: Duke University Press, 2000).

29. Steven Shaviro complains that post-singularity fiction wants to transform the world but ignores the need to transform capitalism as well. See "The Singularity Is Here," in *Red Planets: Marxism and Science Fiction*, ed. Mark Bould and China Miéville (Middletown, CT: Wesleyan University Press, 2009), 103–17.

30. Rudy Rucker, *Postsingular* (New York: Tor Books, 2007), 145.

31. Shaviro traces this idea of singularity as equivalent to the Rapture to Ken MacLeod's *The Cassini Division* (New York: Tor, 1999), 90.

Conclusion

1. For demonstrations of how background influences reading, see Norman N. Holland, *5 Readers Reading* (New Haven: Yale University Press, 1975).
2. Lisa Zunshine, *Strange Concepts and the Stories They Make Possible: Cognition, Culture, Narrative* (Baltimore: The Johns Hopkins University Press, 2008), 16.
3. Aside from those I cite specifically, others I found useful were Paul B. Armstrong, *How Literature Plays with the Brain: The Neuroscience of Reading and Art* (Baltimore: The Johns Hopkins University Press, 2013); Patrick Colm Hogan, *Cognitive Science, Literature, and the Arts: A Guide for Humanists* (New York and London: Routledge, 2003); Lisa Zunshine, *Why We Read Fiction: Theory of Mind and the Novel* (Columbus: Ohio State University Press, 2006); and Marek Oziewicz, *One Earth, One People: The Mythopoeic Fantasy Series of Ursula K. Le Guin, Lloyd Alexander, Madeleine L'Engle and Orson Scott Card* (Jefferson, NC: McFarland, 2008).
4. The most nuanced and least oversimplified account of left- and right-brain responses that I have found is Iain McGilchrist's *The Master and His Emissary* (n. 9).
5. See Chapter 6, n. 21.
6. Very young children's altering stories to get the right ending is discussed by Hugh Crago in *Entranced by Story: Brain, Tale and Teller, from Infancy to Old Age* (New York and London: Routledge, 2014), 175.
7. See Robin Headlam Wells, *Elizabethan Mythologies: Studies in Poetry, Drama, and Music* (Cambridge: Cambridge University Press, 1994).
8. John A. McClure, *Partial Faiths: Postsecular Fiction in the Age of Pynchon and Morrison* (Athens, GA: University of Georgia Press, 2007).

BIBLIOGRAPHY

Acker, Kathy. *Blood and Guts in High School*. 1984. New York: Grove Weidenfeld, 1978.
Acker, Kathy. *Empire of the Senseless*. New York: Grove Weidenfeld, 1988.
Acker, Kathy. "Eurydice in the Underworld." In *Eurydice in the Underworld*. London: Arcadia Books, 1997.
Acker, Kathy. *Pussy, King of the Pirates*. New York: Grove Press, 1996.
Anon. *Saga of the Volsungs*. Edited and translated by R. G. Finch. London: Nelson, 1965.
Anon. *Sir Gawain and the Green Knight*. 2nd edition. Edited by Norman Davis. Oxford: Oxford University Press, 1967.
Anon. *Song of the Nibelungs*. See *The Nibelungenlied: The Lay of the Nibelungs*. Translated by Cyril Edwards. Oxford: Oxford University Press, 2010.
Armor, Brian, John Chambers, Genevieve Cogman, Richard Dansky, B. D. Flory, Harry Heckel IV, Ellen Kiley, James Kiley, Matthew McFarland, Dean Shomshak, and C. A. Suleiman. *Orpheus*. Stone Mountain, CA: White Wolf Press, 2003.
Armstrong, Paul B. *How Literature Plays with the Brain: The Neuroscience of Reading and Art*. Baltimore: The Johns Hopkins University Press, 2013.
Atwood, Margaret. *MaddAddam*. 2013. New York: Anchor, 2014.
Atwood, Margaret. *Oryx and Crake*. New York: Doubleday, 2003.
Atwood, Margaret. *The Penelopiad*. Edinburgh: Canongate, 2005.
Atwood, Margaret. *The Year of the Flood*. 2009. New York: Anchor, 2010.
Austen, Jane. *Pride and Prejudice*. Edited by Pat Rogers. Cambridge: Cambridge University Press, 2006.
Austen, Jane, and Seth Grahame-Smith. *Pride and Prejudice and Zombies*. Philadelphia: Quirk Books, 2009.
Austen, Jane, and Seth Grahame-Smith, Pamela Jane, and Deborah Guyol. *Pride and Prejudice and Kitties: A Cat-Lover's Romp through Jane Austen's Classic*. New York: Skyhorse Publishing, 2013.
Ayers, David. "The Long Last Goodbye: Control and Resistance in the Work of William Burroughs." *Journal of American Studies* 27, no. 2 (1993): 223–36.
Barker, Pat. *The Silence of the Girls: A Novel*. New York: Doubleday, 2018.
Barthelme, Donald. *The Dead Father*. 1975. New York: Penguin, 1986.
Barthes, Roland. "The Reality Effect." Original French, 1968. *The Rustle of Language*. Translated by Richard Howard. New York: Hill and Wang, 1986, 141–48.
Begiebing, Robert J. *Toward a New Synthesis: John Fowles, John Gardner, Norman Mailer*. Ann Arbor: UMI Research Press, 1989.

Beidler, Peter G., and Robert M. Nelson. "Grandma's Wicker Sewing Basket: Untangling the Narrative Threads in Silko's *Ceremony*." *American Indian Culture and Research Journal* 28, no. 1 (2004): 5-13.

Blanchot, Maurice. "Orpheus' Gaze." 1955. In *The Sirens' Song: Selected Essays by Maurice Blanchot*, edited by Gabriel Josipovici and translated by Sacha Rabinovitch. Bloomington: Indiana University Press, 1982, 177-81.

Bloom, Harold. "Norman in Egypt." *New York Review of Books*, April 28, 1983.

Bourdieu, Pierre. *Distinction: A Social Critique of the Judgement of Taste*. Original French, 1979. Translated by Richard Nice. Cambridge, MA: Harvard University Press, 1984.

Boyer, Pascal. *Religion Explained: The Evolutionary Origins of Religious Thought*. New York: Basic Books, 2001.

Bradley, Marion Zimmer. *The Mists of Avalon*. New York: Ballantine, 1982.

Brinkley, Roberta Florence. *Arthurian Legend in the Seventeenth Century*. Baltimore: The Johns Hopkins Press, 1932.

Bull, Malcolm. "Make Me a God." http://www.theguardian.com/artanddesign/2005/apr/30/art.

Bull, Malcolm. *The Mirror of the Gods*. Oxford: Oxford University Press, 2005.

Burroughs, William S. *Mythology and the Renaissance Tradition in English Poetry*. 1932. Rev ed. New York: W. W. Norton, 1963.

Burroughs, William S. *The Adding Machine: Collected Essays*. London: John Calder, 1985.

Burroughs, William S. *The Place of Dead Roads*. 1983. New York: Henry Holt/Owl Book, 1995.

Burroughs, William S. *The Western Lands*. 1987. New York: Penguin, 1988.

Butler, Octavia E. *Dawn*. New York: Warner, 1987.

Byatt, A. S. *Ragnarok: The End of the Gods*. Edinburgh: Canongate, 2011.

Calvino, Italo. *The Complete Cosmicomics*. Translated by Martin McLaughlin, Tim Parks, and William Weaver. London: Penguin, 2002.

Campbell, Joseph. *The Hero with a Thousand Faces*. 1949. Bollingen Series xvii. 2nd edition. Princeton: Princeton University Press, 1968.

Chaney, Michael A. "Slave Cyborgs and the Black Infovirus: Ishmael Reed's Cybernetic Aesthetics." *Modern Fiction Studies* 49, no. 2 (2003): 261-83.

Chaucer, Geoffrey. *Troilus and Criseyde: The Riverside Chaucer*. 3rd edition. General Editor Larry D. Benson. Boston: Houghton Mifflin, 1987.

Coffman, Christopher K. "Bogomilism, Orphism, Shamanism: The Spiritual and Spatial Grounds of Pynchon's Ecological Ethic." *Pynchon's Against the Day: A Corrupted Pilgrim's Guide*. Edited by Jeffrey Severs and Christopher Leise. Newark: University of Delaware Press, 2006, 91-114.

Cole, Merrill. *The Other Orpheus: A Poetics of Modern Homosexuality*. New York: Routledge, 2003.

Collins, Suzanne. *The Hunger Games*. New York: Scholastic, 2008.

Cooper, Helen. "Milton's King Arthur." *The Review of English Studies* n.s. 65, no. 269 (2014): 252-65.

Coover, Robert. *The Universal Baseball Association, Inc., J. Henry Waugh, Prop.* 1968. New York: Plume Books, 1971.

Cowart, David. *History and the Contemporary Novel*. Carbondale: Southern Illinois University Press, 1989.

Crago, Hugh. *Entranced by Story: Brain, Tale and Teller, from Infancy to Old Age.* New York and London: Routledge, 2014.
Delany, Samuel R. *The Einstein Intersection.* New York: Ace, 1967.
De Mott, Benjamin. "Norman Mailer's Egyptian Novel." *New York Times Book Review.* April 10, 1983.
Doctorow, Cory. *Down and Out in the Magic Kingdom.* New York: Tor, 2003.
Dowling, David. "Russell Hoban's *Riddley Walker*: Doing the Connections." *Critique* 29, no. 3 (1988): 179–87.
Ducornet, Rikki. *Gazelle.* New York: Knopf, 2003.
Ducornet, Rikki. *The Jade Cabinet.* Normal, IL: Dalkey Archive Press, 1993.
Egan, Greg. *Permutation City.* 1994. New York: HarperPrism, 1995.
Elam, Diane. *Romancing the Postmodern.* London and New York: Routledge, 1992.
Eliade, Mircea. *Myths, Dreams, and Mysteries: The Encounter between Contemporary Faiths and Archaic Realities.* 1957. Translated from French by Philip Mairet. New York and Evanston: Harper Torchbooks, 1967.
Eliade, Mircea. *The Quest: History and Meaning in Religion.* Chicago and London: University of Chicago Press, 1969.
Eliot, T. S. "Ulysses, Order, and Myth." 1923. http://people.virginia.edu/~jdk3t/eliotulysses.htm (consulted September 6, 2015).
Evans-Wentz, Walter. *The Tibetan Book of the Dead, or, the After-Death Experiences on the Bardo Plane.* 1927. 3rd edition. New York: Oxford University Press, 1960.
Evasdaughter, Elizabeth N. "Leslie Marmon Silko's *Ceremony*: Healing Ethnic Hatred by Mixed-Breed Laughter." *MELUS* 15, no. 1 (1988): 83–95.
Faber, Michel. *The Fire Gospel.* Edinburgh: Canongate, 2008.
Franklin, H. Bruce. *War Stars: The Superweapon and the American Imagination.* New York: Oxford University Press, 1988.
Frye, Northrop. *Anatomy of Criticism: Four Essays.* Princeton: Princeton University Press, 1957.
Frye, Northrop. "Literature and Myth." In *Relations of Literary Study: Essays on Interdisciplinary Contributions*, edited by James Thorpe. New York: MLA, 1967, 27–55.
Gaiman, Neil. *American Gods.* 2001. New York: Harper Torch, 2002.
Gaiman, Neil. *The Ocean at the End of the Lane.* New York: William Morrow, 2013.
Gaiman, Neil. *The Sandman.* 1989–1006. Published as *The Absolute Sandman* in 4 volumes. New York: Vertigo, 2006, 2007, 2008, 2009.
Gaiman, Neil, and Dave McKean. *The Tragical Comedy or Comical Tragedy of Mr Punch.* 1994. New York: Vertigo, 1995.
Gardner, John. *Grendel.* New York: Alfred A. Knopf, 1971.
Gibson, William. *Count Zero.* 1986. New York: Ace, 1987.
Gibson, William. *Neuromancer.* 1984. New York: Ace, 2000.
Gilligan, Carol. *In a Different Voice: Psychological Theory and Women's Development.* Cambridge, MA: Harvard University Press, 1982.
Gower, Daniel H. *The Orpheus Process.* New York: Dell, 1992.
Grossman, David. *Lion's Honey: The Myth of Samson.* Original Hebrew 2005. Translated by Stuart Schoffman. Edinburgh: Canongate, 2006.

Hamilton, Ian. "Mummies." *London Review of Books*, June 15–July 6, 1983, 6.
Haraway, Donna J. *A Cyborg Manifesto: Science, Technology, and Socialist-Feminism in the Late Twentieth Century*. http://ebookcentral.proquest.com/lib/warw/detail.action?docID=4392065.
Harde, Roxanne. "'We Will Make Our Own Future TEXT': Allegory, Iconoclasm, and Reverence in Ishmael Reed's Mumbo Jumbo." *Critique* 43, no. 4 (2002): 361–77.
Harris, Oliver. "Can You See a Virus? The Queer Cold War of William Burroughs." *Journal of American Studies* 33, no. 2 (1999): 243–66.
Hassan, Ihab. *The Dismemberment of Orpheus*. 1971. 2nd edition. Madison: University of Wisconsin Press, 1982.
Haynes, Natalie. *A Thousand Ships*. London: Mantle, 2019.
Headley, Maria Dahvana. *The Mere Wife*. New York: Farrar, Straus and Giroux, 2018.
Herbert, Frank. *Dune*. 1965. New York: Ace Classics of Modern Literature, 2002.
Herodotus, *The History of Herodotus*. http://classics.mit.edu/Herodotus/history.html.
Heinlein, Robert A. *The Moon Is a Harsh Mistress*. 1966. New York: Orb, 1997.
Heller, Joseph. *God Knows*. 1984. New York: Simon and Schuster, 1997.
Herrick, James A. *Scientific Mythologies: How Science and Science Fiction Forge New Religious Beliefs*. Downers Grove, IL: IVP Academic, 2008.
Hoban, Russell. "An Interview with Edward Myers." *Literary Review* 28, no. 1 (1984): 5–16.
Hoban, Russell. *Riddley Walker*. 1980. New York: Washington Square, 1982.
Hoban, Russell. *The Medusa Frequency*. London: Jonathan Cape, 1987.
Hoffman, Donald L. "A Darker Shade of Grail: Questing at the Crossroads in Ishmael Reed's *Mumbo Jumbo*." *Callaloo* 17, no. 4 (1994): 1245–56.
Hogan, Patrick Colm. *Cognitive Science, Literature, and the Arts: A Guide for Humanists*. New York and London: Routledge, 2003.
Hogue, W. Lawrence. "Postmodernism, Traditional Cultural Forms, and the African American Narrative: Major's *Reflex*, Morrison's *Jazz, and Reed*'s *Mumbo Jumbo*." *Novel* 35, nos. 2–3 (2002): 169–92.
Holland, Norman N. *5 Readers Reading*. New Haven: Yale University Press, 1975.
Hospital, Janette Turner. *Orpheus Lost*. London, New York, Sydney and Auckland: Fourth Estate, 2007.
Houen, Alex. "William S. Burroughs's Cities of the Red Night Trilogy: Writing Outer Space." *Journal of American Studies* 41, no. 3 (2006): 523–49.
Howley, Ashton. "Imperial Mailer: *Ancient Evenings*." In *Norman Mailer's Later Fictions: Ancient Evenings through Castle in the Forest*, edited by John Whalen-Bridge. New York: Palgrave Macmillan, 2010, 105–22.
Huisman, David. "'Hoap of a Tree' in Riddley Walker." *Christianity and Literature* 43, nos. 3–4 (1994): 347–73.
Hume, Kathryn. *Aggressive Fictions: Reading the Contemporary American Novel*. Ithaca: Cornell University Press, 2012.
Hume, Kathryn. "Books of the Dead: Postmortem Politics in Novels by Mailer, Burroughs, Acker, and Pynchon." *Modern Philology* 97, no. 3 (2000): 417–44.
Hume, Kathryn. *Calvino's Fictions: Cogito and Cosmos*. Oxford: Clarendon Press, 1992.

Hume, Kathryn. *Fantasy and Mimesis: Responses to Reality in Western Literature.* New York and London: Methuen, 1984.
Hume, Kathryn. "Neil Gaiman's *Sandman* as Mythic Romance." *Genre: Forms of Discourse and Culture* 46, no. 3 (2013): 345-65.
Hume, Kathryn. "Novelty, Pattern, and Power in Richard Powers's *Orfeo.*" *Orbit: A Journal of American Literature* 5, no. 1 (January 18, 2017): 1-19, Doi: https://doi.org/10.16995/orbit.202.
Hume, Kathryn. "The Semiotics of Fantasy in William Kennedy's Fiction." *Philological Quarterly* 79, no. 4 (2000): 523-48.
Hume, Kathryn. "Voice in Kathy Acker's Fiction." *Contemporary Literature* 42, no. 3 (2001): 485-513.
Hume, Kathryn. "William Burroughs's Phantasmic Geography." *Contemporary Literature* 40, no. 1 (1999): 111-35.
Hume, Kathryn, and Thomas J. Knight. "Orpheus and the Orphic Voice in *Gravity's Rainbow.*" *Philological Quarterly* 64, no. 3 (1985): 299-315.
Hutcheon, Linda. *A Theory of Adaptation.* New York: Routledge, 2006.
Huxley, Aldous. *Island.* London: Chatto and Windus, 1962.
Jaynes, Julian. *The Origin of Consciousness in the Breakdown of the Bicameral Mind.* Boston: Houghton Mifflin, 1976.
Jessee, Sharon A. "Laughter and Identity in Ishmael Reed's *Mumbo Jumbo.*" *MELUS* 21, no. 4 (1996): 127-39.
Jewett, Robert, and John Shelton Lawrence. *The American Monomyth.* New York: Anchor Press, 1977.
Kahneman, Daniel. *Thinking Fast and Slow.* New York: Farrar, Straus and Giroux, 2011.
Kaminsky, Inbar. "Epidemic Judaism: Plagues and Their Evocation in Philip Roth's *Nemesis* and Ben Marcus's *The Flame Alphabet.*" *Philip Roth Studies* 10, no. 1 (2014): 109-24.
Kennedy, Edward Donald. "Visions of History: Robert de Boron and English Arthurian Chroniclers." *The Fortunes of King Arthur.* Ed. Norris J. Lacy. Cambridge: D. S. Brewer, 2005, 29-46.
Kennedy, William. *Legs.* 1975. New York: Penguin, 1983.
Kitt, Selena. *The Song of Orpheus.* Alpena, MI: Excessica LCC, 2010.
Kohn, Robert E. "Seven Buddhist Themes in Pynchon's 'The Crying of Lot 49.'" *Religion & Literature* 35, no. 1 (2003): 73-96.
Kuberski, Philip. "The Metaphysics of Postmodern Death: Mailer's *Ancient Evenings* and Merrill's *The Changing Light of Sandover.*" *ELH* 56, no. 1 (1989): 229-54.
Kurzweil, Ray. *The Singularity Is Near: When Humans Transcend Biology.* New York: Penguin, 2005.
LaHaye, Tim, and Jerry B. Jenkins. *Left Behind.* Carol Stream, IL: Tyndale House, 1995.
Langeteig, Kendra. "*Horror Autotoxicus* in the Red Night Trilogy: Ironic Fruits of Burroughs's Terminal Vision." *Configurations* 5, no. 1 (1997): 135-69.
Lawrence, John Shelton, and Robert Jewett. *The Myth of the American Superhero.* Grand Rapids, MI: Eerdmans, 2002.
Leiber, Justin. *An Invitation to Cognitive Science.* Oxford: Basil Blackwell, 1991.

Leiber, Justin. *Can Animals and Machines be Persons?* Indianapolis: Hackett Publishing Company, 1985.
Lennon, John Michael. "Mailer's Cosmology." *Modern Language Studies* 12, no. 3 (1982): 18-29.
Lewis, C. S. *Mere Christianity*. London: Collins, 1953.
Lindner, Robert Mitchell. http://harpers.org/archive/1954/12/the-jet-propelled-couch/ and http://harpers.org/archive/1955/01/the-jet-propelled-couch-2/
Loomis, Roger Sherman. *Celtic Myth and Arthurian Romance*. 1927. New York: Haskell House, 1967.
Luhrmann, T. M. *When God Talks Back: Understanding the American Evangelical Relationship with God*. New York: Knopf, 2012.
Maclean, Mary. "The Signifier as Token: The Textual Riddles of Russell Hoban." *AUMLA* 70 (1988): 211-19.
MacLeod, Ken. *The Cassini Division*. New York: Tor Books, 1999.
Mailer, Norman. *Ancient Evenings*. 1983. New York: Warner, 1984.
Mailer, Norman. "An Interview with Norman Mailer: With Eve Auchincloss and Nancy Lynch," in *Conversations with Norman Mailer*, edited by J. Michael Lennon. Jackson and London: University Press of Mississippi, 1988, 39-51.
Mailer, Norman. "Norman Mailer on *An American Dream*." 1965. Reprinted in *Conversations with Norman Mailer*, edited by J. Michael Lennon. Jackson and London: University Press of Mississippi, 1988, 100-103.
Mailer, Norman. *On God: An Uncommon Conversation*. With Michael Lennon. New York: Random House, 2007.
Mailer, Norman. "On Waste." *The Presidential Papers*. New York: G. P. Putnam's, 1963, 269-302.
Malouf, David. *Ransom*. New York: Pantheon, 2009.
Malory, Thomas, Sir. *Malory: Complete Works*. 2nd edition. Edited by Eugene Vinaver. Oxford: Oxford University Press, 1977.
Marcus, Ben. *The Flame Alphabet*. New York: Knopf, 2012.
Maynor, Natalie, and Richard F. Patteson. "Language as Protagonist in Russell Hoban's *Riddley Walker*." *Critique* 26, no. 1 (1984): 18-25.
McCaffrey, Anne. *The Ship Who Sang*. New York: Ballantine Books, 1970.
McCarthy, Cormac. *Blood Meridian: Or the Evening Redness in the West*. 1985. New York: Vintage, 1992.
McClure, John A. *Partial Faiths: Postsecular Fiction in the Age of Pynchon and Morrison*. Athens, GA: University of Georgia Press, 2007.
McGilchrist, Iain. *The Master and His Emissary: The Divided Brain and the Making of the Western World*. 2009. New Haven and London: Yale University Press, 2012.
McHale, Brian. "Modernist Reading, Post-Modern Text: The Case of *Gravity's Rainbow*." *Poetics Today* 1, nos. 1-2 (1979): 85-110.
McIntyre, Vonda. *Superluminal*. 1983. New York: Pocket Books, 1984.
Melley, Timothy. *Empire of Conspiracy: The Culture of Paranoia in Postwar America*. Ithaca: Cornell University Press, 1999.
Mey, Jacob. "The Last of the Canterbury Tales: Artificial Intelligence in the Fifth Millennium." *Prague Linguistic Circle Papers* 1 (1995): 261-94.
Miller, Madeline. *Circe*. New York: Little, Brown and Company, 2018.

Miller, Madeline. *The Song of Achilles*. New York: Eeco, 2012.
Miller, Walter M., Jr. *A Canticle for Leibowitz*. 1959. New York: Bantam, 1982.
Moddelmog, Debra A. *Readers and Mythic Signs: The Oedipus Myth in Twentieth-Century Fiction*. Carbondale and Edwardsville: Southern Illinois University Press, 1993.
Momaday, N. Scott. *House Made of Dawn*. 1968. New York: HarperPerennial, 1999.
Monaghan, Patricia. *The Encyclopedia of Celtic Mythology and Folklore*. New York: Facts on File, Inc., 2004.
Moore, Alan, and Dave Gibbons. *Watchmen*. New York: DC Comics, 1987.
Morrison, Toni. *Song of Solomon*. 1977. New York: Signet, 1978.
Morrow, James. *Blameless in Abaddon*. 1996. San Diego: Harvest, 1997.
Morrow, James. *Only Begotten Daughter*. 1990. San Diego, New York, and London: Harvest Book, 1996.
Morrow, James. *The Eternal Footman*. New York: Harcourt Brace, 1999.
Morrow, James. *Towing Jehovah*. New York: Harcourt Brace/Harvest, 1994.
Mullen, R. D. "Dialect, Grapholect, and Story: Russell Hoban's 'Riddley Walker' as Science Fiction." *Science Fiction Studies* 27, no. 3 (2000): 391–417.
Naylor, Gloria. *Mama Day*. 1988. New York: Vintage, 1989.
Nelson, Robert M. "Settling for Vision in Silko's *Ceremony*: Sun Man, Arrowboy, and Tayo." *American Indian Culture and Research Journal* 28, no. 1 (2004): 67–73.
Nelson, Robert M. "The Kaupata Motif in Silko's *Ceremony*: A Study of Literary Homology." *Studies in American Indian Literatures Series* 2, 11, no. 3 (1999): 2–21.
Nolan, Amy. "'A New Myth to Live By': The Graphic Vision of Kathy Acker." *Critique* 53, no. 3 (2012): 201–13.
O'Donnell, Patrick. *Latent Destinies: Cultural Paranoia and Contemporary U.S. Narrative*. Durham: Duke University Press, 2000.
Östergren, Klas. *The Hurricane Party*. Original Swedish, 2007. Translated by Tiina Nunnally. Edinburgh: Canongate, 2009.
Oziewicz, Marek. *One Earth, One People: The Mythopoeic Fantasy Series of Ursula K. Le Guin, Lloyd Alexander, Madeleine L'Engle and Orson Scott Card*. Jefferson, NC: McFarland, 2008.
Paffenroth, Kim. *Orpheus and the Pearl*. Salt Lake City: Magus Press, 2008.
Phillips, J. J. *Mojo Hand: An Orphic Tale*. Berkeley: City Miner Books, 1966.
Piercy, Marge. *He, She and It*. 1991. New York: Fawcett Crest, 1993.
Poirier, Richard. "In Pyramid and Palace." *Times Literary Supplement*. June 10, 1983, 591–92.
Pounds, Wayne. "The Postmodern Anus: Parody and Utopia in Two Recent Novels by William Burroughs." *Poetics Today* 8 (1987): 611–29.
Powers, Richard. *Galatea 2.2*. 1995. New York: HarperPerennial, 1996.
Powers, Richard. *Generosity: An Enhancement*. New York: Farrar, Straus and Giroux, 2009.
Powers, Richard. *Orfeo: A Novel*. New York: W. W. Norton, 2014.
Powers, Richard. *Prisoner's Dilemma*. 1988. New York: Collier, 1989.
Powers, Richard. *The Gold Bug Variations*. 1991. New York: HarperPerennial, 1992.

Prince, Michael J. "The Master Film Is a Western: The Mythology of the American West in the *Cities of the Red Night* Trilogy." *European Journal of American Studies* 2011. http://ejas.revues.org/9412. Document 3.
Pullman, Philip. *The Amber Spyglass*. New York: Knopf, 2000.
Pullman, Philip. *The Golden Compass* (Original British title, *Northern Lights*). 1995. New York: Knopf, 1998.
Pullman, Philip. *The Good Man Jesus and the Scoundrel Christ*. Edinburgh: Canongate, 2010.
Pullman, Philip. *The Subtle Knife*. London: Scholastic, 1997.
Punday, Daniel. "Ishmael Reed's Rhetorical Turn: Uses of 'Signifying' in *Reckless Eyeballing*." *College English* 54, no. 4 (1992): 446-61.
Pynchon, Thomas. *Bleeding Edge*. New York: Penguin, 2013.
Pynchon, Thomas. *Gravity's Rainbow*. 1973. New York: Penguin, 2006.
Pynchon, Thomas. *Inherent Vice*. New York: Penguin, 2009.
Pynchon, Thomas. *Vineland*. Boston: Little Brown, 1990.
Raglan, Major FitzRoy Richard Somerset (4th Baron Raglan). *The Hero: A Study in Tradition, Myth, and Drama*. London: Methuen, 1936.
Réage, Pauline. *Story of O*. London: Corgi, 1972.
Reed, Ishmael. *Mumbo Jumbo*. 1972. New York: Atheneum, 1988.
Reed, Ishmael. *Reckless Eyeballing*. 1986. New York: Atheneum, 1988.
Renault, Mary. *The King Must Die*. New York: Pantheon, 1958.
Rice, David A. "Witchery, Indigenous Resistance, and Urban Space in Leslie Marmon Silko's *Ceremony*." *Studies in American Indian Literatures*, Series 2, 17, no. 4 (2005): 114-43.
Ricoeur, Paul. *The Symbolism of Evil*. Trans. Emerson Buchanan. Boston: Beacon Press, 1967.
Robertson, Pat. *The End of the Age*. 1995. Nashville, TN: Thomas Nelson, 2002.
Robinson, Spider, and Jeanne Robinson. *Stardance*. New York: Baen, 1991.
Robinson, Spider, and Jeanne Robinson. *Starmind*. New York: Ace, 1995.
Robinson, Spider, and Jeanne Robinson. *Starseed*. New York: Ace, 1991.
Roppolo, Kimberly. "Vision, Voice, and Intertribal Metanarrative: The American Indian Visual-Rhetorical Tradition and Leslie Marmon Silko's *Almanac of the Dead*." *American Indian Quarterly* 31, no. 4 (2007): 534-58.
Roth, Philip. *Nemesis*. New York: Houghton Mifflin, 2010.
Rucker, Rudy. *Postsingular*. New York: Tor Books, 2007.
Sanders, Julie. *Adaptation and Appropriation*. London: Routledge, 2006.
Sewell, Elizabeth. *The Orphic Voice: Poetry and Natural History*. New Haven: Yale University Press, 1960.
Shaviro, Steven. "The Singularity Is Here." In *Red Planets: Marxism and Science Fiction*, edited by Mark Bould and China Miéville. Middletown, CT: Wesleyan University Press, 2009, 103-17.
Shippey, Thomas A. *Heroes and Legends: The Most Influential Characters of Literature*. Chantilly, VA: The Great Courses, 2014.
Shippey, Tom. *Laughing Shall I Die: Lives and Deaths of the Great Vikings*. London: Reaktion Books, 2018.
Shute, Nevil. *On the Beach*. London: Heinemann, 1957.
Shute, Nevil. *Round the Bend*. 1951. London: Pan, 1968.
Silko, Leslie Marmon. *Almanac of the Dead*. 1991. New York: Penguin, 1992.

Silko, Leslie Marmon. *Ceremony*. 1977. New York: Penguin, 1986.
Silko, Leslie Marmon. "Notes on *Almanac of the Dead*." In *Yellow Woman and a Beauty of the Spirit*. New York: Simon and Schuster, 1996, 135–45.
Simmons, Dan. *Hyperion*. 1989. New York: Bantam, 1995.
Simmons, Dan. *The Fall of Hyperion*. New York: Foundation, 1990.
Slochower, Harry. *Mythopoesis: Mythic Patterns in the Literary Classics*. Detroit: Wayne State University Press, 1970.
Smith, Evans Lansing. *Thomas Pynchon and the Postmodern Mythology of the Underworld*. New York: Peter Lang, 2012.
Stallings, A. E. *Archaic Smile*. Evansville, IN: University of Evansville Press, 1999.
Stewart, Mary. *Airs above the Ground*. London: Hodder and Stoughton, 1965.
Stewart, Mary. *Nine Coaches Waiting*. 1958. New York: M. S. Mill Co. and William Morrow, 1959.
Stewart, Mary. *The Crystal Cave*. New York: William Morrow, 1970.
Stoppard, Tom. *Rosencrantz and Guildenstern Are Dead*. 1967. New York: Grove/Evergreen, 1968.
Strauss, Walter A. *Descent and Return: The Orphic Theme in Modern Literature*. Cambridge, MA: Harvard University Press, 1971.
Strombeck, Andrew. "The Conspiracy of Masculinity in Ishmael Reed." *African American Review* 40, no. 2 (2006): 299–311.
Stross, Charles. *Accelerando*. 2005. New York: Ace, 2006.
Swan, Edith. "Healing via the Sunwise Cycle in Silko's *Ceremony*." *American Indian Quarterly* 12, no. 4 (1988): 313–28.
Tidhar, Lavie. *Central Station*. San Francisco: Tachyon, 2016.
Tolkien, J. R. R. *The Hobbit*. 1937. 2nd edition. London: George Allen and Unwin, 1951.
Tolkien, J. R. R. *The Silmarillion*. Edited by Christopher Tolkien. Boston: Houghton Mifflin, 1977.
Unsworth, Barry. *The Songs of the Kings*. 2003. New York: Norton, 2004.
Veyne, Paul. *Did the Greeks Believe in Their Myths? An Essay on Constitutive Imagination*. Original French, 1983. Translated by Paula Wissing. Chicago: University of Chicago Press, 1988.
Vinaver, Eugène. "The Waste Land." *The Rise of Romance*. Oxford: Clarendon Press, 1971, 53–67.
Von Hendy, Andrew. *The Modern Construction of Myth*. Bloomington: Indiana University Press, 2002.
Vonnegut, Kurt. *Galápagos*. New York: Delacorte, 1985.
Wade, James. *Fairies in Medieval Romance*. New York: Palgrave Macmillan, 2011.
Washington, Salim. "The Avenging Angel of Creation/Destruction: Black Music and the Afro-Technological in the Science Fiction of Henry Dumas and Samuel R. Delany." *Journal of the Society for American Music* 2, no. 2 (2008): 235–53.
Wells, H. G. *The War of the Worlds*. London: Heinemann, 1898.
Wells, Robin Headlam. *Elizabethan Mythologies: Studies in Poetry, Drama, and Music*. Cambridge: Cambridge University Press, 1994.
White, John J. "Mythological Fiction and the Reading Process." In *Literary Criticism and Myth*, edited by Joseph P. Strelka. *Yearbook of Comparative Criticism* 9 (1980): 72–92.

White, John J. *Mythology in the Modern Novel*. Princeton: Princeton University Press, 1971.
White, T. H. *The Once and Future King*. London: Collins, 1958.
Whyte, Jack. *The Skystone*. New York: Forge, 1996.
Winterson, Jeanette. *Weight*. Edinburgh: Canongate, 2005.
Xue, Katherine. "Synthetic Biology's New Menagerie: Life, Reengineered." *Harvard Magazine* September–October (2014): 42–49.
Zelazny, Roger. *Creatures of Light and Darkness*. 1969. New York: Eos, 2010.
Zunshine, Lisa. *Strange Concepts and the Stories They Make Possible: Cognition, Culture, Narrative*. Baltimore: The Johns Hopkins University Press, 2008.
Zunshine, Lisa. *Why We Read Fiction: Theory of Mind and the Novel*. Columbus: Ohio State University Press, 2006.

INDEX

Acker, Kathy   1, 3, 8, 10, 13, 39, 98, 106
   *Blood and Guts in High
      School*   33–6, 80, 169, 172
   Empire of the Senseless   80, 172
   "Eurydice in the Underworld"
      83, 172
   Pussy, King of the Pirates   1, 80–4,
      165, 172
Althusser, Louis   16
Armor, Bryan et al.
   Orpheus   58, 170
Armstrong, Paul B.   177
Arthurian myth   7–8, 13, 112, 162
Atwood, Margaret
   Maddaddam   140
   Oryx and Crake   99, 140
   Penelopiad   148, 150–1, 176
   The Year of the Flood   140
Auchincloss, Eve   167
Austen, Jane
   Pride and Prejudice   12
Austen, Jane and Pamela Jane and
      Deborah Guyol
   Pride and Prejudice and Kitties   12
Austen, Jane and Seth Grahame-Smith
   Pride and Prejudice and Zombies   12
Ayers, David   168

Barker, Pat
   The Silence of the Girls   176
Barthelme, Donald
   The Dead Father   13, 80,
      84–6, 172
Barthes, Roland   144, 175
Begiebing, Robert J   167
Beidler, Peter G.   175
Beowulf (anon.)   158
Bernstein, Leonard
   West Side Story   12

Bible   4
Blake, William   7, 13
Blanchot, Maurice   66, 170
Bloom, Harold   168
Bourdieu, Pierre   165
Botticelli, Sandro   6
Boyer, Pascal   176, 177
Bradley, Marion Zimmer
   The Mists of Avalon   132
Brinkley, Roberta Florence   166
Bull, Malcolm   165
Burroughs, William S.   17, 39
   The Western Lands   23–6, 168
Butler, Octavia   99
   Dawn   173
Byatt, A. S.
   Ragnarok: The End of the Gods   4,
      44–7, 146, 169

Calvino, Italo   80, 127
   The Complete Cosmicomics   8, 13,
      68, 76, 101–6, 173
   "The Other Eurydice"   106
   solution to the problem of
      power   110
   "The Stone Sky"   106
Campbell, Joseph   167
Canongate Myth series   134, 147, 148
Celtic myth   94
Chaney, Michael A.   169
Coffman, Christopher K.   174
Cole, Merrill   170
Collins, Suzanne
   The Hunger Games   11
Cooper, Helen   166
Coover, Robert
   *The Universal Baseball Association,
      Inc., J. Henry Waugh,
      Prop.*   7, 8, 10, 14

Cowart, David   173
Crago, Hugh   177

Dares Phrygius   4, 112
Delany, Samuel
  The Einstein Intersection
    69–71, 171
De Mott, Benjamin   168
Derrida, Jacques   16
Dictys Cretensis   4, 112
Doctorow, Cory   154
  *Down and Out in the Magic
    Kingdom*   118–19, 124
Dowling, David   172
Ducornet, Rikki
  Gazelle   138
  The Jade Cabinet   137–9,
    175
Dugas, Don-John   173

Egan, Greg
  Permutation City   154
Elam, Diane   x
Eliade, Mircea   3
Eliot, T. S.   167
Evasdaughter, Elizabeth N.   175

Faber, Michel
  The Fire Gospel   134
Feist, Raymond   113, 133
Foucault, Michel   16
Franklin, H. Bruce   174
Frye, Northrop   13, 165, 167

Gaiman, Neil   55, 80
  American Gods   42–4, 148
  The Graveyard Book   72
  The Ocean at the End of the Lane
    107–9, 173
  The Sandman   69, 71–3, 107, 109,
    113, 171
Gaiman, Neil, and Dave McKean
  *The Tragical Comedy or Comical
    Tragedy of Mr Punch*   173
Gardner, John
  Grendel   158
Gibson, William
  Count Zero   40–2, 169
  Neuromancer   36–8, 120, 169

Gilligan, Carol   60, 170
Gower, Daniel H.
  The Orpheus Process   58, 170
Grossman, David
  *Lion's Honey: The Myth of
    Samson*   149–50, 176

Hamilton, Ian   168
Haraway. Donna J.   126, 174, 175
Harde, Roxanne   168
Harris, Oliver   168
Hassan, Ihab   66, 170
Haynes, Natalie
  A Thousand Ships   176
Headley, Maria Dahvana
  The Mere Wife   158
Heinlein, Robert
  The Moon is a Harsh Mistress   122
Heller, Joseph
  God Knows   6
Herbert, Frank
  Dune   8, 10
Herrick, James A.   166
Higden, Ranulf   166
Hoban, Russell   98, 172
  The Medusa Frequency   65–9, 74,
    106, 171
  Riddley Walker   69, 80, 86–97,
    131, 171, 172
Hoffman, Donald L.   169
Hogan, Patrick Colm   177
Hogue, W. Lawrence   169
Holland, Norman N.   177
Hospital, Janette Turner
  Orpheus Lost   60–4
Houen, Alex   168
Howley, Ashton   167
Huisman, David   173
Hume, Kathryn
  on Acker   169
  on Burroughs   168
  on Calvino   173
  on Gaiman   171
  on Kennedy   175
  on Mailer   167
  on Morrow   170
  on Powers   171
  on Pynchon   170
Hume, Kathryn   ix, 174

Hutcheon, Linda   167
Huxley, Aldous
    Island   106

invented myth
    post-singularity   112
    the problem of power   161

Jaynes, Julian   172
Jessee, Sharon A.   168
Jewett, Robert   172
Jordan, Robert   113
Judeo-Christian myth
    minority myth used to
        attack   143–6
Jung, Carl   167

Kahneman, Daniel   99
Kaminsky, Inbar   175
Kennedy, William
    Legs   47–9, 169
Kerr, Katharine   11, 113, 133
Kitt, Selena
    The Song of Orpheus   58, 170
Knight, Thomas J.   174
Kohn, Robert E.   169
Kuberski, Philip   167
Kurzweil, Ray   9, 114, 115–16, 166, 174

Lacan, Jacques   16
Lackey, Mercedes   133
    Valdemar series   113
LaHaye, Tim and Jerry B. Jenkins
    Left Behind fantasies   6
Langeteig, Kendra   168
Lawrence, John Shelton   172
Leiber, Justin   174
Lennon, John Michael   167
Lewis, C. S.   135, 174
Lindner, Robert   7, 166
Loomis, Roger Sherman   166
Luhrmann, T. M.   172
Lynch, Nancy   167

McCaffrey, Anne   133
    The Ship Who Sang   116–17
McCarthy, Cormac   viii

Maclean, Mary   172
McClure, John   x, 161, 177
McGilchrist, Iain   172, 175, 177
McHale, Brian   174
McIntyre, Vonda
    Superluminal   117
MacLeod, Ken
    The Cassini Division   166, 176
Mailer, Norman   15, 17, 129, 174
    Ancient Evenings   17–23, 167
    *On God: An Uncommon
        Conversation, Norman
        Mailer with Michael
        Lennon*   167
    The Presidential Papers   167
Malory, Thomas
    Le Morte D'Arthur   112, 132
Malouf, David
    Ransom   4, 6
Marcus, Ben
    The Flame Alphabet   139–40, 175
Maynor, Natalie   173
Melley, Timothy   176
Mey, Jacob   173
Miller, Madeleine
    Circe   176
    The Song of Achilles   4
Miller, Walter M., Jr.
    A Canticle for Leibowitz   91, 92, 100, 173
Moddelmog, Debra A.   165
Momaday, N. Scott
    House Made of Dawn   146
Monaghan, Patricia   173
Monteverdi, Claudio
    L'Orfeo   6
Moore, Alan
    Watchmen   80, 97–100, 113
Morrison, Toni
    Song of Solomon   143, 175
Morrow, James
    Blameless in Abaddon   51–3, 136, 170
    The Eternal Footman   53–4
    Only Begotten Daughter   135–7, 175
    Towing Jehovah   6, 13, 50–1, 84, 136, 170
Mullen, R. D.   173

Myers, Edward   172, 173
myth
    as artistic tool   2, 129–55
    attacking myth   146–8
    criticizing Christian myth   134–7
    as cultural capital   130–1
    as cultural compensation   131–4
    and death   54–6
    definition   2–3, 111
    a feeling of meaning   162
    Greco-Roman   2
    invented myth   1, 6–8, 79–110
    invented myth versus
        fantasy   112–15
    Judeo-Christian myth   137–42
    mapping the mythic   13–14
    metamorphosis in the post-
        singularity era   160
    origin in religion   5
    the problem of power   79–110
    sense of meaning   157–63
        cultural compensation   158
        linkage to the past   157–8
        pattern recognition   157
        rightness   157
    situational myth   1, 8, 111–27, 161
    in technological form   151–5
    versus fantasy   8, 9–13, 131
mythic worlds   151
    definition   4–5, 112
mythology
    collaborative nature of   112–13
    definition   3–4, 111
    as multiple self   16

Naylor, Gloria
    Mama Day   143, 175
Nelson, Robert M.   175
neurocognitive theory   158–9
Nibelungenlied (anon.)   4
Nolan, Amy   172

O'Donnell, Patrick   176
Orpheus   85, 94, 130, 157, 158
Orpheus and Eurydice   57–8, 83, 106
    mythemes   2, 57
Östergren, Klas
    The Hurricane Party   147–8, 176
Oziewicz, Marek   177

Paffenroth, Kim
    Orpheus and the Pearl   58, 170
Patteson, Richard F.   173
Phillips, J. J.
    Mojo Hand   64–5
Piercy, Marge
    He, She and It   119–22
Poirier, Richard   168
post-singularity   8, 114–15
    myth of metamorphosis   160
Pounds, Wayne   168
Powers, Richard
    Galatea 2.2   75
    Generosity   106
    The Gold Bug Variations   106
    Orfeo   74–6, 106, 171
    Prisoner's Dilemma   106
    solution to the problem of power
        110
Pratchett, Terry   13
Prince, Michael J.   168
Pullman, Philip
    *The Good Man Jesus and the
        Scoundrel Chris*t   134
    His Dark Materials trilogy   135
Punch and Judy   93
Punday, Daniel   168
Pynchon, Thomas
    Bleeding Edge   8, 152
    The Crying of Lot 49   169
    Gravity's Rainbow   130–1,
        160
    Inherent Vice   141–142, 175
    Vineland   49–50, 169, 170

Raglan, Lord   167
Réage, Pauline
    Story of O   172
Reed, Ishmael   17, 168, 169
    Mumbo Jumbo   26–9, 169
    Reckless Eyeballing   168
Renault, Mary
    The King Must Die   6
Rice, David A.   176
Ricoeur, Paul   3, 165
Robertson, Pat
    The End of the Age   6, 137
Robinson, Spider and Jeanne
    Stardance   137

Starmind   137
Starseed   137
Roppolo, Kimberly   176
Roth, Philip
  Nemesis   139
Rowling, J. K.
  Harry Potter series   11
Rucker, Rudy
  Postsingular   124–6, 151, 152–5, 174, 176
Rushdie, Salman   6

Saga of the Volsungs (anon.)   112
Sanders, Julie   166
Sewell, Elizabeth   170
Shakespeare, William
  Venus and Adonis   6
Shaviro, Steven   166, 176
Shippey, Thomas A.   174, 176
Shute, Nevil
  On the Beach   100, 112
  Round the Bend   8
Silko, Leslie Marmon
  Almanac of the Dead   146, 160, 169
  Ceremony   144–6, 160, 175
  Yellow Woman and a Beauty of the Spirit   176
Simmons, Dan
  Hyperion   117
Sir Gawain and the Green Knight (anon.)   11
Slochower, Harry   3, 165
Smith, Evans Lansing   174
Song of the Nibelungs (anon.)   112
Stallings, A. E.
  Archaic Smile   170
  "Eurydice Reveals Her Strength"   59
  "Eurydice's Footnote"   59
Stewart, Mary
  The Crystal Cave   132
Stoppard, Tom
  Rosencrantz and Guildenstern are Dead   12
Strauss, Walter A.   170
Strombeck, Andrew   168
Stross, Charles
  Accelerando   122–4, 154, 174

superheroes   79
Swan, Edith   175

Tennyson, Alfred
  "The Lotos-Eaters"   6
Tidhar, Lavie
  Central Station   126–7
Tolkien, J. R. R.   13, 113, 133
  The Hobbit   158
  The Silmarillion   7

Unsworth, Barry
  Songs of the Kings   4
Updike, John   129

Veyne, Paul   165
Vinaver, Eugène   166
Völsunga saga (anon.)   4
Von Hendy, Andrew   3
Vonnegut, Kurt
  Galápagos   99, 140

Wagner, Richard
  Der Ring des Nibelungen   46, 112, 158
Washington, Salim   171
Wells, H. G.
  The War of the Worlds   9, 114, 134
Wells, Robin Headlam   173, 177
White, John J.   167
White, T. H.
  The Once and Future King   133
Whyte, Jack
  The Skystone   133
Winterson, Jeanette
  Weight   148–9, 176

Xue, Katherine   171

Zelazny, Roger   10, 17
  Creatures of Light and Darkness   29–31
Zemeckis, Robert
  Beowulf (film)   158
Zombies   12, 58
Zunshine, Lisa   157, 177

www.ingramcontent.com/pod-product-compliance
Lightning Source LLC
Chambersburg PA
CBHW052044300426
44117CB00012B/1966